The Logic of Real Arguments

This new and expanded edition of *The Logic of Real Arguments* explains a distinctive method for analysing and evaluating arguments. It discusses many examples, ranging from newspaper articles to extracts from classic texts, and from easy passages to much more difficult ones. It shows students how to use the question 'What argument or evidence would justify me in believing P?', and also how to deal with suppositional arguments beginning with the phrase 'Suppose that X were the case.' It aims to help students to think critically about the kind of sustained, theoretical arguments which they commonly encounter in the course of their studies, including arguments about the natural world, about society, about policy and about philosophy. It will be valuable for students and their teachers in a wide range of disciplines including philosophy, law and the social sciences.

Alec Fisher

School of Economic and Social Studies
University of East Anglia

The
logic
of
real
arguments

CAMBRIDGE
UNIVERSITY PRESS

CAMBRIDGE UNIVERSITY PRESS
Cambridge, New York, Melbourne, Madrid, Cape Town, Singapore, São Paulo

Cambridge University Press
The Edinburgh Building, Cambridge, CB2 8RU, UK

Published in the United States of America by Cambridge University Press, New York

www.cambridge.org
Information on the title: www.cambridge.org/9780521654814

First edition © Cambridge University Press 1988
Second edition © Alec Fisher 2004

First published 1988
Second edition 2004
Fourth printing 2007

Printed in the United Kingdom at the University Press, Cambridge

A catalogue record for this publication is available from the British Library

ISBN 978-0-521-65241-4 hardback
ISBN 978-0-521-65481-4 paperback

Contents

Preface to the first edition

This book arose out of my experience of teaching logic. Like many others I hoped that teaching logic would help my students to argue better and more logically. Like many others, I was disappointed. Students who were well able to master the techniques of logic seemed to find that these were of very little help in handling real arguments. The tools of classical logic – formalisation, truth-tables, Venn diagrams, semantic tableaux, etc. – just didn't seem to apply in any straightforward way to the reasoning which students had to read in courses other than logic. At the same time I felt that it ought to be possible to give students some guidance – some procedure – which would help them to extract and to evaluate arguments from written texts and which would help them to write good arguments of their own. I wanted the procedure to be non-formal but to build upon the insights of traditional logic; this book attempts to realise that objective.

Many other teachers of logic and philosophy have had much the same experience in the past two decades and the result has been the emergence of what is now called the 'informal logic and critical thinking movement' in North America. One of the first books in this tradition was Monroe Beardsley's *Practical Logic*, a book which is still well worth reading over thirty years on. Stephen Toulmin's *The Uses of Argument* is another classic attempt at providing an alternative framework for understanding reasoning. However, Michael Scriven's *Reasoning* has probably been the most influential contribution to the field: it marks a watershed since which interest in the subject has grown very rapidly. For a very useful bibliography, see *Informal Logic: The First International Symposium*, edited by J. Anthony Blair and Ralph H. Johnson.

The Logic of Real Arguments is a contribution to the literature in a field which is already very extensive and it makes no attempt to be comprehensive. However, it is distinctive in various ways. For example the focus of interest is not so much on everyday reasoning as on theoretical argument of the kind that university and college students encounter in the course of their work. The book considers mainly sustained theoretical arguments about the natural world, about society, about policy or about philosophy – the sort of argument which is *complex, important* but *hard to handle*.

The general method of argument analysis which is presented (see especially Chapter 2) is intended to apply to a wide range of such written arguments – expressed in ordinary language. The method employs diagramming techniques to represent the structure of arguments, and an alternative, linear representation, is provided for those who hate diagrams. However, the distinctive feature of the method explained here is its use of the Assertibility Question,

> What argument or evidence would justify me in asserting the conclusion C?

This question is used both in discovering an author's intended argument and in evaluating that argument. It is used and discussed extensively throughout the book and the philosophical assumptions underlying its use are explained in Chapter 11.

Another distinctive feature of this book is its treatment of 'suppositional reasoning'. Most informal logic/critical thinking texts make no mention of this at all (though Stephen Thomas's *Practical Reasoning in Natural Language* (3rd edn) is a notable exception). The reasoning considered in most texts employs only *assertions*, i.e. propositions which have been presented as being true. However, many arguments (particularly in theoretical contexts) reach their conclusion not by asserting their starting points but by assuming or supposing something 'for the sake of argument' – as when an atheist says, 'Suppose there is a God . . .' In Chapter 8 we explain how to handle such reasoning and how to diagram it, using ideas due originally to Gottlob Frege. This necessitates revising what is normally said about reason and conclusion indicators; these are systematically ambiguous in a way that most texts fail to notice.

Since it will be clear that many of the theoretical contexts in which we are interested are scientific or pseudo-scientific we also have a chapter on scientific argument. This involves giving an account of Hume's ideas on the role of observation and induction, of Popper's conception of scientific method in terms of conjectures and refutations and of Thomas Kuhn's work on paradigms, normal science and scientific revolutions. Since the message of this book is that one cannot escape epistemology (in evaluating reasoning) the teacher who wishes to employ the approach of this book further in, say, the historical domain might wish to supply a similar chapter on historical method.

Much of the book consists in discussing particular examples of reasoning: the sources range from Thomas Malthus to Karl Marx and from Caspar Weinberger to Charles Darwin. There is also an Appendix which outlines some of the basic ideas of classical elementary formal logic. This contains an extensive explanation of the notion of (deductive) validity in terms of the notion of 'logical form' (logical structure). Furthermore, the notation of propositional and predicate logic, truth-tables and semantic tableaux are all introduced in so far as they are relevant to what has gone before. The book concludes with a large number of carefully selected exercises. Those who are sceptical of the value of methods like the ones expounded in this book tend to underestimate how hard students find it to grasp and evaluate arguments. One way to see this is to choose an exercise from the book and see how well students can handle it with and without the methods explained here. No doubt there is room for extending and improving these methods but experience strongly suggests that they are a real help.

I have enjoyed writing this book. Many people have helped and encouraged me in the course of writing it and it is a pleasure to thank them now. The Nuffield Foundation and the University of East Anglia generously supported work on an earlier draft of the text and this enabled Dr Anne Thomson to help me with much of the initial work. This got the project off to a good start. Many colleagues and students have supplied me with examples and have helped to clear my thoughts in the course of presenting these ideas at UEA over recent years. I should like to thank them all, especially Martin Hollis, for his unflagging encouragement. Muriel Parke, Pat Earl and Val Striker produced beautiful typescript from my messy manuscript. My University and Cambridge University Press have been helpful and supportive throughout. More recently I have learned a great deal from Professor John Hoaglund's excellent conference at Christopher Newport College, Newport News, Virginia, from Professor Frans van Eemeren's wide-ranging work on argumentation in Amsterdam and from Professor Richard Paul's pioneering work on 'strong critical thinking'. Ideas in this field are developing very rapidly and I am conscious of how much I owe to many valuable conversations with all of them.

Finally, affectionate thanks to my wife Sarah and to my children Daniel, Max and Susannah for extensive practice in arguing my case.

Preface to the second edition

This second edition differs from the first mainly by the addition of two new chapters. These deal with some fascinating arguments about the existence of God and about how our minds and bodies interact. Although this approach to teaching students how to analyse and evaluate arguments was first published in 1988, many students and teachers still find it useful and instructive, and this seems to be especially true in Philosophy departments, hence the choice of new topics. The general approach has not been changed here, but the new examples illustrate applications of my approach in particular contexts – some especially philosophical and one which is rhetorically powerful. It has been a pleasure to write this second edition and I particularly want to thank Nicholas Everitt for reading the new chapters and making very helpful suggestions; I often accepted these but, needless to say, the resulting work is my responsibility. Again I also wish to thank Cambridge University Press for their help and patience and my wife and family for theirs too.

Acknowledgements

We gratefully acknowledge the permission of the authors, editors and publishers to reproduce the extracts used in this book:

p. 66, from a speech delivered in Bristol in 1982 by Enoch Powell; p. 100, from 'The Physical Basis of Mind' by A. J. Ayer in *The Physical Basis of Mind: A Series of Broadcast Talks* edited by Peter Laslett, published by Basil Blackwell 1957; p. 82, from 'The more you understand evolution, the more you move towards atheism', an edited version of a speech by Dr Richard Dawkins to the Edinburgh International Science Festival on 15 April 1992 and printed in the *Independent* newspaper; p. 147, from *Conjectures and Refutations* by Karl Popper (pp. 36–7), published in the United Kingdom by Routledge and Kegan Paul and in the United States by Basic Books, 1963; pp. 152ff, from *The Structure of Scientific Revolutions* by T. S. Kuhn, published in 1970 by University of Chicago Press; p. 166, from 'Truth', by M. A. E. Dummett, in *Proceedings of the Aristotelian Society*, vol. 59 (1958–9, pp. 141–62), © The Aristotelian Society 1959, reprinted by courtesy of the editor; p. 167, from *Language, Truth and Logic* by A. J. Ayer (pp. 35, 37), published by Victor Gollancz Ltd; p. 168, from *Frege: Philosophy of Language* by M. A. E. Dummett (p. 590), published in the United Kingdom by Gerald Duckworth and Co. Ltd and in the United States by Harvard University Press; p. 189, from a letter to *The Guardian* by Ken Booth (2 September 1982); p. 190, from 'How to think sceptically about the bomb' by Bernard Williams, in *New Society* (18 September 1982); p. 193, from *The Last Days of Hitler* by Hugh Trevor-Roper. Copyright 1947 by H. R. Trevor-Roper, renewed 1975 by H. R. Trevor-Roper. Reprinted with permission of Macmillan Publishing Company; p. 195, from 'Riddles of Public Choice' by M. Hollis, R. Sugden and A. Weale, in *The Times Higher Education Supplement* (25 October 1985); p. 196, from *Miracles: A Preliminary Study* by C. S. Lewis (p. 27), published 1947 by Geoffrey Bles, © William Collins, Sons & Co. Ltd; p. 210, from *The Foundations of Scientific Inference* by Wesley C. Salmon, published by University of Pittsburgh Press; p. 212, from *Darwin and the Beagle* by A. Moorehead (pp. 236–40), published by Hamish Hamilton, reprinted by courtesy of The Rainbird Publishing Group Limited.

Other extracts:

p. 4, from an essay 'On the Balance of Trade' by David Hume, published in *David Hume: The Philosophical Works*, edited by T. H. Green and T. H. Grose, vol. 3, published by Scienta Verlag Aalen, 1964 (p. 333); p. 29, from *An Essay on the Principle of Population* by Thomas Malthus, edited with an introduction by Anthony Flew, published by Penguin, 1970 (Chapter 1); pp. 44, 45, 46, from *Outlines of a Critique of Political Economy* by Friedrich Engels, taken from *Marx and Engels on Malthus*, edited by Ronald L. Meek, published by Lawrence and Wishart, 1953 (pp. 59, 63); p. 70, from *Autobiography* by John Stuart Mill, edited with an introduction by Jack Stillinger, published by Oxford University Press (Chapter 1); p. 71, from *Principles of Political Economy* by John Stuart Mill, edited with an introduction by Sir J. W. Ashley, published by Longmans Green & Co., 1920 (pp. 963–5); p. 95, from *Language, Truth and Logic* by A. J. Ayer, published by Gollancz, 2nd edition 1960, pp. 115–16; pp. 124, 197–202, from *Dialogues Concerning Two New Sciences* by Galileo Galilei, translated by Henry Crew and Alfonso de Salvio with an introduction by Antonio Favaro, published by Dover Publications 1914 (pp. 62ff, 168); p. 133, from *Value, Price and Profit* by Karl Marx, edited by Eleanor Marx Aveling, published by George Allen and Unwin Ltd; pp. 202–4, from *Dialogues Concerning Natural Religion* by David Hume, edited with an introduction by Henry D. Aiken, published by Hafner Press, 1948 (pp. 17, 57–8, 66); p. 214, from *An Anatomical Disquisition on the Motion of the Heart and Blood in Animals* by William Harvey, published by Everyman 1907 (Chapter 13).

1 · Introduction

We learn most of what we know from teachers and experts of one kind and another and this is not surprising in a highly specialised modern society. However, it is possible to rely too heavily on experts and this approach to learning and knowledge tends to encourage passivity and receptiveness rather than inventiveness and imagination. We tend to think that because the teachers and experts *know more* about the subject than the rest of us we must ask for their judgement and we must rely on it. One object of this book is to combat this attitude and to impress on the reader what a long way one can get in understanding any subject by thinking it through for oneself, by being imaginative and inventive rather than by simply accepting expert opinion. We shall do this by concentrating on the arguments experts have produced for believing a wide range of things and showing how it requires only a relatively slight knowledge of the subject to evaluate these arguments oneself. (When we speak of an argument in this book, we mean a train of reasoning – not a quarrel!) Confidence in one's own judgement is another key to understanding and a secondary objective of this book is to give the reader such confidence. It's like learning to ride a bicycle – you will have some falls on the way but once you can do it you'll realise you can do a great deal on your own.

It is surprising how far one can get by thinking things through. Here is an example: it is an argument about how bodies of different mass/weight fall under the influence of gravity.

Suppose (as Aristotle believed) that the heavier a body is, the faster it falls to the ground and suppose that we have two bodies, a heavy one called $\boxed{M}$ and a light one called $\boxed{m}$. Under our initial assumption $\boxed{M}$ will fall faster than $\boxed{m}$. Now suppose that $\boxed{M}$ and $\boxed{m}$ are joined together thus $\boxed{\frac{m}{M}}$. Now what happens? Well, $\boxed{\frac{m}{M}}$ is heavier than $\boxed{M}$ so by our initial assumption it should fall *faster* than $\boxed{M}$ alone. But in the joined body $\boxed{\frac{m}{M}}$, $\boxed{m}$ and $\boxed{M}$ will each tend to fall just as fast as before they were joined, so $\boxed{m}$ will act as a 'brake' on $\boxed{M}$ and $\boxed{\frac{m}{M}}$ will fall *slower* than $\boxed{M}$ alone. Hence it follows from our initial assumption that $\boxed{\frac{m}{M}}$ will fall both *faster* and *slower* than $\boxed{M}$ alone. Since this is absurd our initial assumption must be *false*.

This beautiful piece of reasoning shows – *if it is correct* – that heavier bodies *cannot* fall faster under gravity than lighter ones. It illustrates what can be discovered by *thinking things through* (if it is correct). Of course the big question is whether it is correct and we shall consider how to answer that question later in the book. We introduce it now because it is a lovely example of the kind of reasoning – thinking things through – to which this book is addressed. It is a fairly *complex* piece of reasoning: it is not too easy to say exactly what the structure of the reasoning is and it is not easy to see whether the reasoning is correct. But it is also an *important* argument, because if it is correct it establishes a substantial, scientific conclusion which has very considerable implications (as we show in Chapter 8). Last, but not least, it is the sort of *complex* and *important* reasoning which most people feel unable to handle. They tend to give up on it and to ask someone they regard as an expert, 'Well, is it right?' The object of this book is to *show* the reader how to extract and evaluate such complex and important arguments and to demonstrate that one does not need to be an expert in the field to make significant progress in doing this.

Here is another, rather different example.

> Either there is a Christian God or there isn't. Suppose you believe in His existence and live a Christian life. Then, *if He does exist* you will enjoy eternal bliss and if He doesn't exist you will lose very little. But suppose you don't believe in His existence and don't live a Christian life. If He doesn't exist you will lose nothing, but *if He does exist* you will suffer eternal damnation! So it is rational and prudent to believe in God's existence and to live a Christian life.

Again, this is a fascinating piece of reasoning. It is complex and important and hard to handle. In this case furthermore, it is the sort of argument which tends to stop the non-believer in his tracks: *if it is right* it seems to provide a very compelling reason for reforming his ways because the consequences of his being mistaken are so appalling. And yet one can't help feeling that one's beliefs are not things which can be adapted simply to avoid some awful consequence. Again this book tries to help.

As it happens both the examples we have considered so far are of great historical importance. The first was due to Galileo and the second is known as Pascal's Wager after the French philosopher and mathematician. Many of the examples of reasoning which we shall consider in this book are historical classics in the same way. We have chosen them because, being classics, they tend to be of interest in their own right (apart, that is, from their interest in argument analysis). They also tend to have a history and a contemporary relevance which is instructive. But they are also usually backed by some 'authority', for example Galileo or Pascal, and it is precisely the tendency to rely on the expert authority that we wish to combat – up to a point!

Here is another example. Most people who struggled with the proof of Pythagoras' Theorem at school never came anywhere near to understanding it, but here is a much simpler 'proof' (*if it is correct*). Pythagoras' Theorem is about any right-angled triangle in the Euclidean plane (i.e. on a flat surface like this page). The 'hypotenuse' in such a triangle is the side opposite the right angle and Pythagoras' Theorem says that for any right-angled triangle the square on the hypotenuse equals the sum of the squares on the other two sides, i.e. the area A = the area B + the area C.

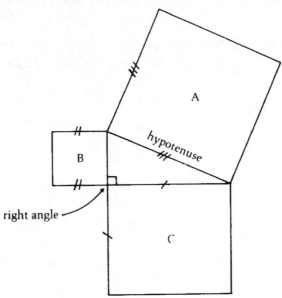

Few people grasp the standard Euclidean proof, but here is a much simpler one. The same large square can be formed by arranging four copies of the given triangle with B and C or with A as shown below:

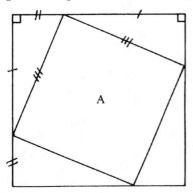
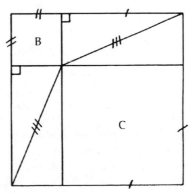

Do these diagrams prove Pythagoras' Theorem? Or is there a catch? One only has to think about it to realise that any reader can judge this – and yet most will lack the confidence to do so.

Here is a last example – for the time being.

> Suppose four-fifths of all the money in Great Britain to be annihilated in one night, and the nation reduced to the same condition, with regard to specie [cash], as in the reigns of the Harrys and Edwards, what would be the consequence? Must not the price of all labour and commodities sink in proportion, and everything be sold as cheap as they were in those ages? What nation could then dispute with us in any foreign market, or pretend to navigate or to sell manufactures at the same price, which to us would afford sufficient profit? In how little time, therefore, must this bring back the money which we had lost, and raise us to the level of all the neighbouring nations? Where, after we had arrived, we immediately lose the advantage of the cheapness of labour and commodities; and the farther flowing in of money is stopped by our fulness and repletion.
>
> Again, suppose, that all the money of Great Britain were multiplied five-fold in a night, must not the contrary effect follow? Must not all labour and commodities rise to such an exorbitant height, that no neighbouring nations could afford to buy from us; while their commodities, on the other hand, become comparatively so cheap, that, in spite of all the laws which could be formed, they would be run in upon us, and our money flow out; till we fall to a level with foreigners, and lose that great superiority of riches, which had laid us under such disadvantages?
>
> Now it is evident, that the same causes, which would correct these exorbitant inequalities, were they to happen miraculously, must prevent their happening in the common course of nature, and must forever, in all neighbouring nations, preserve money nearly proportionable to the art and industry of each nation.

This argument is again quite complex, quite hard to unravel, and of considerable historical and theoretical importance. Its author was David Hume, the philosopher, and it was first published over two centuries ago. However, it is not of purely historical significance: in short it is a classic statement of the case for what we now call 'monetarism'. If the reasoning is correct it has important implications for government policy. If it is incorrect many Western governments have based their economic policies in recent years on a fallacy! But again it is the kind of argument most people shy away from. They feel that it is a matter for the experts – in this case economists. But since economists disagree strongly over this and many other issues why should we rely on them and not on ourselves?

In this book we shall try to show that it is possible to get quite a long way in handling arguments like those above just by thinking things through. All that is needed is a fairly simple intellectual framework within which to organise one's thoughts plus the confidence to be imaginative and inventive instead of waiting for the expert. A little practice at riding this particular bicycle will show you what you can do and what your limitations are and most people can get further than they realise.

The methods which work for these relatively difficult arguments will of course work for easier arguments, but the *test* of any method which aims to help people in reasoning is how it handles difficult cases, which is why we tend to concentrate on these in this book. We cannot of course start with difficult cases, so we begin with some basic elements of the intellectual framework we need and some easier examples which will lead us in the right direction.

First, some basic ideas. Although much of what is said in this book generalises to broader areas than the sort of 'nuggets' of reasoning we have introduced above we shall restrict our attention to such reasoning for the sake of simplicity. By the end the reader should see how to generalise the approach explained in this book in various ways – especially in the light of the last chapter.

So basically we shall be looking at passages quite like those introduced so far (though often rather longer). The key ideas we need to introduce for the moment are *'conclusion'*, *'reason'* and *'establish'*. The passages in which we are interested all contain reasoning, they are all arguing a case. We argue a case by presenting grounds or *reasons* for accepting some *conclusion* (which need not come at the 'end' of the passage of course!) and the reasons are put forward in order to *establish* the conclusion, to *justify* it, *prove* it, *support* it, *demonstrate* it – or some such word. For present purposes we do not need to define these terms. The reader will be used to using such terms and for the present we want to rely on, and draw out, the reader's logical intuitions.

Of course the interesting question is always whether the reasons given *do* justify the conclusion, but it is impossible to answer that question until you have identified the conclusion and the reasons presented for it, so we now set a few simple exercises in doing this. It will help the reader to see what the problems are and to see why the 'machinery' introduced later in this book (especially in Chapters 2 and 8) is necessary if he or she writes out careful answers to each of the questions below before reading the answer which immediately follows.

The general form of the exercise is the same in each case. For each of the following passages the reader should first say whether it is an argument (whether it contains reasoning to a conclusion). For those which are arguments the reader should next say what their conclusion is, and then what reasons are given for that conclusion. Finally the reader should attempt to decide whether the reasoning establishes its conclusion in each case. It is important of course to say *why* you reach your decision.

Example (1)

If the money supply were to increase at less than 5% the rate of inflation would come down. Since the money supply is increasing at about 10% inflation will not come down.

This clearly is a piece of reasoning. It is the sort of argument which has been all too familiar in Britain in recent years, but, discounting this, the use of the word 'since' shows that what we have here is reasoning. The conclusion is,

inflation will not come down

and the reasons given are,

if the money supply were to increase at less than 5% the rate of inflation would come down

and,

the money supply is increasing at 10%.

This reasoning does *not* establish its conclusion: the reasons could both be true and the conclusion false. Something else could bring inflation down – for example a fall in the price of imports. There is nothing in the argument *as it is presented* to suggest that *only* a reduction in the rate of increase of the money supply will bring down inflation. Many people, perhaps under the influence of monetarism, construe this as a *good* argument (it has been used often by British politicians in recent years), but it isn't. In fact it is an example of a classical logical fallacy: this will become obvious later if it is not already.

Example (2)

If Russia were unsure about American reactions to an attack on Western Europe, and if her intention were to conquer Western Europe, she would create local *casus belli* (causes of war) but since she has not done this, she cannot intend to conquer Western Europe.

Again this is clearly a piece of reasoning to a conclusion; again the word 'since' is the linguistic clue that we have an argument here. The conclusion in this case is,

> [Russia] cannot intend to conquer Western Europe

and the reasons given for this conclusion are,

> If Russia were unsure about American reactions to an attack on Europe, and if her intention were to conquer Western Europe, she would create local *casus belli* but . . . she has not done this.

Again, this reasoning does *not* establish its conclusion: the reasons could be true and the conclusion false. Suppose the reasons *are true*, then it does follow that *either*,

> Russia cannot intend to conquer Western Europe

or,

> Russia is *not* at all unsure about American reactions to an attack on Europe.

But it may be that Russia is very sure about American reactions to such an attack, that Russia has no doubt at all that America is ready and willing to fight a European war if the Russians are so foolish as to provoke one. So it may be that the Russians would dearly love to conquer Western Europe but that they carefully avoid creating *casus belli* knowing only too well what the American reaction would be. Hence the reasons could be true and the conclusion false, so the reasoning does not establish its conclusion. This example is very like one which is considered later in this book and which is due to Enoch Powell, the British politician. He takes it to be a good argument. He would probably say in response to the above criticism that the argument has an *implicit* assumption, namely that,

> The Russians must be unsure about American reactions to an attack on Western Europe.

With this addition to the reasoning the conclusion would indeed be established if all the reasons were true: that is to say, there would be no way in which all the reasons could be true and the conclusion false. When people produce real arguments which are aimed at convincing others, there are nearly always *some* relevant *implicit* assumptions – as Powell would no doubt point out in this case. The only way to deal with such arguments is to handle them initially *as they are presented*, to extract and evaluate the argument on the basis of what is actually said or written. This process may reveal implicit assumptions and we shall explain how to deal with these in the course of considering examples throughout the book. In this case the soundness of the argument hinges on whether it is reasonable to assume that,

> the Russians must be unsure about American reactions to an attack on Western Europe

and we leave that question open.

> Example (3)
> If the civil population cannot be defended in the event of nuclear war, we do not need a civil defence policy. But, we *do* need a civil defence policy if 'deterrence' is to be a convincing strategy. Therefore deterrence is *not* a convincing strategy.

This is clearly a piece of reasoning: the word 'therefore' is the linguistic clue. The conclusion is,

> deterrence is not a convincing strategy

and the reasons given are,

> If the civil population cannot be defended in the event of nuclear war, we do not need a civil defence policy

and (but),

> we *do* need a civil defence policy if deterrence is to be a convincing strategy.

In this example the reasoning is a bit more complex. It contains two separate hypotheticals (a hypothetical is a sentence of the form '*if* this *then* that') and it can be tricky to put them together. (The notation of classical formal logic makes it easy but for that see the Appendix.) Once again, however, the reasoning (as it is presented) does *not* establish its conclusion: the reasons could be true and the conclusion false. It could well be true that,

> If the civil population cannot be defended in the event of nuclear war we do not need a civil defence policy

whilst *as a matter of fact* the civil population *can* be defended in the event of nuclear war (for example by having shelters for everyone, as in Switzerland). In that case the reasons given in this argument could well be true whilst the conclusion was false.

This example is adapted from a CND (Campaign for Nuclear Disarmament) pamphlet. No doubt CND would respond to the above by saying that the argument rests on the *implicit* assumption that,

> the civil population cannot be defended in the event of nuclear war.

No doubt they would also point out that since this is official government policy it is a reasonable assumption to make (in Britain). With this additional reason the argument does indeed become watertight if the reasons are all true.

Suppose it is true that,

> If the civil population cannot be defended in the event of nuclear war we do not need a civil defence policy

and suppose it is also true that,

> the civil population cannot be defended in the event of nuclear war

then it does indeed follow that,

> we do not need a civil defence policy.

But from this conclusion and the truth of the second reason (slightly re-written for convenience),

> if deterrence is to be a convincing strategy we *do* need a civil defence policy

it follows immediately that,

> deterrence is *not* a convincing strategy.

One could say much more about this little argument but for our present purposes it is sufficient to say that *as it stands* it does *not* prove its conclusion, but with its additional reason it does if all the reasons are true. If you really want to establish the conclusion by means of this argument you must also establish the truth of its reasons and it is a useful exercise to consider how you would do this. For example to show that,

> If the civil population cannot be defended in the event of nuclear war we do not need a civil defence policy

is true, presumably you have to show that no useful purpose would be served by having a civil defence policy – the civil population would not be defended, they would not be reassured, the enemy would not be deceived, and such like.

Example (4)

The materials of nature (air, earth, water) that remain untouched by human effort belong to no one and are not property. It follows that a thing can become someone's property only if he works and labours on it to change its natural state. From this I conclude that whatever a man improves by the labour of his hand and brain belongs to him and to him alone.

9

This is clearly a piece of argument. The linguistic clues are 'it follows that' and 'from this I conclude that': in fact it is a very famous argument from John Locke's *Second Treatise of Government*. He starts with a basic reason,

> The materials of nature (air, earth, water) that remain untouched by human effort belong to no-one and are not property

and from this he draws the conclusion (he says 'it follows that'),

> a thing can become someone's private property only if he works and labours on it to change its natural state.

We might call this an *intermediate* conclusion in Locke's argument because he then goes on to use it as a reason for a further conclusion – what we might call the *main* conclusion of the passage, namely,

> whatever a man improves by the labour of his hand and brain belongs to him and to him alone.

In fact this is a 'chain' of reasoning. A basic reason is presented and a conclusion is drawn from this: that conclusion is then the reason for a further conclusion, so the reasoning has a structure which might be pictured like this,

Basic reason
↓
Intermediate conclusion
↓
Main conclusion.

Such chains of reasons are very common in arguments and may be a good deal longer.

Again, the reasoning does *not* establish its main conclusion. The basic reason could be true and the main conclusion false. To see this let us suppose that the basic reason is true, that,

> The materials of nature (air, earth, water) that remain untouched by human effort belong to no-one and are not property.

Let us also suppose that it does indeed follow that,

> a thing can become someone's private property only if he works and labours on it to change its natural state.

(Some might want to criticise this move in the argument by insisting that something can become your private property if you are *given* it by someone else whose property it was, but we ignore this objection for the moment and assume Locke's intermediate conclusion is true.) Even so, Locke's main conclusion that,

> whatever a man improves by the labour of his hand and brain belongs to him and to him alone

does not follow. It does *not* follow from the fact that 'a thing can become someone's private property *only if* he labours on it' that '*if* he labours on something it becomes his private property'. It does not follow from the fact that 'you will get a good degree *only if* you are clever' that '*if* you are clever you will get a good degree' – you will have to work too! In general it doesn't follow from 'A will happen only if B does' that 'if B happens A will' – other conditions may have to be satisfied too. (As it might be put: B may be a *necessary* condition for A without being a *sufficient* condition.)

> Example (5)
> The only freedom which deserves the name is that of pursuing our own good in our own way, so long as we do not attempt to deprive others of theirs, or impede their efforts to obtain it. Each is the proper guardian of his own health, whether bodily, or mental and spiritual. Mankind are greater gainers suffering each other to live as seems good to themselves, rather than by compelling each to live as seems good to the rest.

This passage comes from John Stuart Mill's marvellous book *On Liberty*. Is it an argument? It is hard to say. What is the conclusion and which are the reasons? There are none of those words like 'therefore' and 'since' which indicate conclusions and reasons and yet one can't help feeling Mill is trying to persuade us of something! As it stands we have no way of telling which are reasons and which is conclusion though we might be able to do so if we looked at its larger context.

> Example (6)
> Radioactive elements disintegrate and eventually turn into lead. If matter has always existed there should be no radioactive elements left. The presence of uranium etc. is scientific proof that matter has not always existed.

This is clearly an argument: the linguistic clue is the phrase 'is scientific proof that'. (It comes from a pamphlet published by the Worldwide Church of God.) The conclusion is,

> matter has not always existed

and the reasons are,

(1) Radioactive elements disintegrate and eventually turn to lead.

(2) If matter has always existed there should be no radioactive elements left.

(3) Uranium [and other radioactive elements are still present].

It is not quite so easy to say what the 'structure' of the reasoning is, but a little reflection shows that although the text does not *say* '(1) therefore (2)' that is a very natural way of construing it: if it is true that,

Radioactive elements disintegrate and eventually turn to lead

then,

if all the matter which exists now has always existed there should be no radioactive elements left

seems to follow by impeccable logic (however long the half-life of a radioactive material is, it will disappear over an *infinite* time). The rest of the argument is equally irresistible now:

If matter has always existed there should be no radioactive elements left

but,

there are some

so,

matter has not always existed.

This is a very common move in reasoning: it is of the general shape,

if A then B but B is false

so,

A is false,

and anyone who understands the language knows that it is sound.

This is a beautiful piece of reasoning. It is hard to see how the reasons could be true and the conclusion false, so from a very simple piece of evidence, it seems to show that matter must have been *created* either at some particular time or continuously!

Example (7)

If the 'nuclear winter' scientists are right the population of Britain would be virtually eliminated in a nuclear war between the superpowers *even if Britain suffered no direct nuclear attack*. Quite apart

from the radioactive fall-out, we would suffer the darkness, the
sub-freezing temperatures and the mass starvation of a nuclear
winter.

This is an interesting example: although there are no linguistic cue words
like 'therefore', 'since', 'proves' (etc.) the second sentence is surely giving a
reason for accepting the first. It would read quite naturally if one inserted
'because' between the two sentences. There is, however, another test (besides
what one feels would read naturally) which one can use to decide whether
this is an argument: the test is to ask 'What would show the (apparent)
conclusion to be true?' or 'What would justify me in believing the (apparent)
conclusion?' In this case, 'What would show that,

> If the nuclear winter scientists are right the population of Britain
> * would be virtually eliminated in a nuclear war between the super-
> powers even if Britain suffered no direct nuclear attack

was true?'

The obvious answer is that something else would happen, as a result of
the super-power nuclear war which would eliminate most people in Britain
even if no nuclear weapons fell on Britain. Since that is precisely what the
second sentence in (7) describes,

> Quite apart from the radioactive fall-out, we would suffer the dark-
> ness, the sub-freezing temperatures and the mass starvation of a
> nuclear winter

it is reasonable to construe this as presenting a reason for * in (7) and a *good*
one since it asserts precisely what would be required to show * true.

> Example (8)
> Some people have solved their own unemployment problem by great
> ingenuity in hunting for a job or by willingness to work for less, so
> all the unemployed could do this.

This is clearly a piece of reasoning. The linguistic clue is the word 'so'. The
reason is,

> Some people have solved their own unemployment problem by great
> ingenuity in hunting for a job or by willingness to work for less

and the conclusion is,

> all the unemployed could solve their own unemployment problem
> by (etc.).

13

This argument has been used a good deal by British politicians in recent years, but is it a good argument? Certainly the reason given for the conclusion is *true*, but does the conclusion *follow* from it? Or could the reason be true and the conclusion false? It certainly doesn't follow from the fact that 'some people have done x' that 'everyone *could* do x': some people have run a mile in under four minutes but it doesn't follow that everyone could. Whether this analogous argument shows that our original argument is a bad one depends on whether it really is analogous – whether it exhibits the same logic. Does the original argument assume the principle that 'Some As are Bs so all As could be Bs' (clearly an unsound principle in general) or does it assume 'Some people have done x so everyone *could* do x' (clearly also an unsound principle) or is the argument specifically about unemployment and finding a job so that its justification is some economic truth or principle which is taken for granted (implicit)? Again, the way to proceed is to ask, 'What would *show* that,

> everyone *could* solve their unemployment problem by great in-
> genuity in hunting for a job or by willingness to work for less?'

Presumably the way to show this is by means of sound economic argument, based on well-established economic truths. Since the argument we are considering does not do this – does not do what is *required*, in order to establish its conclusion, it is *not* a good argument and its conclusion (may be true but) does not follow from the reason given. Passage (8) is still an argument, the use of the word 'so' makes that clear, but its reason could be true and its conclusion false – the argument does not establish its conclusion. Interestingly, this argument is discussed by Paul Samuelson in his widely used and influential economics textbook *Economics: An Introductory Analysis* where he presents it in a list of classic economic *fallacies*.

These examples are enough to begin with. We now introduce a more general approach.

2 · A general method of argument analysis

In Chapter 1 we considered several *examples*; most of them were arguing a case and we used them to point up various lessons about reasoning. Having given the reader a taste of argument analysis we now introduce a *general* method for analysing and evaluating arguments. The method lay behind what was said in Chapter 1 but the reader who tried the exercises should now be ready for a general account rather than the piecemeal approach.

The method which we describe applies to reasoning, or argument, as it actually occurs in natural language – in our case, English. We begin by describing how to recognise contexts in which reasoning is taking place (i.e. we say what the 'linguistic clues' are). We then describe how to uncover and display the *structure* of a piece of reasoning (whether it is a 'chain' of reasons etc.). Finally we explain, as far as possible, how to decide whether the reasoning is correct or incorrect.

At this stage we do no more than *outline* the method. We do this so that its essential lines may be boldly drawn and clearly grasped. Too many qualifications at this point might obscure the method's basic simplicity: if it is basically correct the place to develop and refine it is where the problems arise – in applying it to particular examples – and this is what we shall do. In subsequent chapters the basic skeleton will be extended and 'fleshed out' as the need arises. We shall do this in the course of showing how to apply the method to a number of instructive examples.

Nearly all the arguments we study in this book are arguments which have *actually been used* by someone with a view to *convincing* others about some matter. They are *real* arguments – not the 'made-up' kind with which logicians usually deal. They originate from various sources ranging from classic texts to newspapers. And they come from various fields, although broadly speaking they are from the social sciences, some natural sciences and philosophy.

I The language of reasoning

Some clues

Of course we use language for many purposes besides reasoning. We use it to report events, to tell jokes, to extend invitations, to tell stories, to make promises, to give orders, to ask questions, to issue instructions, to evoke emotions, to describe things, to entertain, and a thousand other things. (It is as well to note early on that in this book we are restricting our attention to a quite specific area of human activity, even if it is of very general importance.) Each of the activities mentioned above employs its own characteristic language – a language which helps us to grasp what is happening. For example 'Have you heard the one about . . . ?' is a common way to signal that a joke is coming (rather than a true report, etc.). 'Would you like to come and . . . ?' is a common way of issuing an invitation. 'Don't do that or else . . . !' is a common way of issuing a threat, and so on. Of course these same phrases can be used for quite different purposes and knowing the context in which they are used is often essential to understanding their meaning. It would be a very complex matter to say how in general we identify jokes, or threats or whatever (cf. J. L. Austin, *How To Do Things With Words*) and it should come as no surprise that the language of reasoning is complex too, but there are several helpful things which can be said.

If we are to focus attention on reasoning we must first describe how to distinguish contexts in which reasoning is taking place. Remember, reasoning or arguing a case consists in giving grounds or *reasons* for *conclusions*, and the reasons are put forward in order to *support*, *justify*, *establish*, *prove* or *demonstrate* the conclusion. (The author is trying to *convince* the audience by means of reasoning.) In natural languages it is not always easy to tell when an argument is being presented (remember some of the examples in Chapter 1), but all arguments have a conclusion and in English a conclusion is often signalled by the presence of one of the following words or phrases, which we call 'conclusion indicators':

Conclusion indicators

therefore . . .	I conclude that . . .
so . . .	. . . which implies that . . .
hence . . .	. . . which allows us to
thus . . .	infer that . . .
consequently . . .	it follows that . . .
which proves that . . .	. . . establishes the fact that . . .
justifies the belief that . . .	. . . demonstrates that . . .

We do not suggest that *whenever* these phrases are used a conclusion follows, but that they commonly *indicate* the presence of a conclusion. They are linguistic clues to what is intended in the text. Sometimes of course they have a quite different usage, for example 'It is thirty minutes *since* I started to read this book', 'I can only go *so* far', 'You ride a bicycle *thus*.' The conclusion indicators which we have listed, and similar ones, are only markers. They cannot be used mechanically to find conclusions: it usually requires a little judgement to decide whether they do in fact signal the presence of a conclusion. Of course, conclusions are sometimes presented with no conclusion indicator at all; instead the context shows that a conclusion is being presented.

Every argument also includes grounds or *reasons* for its conclusion. A reason is usually presented as being *true* and as being *a reason for* some conclusion. (For the sake of simplicity we begin with examples in which the reasons are *presented as being true* and we restrict the term 'reason' to such cases. However, in Chapter 8 we shall extend the term to include reasons which are *not* presented as being true but which are 'supposed for the sake of the argument'.) Words and phrases which are used in English to signal the presence of reasons – and which we shall call 'reason indicators' – include the following:

> *Reason indicators*
> because ...   the reason being ...
> for ...   firstly, ... secondly, ... (etc.)
> since ...   may be inferred from the fact that ...
> follows from the fact that ...

Again, we are not saying that *whenever* these words or phrases are used a reason is present, but that they commonly *indicate* the presence of a reason. They serve as markers which enable us, with the aid of a little judgement, to locate reasons. Again it is true that reasons are often presented without reason indicators but that the context shows that a reason is being given.

It will be convenient to have a phrase to refer to both reason and conclusion indicators so we shall call them both 'inference indicators' or 'argument indicators'.

Some complications

(i) The contexts in which we are interested are those in which an author or speaker presents some claim, the conclusion, as being supported or justified by other claims, the reasons. So whether certain claims are to be counted as conclusions or reasons depends solely on the author's apparent intentions – as he or she has expressed them. It does *not* matter whether the claims are *true* or *false*, nor does it matter whether the reasons *succeed* in justifying the conclusion: all that matters at this stage – where we are trying to identify what the argument is – is whether the text presents some claims as *reasons* for *conclusions*.

(ii) Sometimes reasoning takes place without the use of inference indicators to signal the presence of reasons and conclusions. Sometimes it is difficult to decide whether reasoning is taking place in such cases. We shall explain shortly (pp. 22f.) how to make that decision. In general when trying to decide whether a passage contains reasoning one should adopt the Principle of Charity. This says that if interpreting as reasoning a passage which is not *obviously* reasoning yields only bad arguments, assume it is *not* reasoning. (The rationale for this approach is that we are interested in finding out the truth about things rather than in scoring points off people.) Omitting inference indicators is sometimes a rhetorical device, used for purposes of emphasis, and is common with politicians and public speakers (cf. Weinberger's letter in Chapter 4).

(iii) There is an important complication which arises out of the different uses to which some inference indicators can be put. This is best explained by reference to the ambiguity of the word 'because' which sometimes signals the presence of a reason for a conclusion, but which sometimes signals the presence of a *causal claim* or, more generally, an *explanation* of some kind. Here are some examples.

(1) John broke the window because he tripped.

(2) John broke the window because he had forgotten his key.

(3) John must have broken the window because he was the only person in the house.

Assuming the natural context in each case the question is how to understand what is being said. Clearly, in neither case (1) nor case (2) does the use of 'because' signal that a reason is being given for a conclusion. In (1) the whole statement is a *causal* one: what *caused* John to break the window was that he tripped. The whole statement could well be the *conclusion* of some other reasoning but in itself it expresses no argument at all. In (2) the statement *explains* John's *reason* for breaking the window – explains why he did it. Again the whole statement could be the conclusion of further reasoning but in itself it expresses no argument. In (3), on the other hand, the natural way to construe it requires that we treat 'because' as a reason indicator. (The 'must' is a further clue. See below.)

(iv) So-called 'modal' words and phrases like 'must', 'cannot', 'impossible', 'necessarily', and so on are sometimes used to signal reasoning. For example:

The engine won't fire. The carburettor must be blocked.

Assuming the obvious context, the word 'must' is being used by the speaker to signal the fact that he is drawing a conclusion: he could have said, 'Since the engine won't fire, I conclude that the carburettor is blocked' and this would have conveyed much the same message (though rather stuffily!). Here is another example:

The world is full of suffering. God cannot exist.

(v) The conclusion is sometimes omitted from an argument. Here is an example:

All boxers suffer brain damage and Smith had a long career as a boxer. (Need I say more?)

The context usually makes the intended conclusion clear. Similarly, reasons are sometimes omitted from arguments even though they are being assumed as part of the argument. We have discussed several such cases in Chapter 1 and we shall say more about them later.

It follows immediately from paragraphs (i) to (v) that the dividing line between argument and non-argument is not sharp. It is often absolutely clear that a passage expresses an argument. Similarly it is often quite certain that a passage does *not* contain reasoning. But equally, it is often quite unclear whether it does or not.

II   The structure of reasoning

We have explained part of what is necessary in order to decide whether some piece of English contains reasoning, but in real life it is often surprisingly difficult to tell exactly what the argument is supposed to be, so we shall shortly describe a systematic and comprehensive method for extracting an argument from its text. Before we do this, however, we shall find it helpful to introduce some conventions for representing arguments, some terminology, and some elementary ideas about the *structure* of an argument.

Some conventions and terminology

We begin by dealing with the *simplest* cases of reasoning, cases in which the reasons are presented as *being true* and as being reasons for some conclusion. (We shall extend the present treatment to deal with 'suppositional' arguments in Chapter 8.) The notation we are about to introduce is not *essential* to argument analysis: those who hate symbols may stick to words, like 'therefore' etc., but they do need to grasp the ideas behind the notation.

If some claim, R, is presented as being a reason for accepting some conclusion, C, we shall write it like this:

$$R \rightarrow C$$

where the arrow is to be read as 'therefore' or some idiomatically appropriate synonym.

If several reasons are given for some conclusion there are two possibilities: the reasons may be presented as *jointly* supporting the conclusion (taken *together* they support the conclusion but each *in isolation* does not) or they may be presented as *independently* justifying it (so that if you accept *one* of the reasons the author expects you to accept the conclusion). An example of the latter case is the following:

> Russia will not occupy Britain because she does not want to. Anyway, the Americans would not let her.

Another example is this:

> Universities must expect further cuts because they have suffered less than other sectors of education, but even if this were not so, they should expect further cuts because they are not sufficiently vocationally oriented.

Examples where the reasons are presented as *jointly* supporting the conclusion were common in Chapter 1; (1), (2), (3) and (6) were just such examples.

Let us suppose that two reasons, R_1 and R_2, are given for some conclusion C, then we shall represent the cases we have just described as follows. If R_1 and R_2 are *joint* reasons for C we write,

$$\underbrace{R_1 + R_2}_{}$$
$$C$$

but if R_1 and R_2 are *independent* reasons for C we write,

$$R_1 \qquad R_2$$
$$\searrow \quad \swarrow$$
$$C$$

(If it is not easy to judge which the author intends, choose whichever interpretation yields the *better* argument, i.e. whichever is the hardest to fault.)

This is all the notation we need for the moment. We shall extend it as we need to. Of course, complex arguments may combine the cases we have described in a variety of ways. In particular, the conclusion of one part of the argument may be used as a reason for some further conclusion (as in example (4), Chapter 1). We shall call such a conclusion an *intermediate conclusion*: it is presented both as a conclusion from prior reasons and as a reason for a subsequent conclusion. If a reason, R, is given for some conclusion, C, and the argument contains *no* intermediate conclusion between R and C, then we shall call R an *immediate reason* for C. Those reasons which are presented without themselves being supported by other reasons, we shall call the *basic reasons* or *premises* of the argument. A conclusion which is not used in the argument to support any further conclusion will be called a *final conclusion* or *main conclusion*.

So, in summary, one might have an argument whose structure is represented by the following *argument diagram* (as we shall call it):

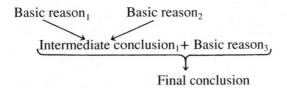

Basic reason$_1$ and basic reason$_2$ are not immediate reasons for the final conclusion, but intermediate conclusion$_1$ and basic reason$_3$ *are*.

Those who hate notation and diagrams can do everything using appropriate words and writing the reasoning in linear form, so the example diagrammed above might look as follows:

    (1) Basic reason$_1$.

    (2) Basic reason$_2$.

Either (1) or (2) is sufficient to justify (3), therefore

    (3) Intermediate conclusion$_1$.

(3) is true and

    (4) Basic reason$_3$.

Therefore

    (5) Final conclusion.

Given a piece of reasoning in ordinary English, it is helpful either to draw its *argument diagram* or to write it in equivalent linear form. Doing so forces us to clarify exactly what the argument is – and that is its main purpose. It is also true however that the structure which is revealed by this process may be important in deciding whether the argument is sound. We shall return to this point later but we have now progressed far enough to outline a method for extracting an argument from its context, so we do this next.

The method of extracting arguments outlined

It is easy to underestimate how difficult it can be to extract an author's intended argument from a written, natural language text, but given a piece of ordinary English the following method will help to determine its conclusion(s), its reason(s) and the structure of its argument(s) if these are not already clear.

    (1) Read through the text to get its sense, circling – |thus| – all the inference indicators as you go.

    (2) Underline – <u>thus</u> – any clearly indicated conclusions, and bracket – ⟨thus⟩ – any clearly indicated reasons. (It helps at this stage if one tries to summarise the argument.)

    (3) Identify what you take to be the main conclusion and mark it C. (There may be more than one.)

(4) Starting with C, ask 'What immediate reasons are presented in the text for accepting C?' or 'Why (in the text) am I asked to believe C?' Use inference indicators to help answer the question. If the question is hard to answer because the author's intentions are not transparent (i.e. they are neither explicitly shown by argument indicators nor obvious from the context), then ask the Assertibility Question,

(AQ) What argument or evidence would justify me in asserting the conclusion C? (What would I have to know or believe to be justified in accepting C?)

Having done this look to see if the author asserts or clearly assumes these same claims (reasons). If he does it is reasonable (and accords with the Principle of Charity) to construe him as having intended the same argument. If he doesn't you have no rational way of reconstructing his argument (on the basis of the text alone).

(5) For each reason, R, already identified, repeat the process described in step (4) above. Do this until you are left with only basic reasons and then display the argument(s) in a clear way (say, by means of a diagram or in linear form).

This is the basic outline of the method, but several further points need to be made if it is to be properly understood. We present some general ones first and reserve some specific ones to the next section.

(a) Notice that the issue is 'What does *the text/author* present as a reason, conclusion, etc.?' not 'What is a good reason, etc.?' But notice also that in order to find the answer to the first question we may have to ask ourselves the second one. To put the point another way,

(b) inference indicators may make an author's intentions completely clear (quite certain); context may do the same; but if this is not the case the only way you can divine the author's intentions (given only the text) is to construct the *best* argument you can and ask whether the author could be construed as presenting it. It follows that in such cases,

(c) this is not a mechanical method which yields an argument automatically; it requires judgement and imagination.

(d) Furthermore, the extent to which you can grasp the author's intended meaning will depend on your understanding of the language and your knowledge of the subject and so will be a matter of degree.

(e) The philosophical justification for the use of the Assertibility Question is based on the assumption that

* If you understand a proposition you must be able to give at least some account of how you could decide whether it was true or false, what argument or evidence would show it to be true or false (otherwise you don't understand it at all).

We shall return to this principle often in what follows, but we leave it unsupported for the moment.

The structure of reasons and conclusions

Just as arguments are logically complex, so are their reasons and conclusions: they too exhibit logical structure. We shall say very little here about these 'internal' structures (see the Appendix for a fuller account) but some things must be said in order to avoid confusion in applying the method just outlined. In short there are cases where the internal structure of a sentence may obscure what is to *count* as a reason or a conclusion.

In order to discuss these cases we shall find it convenient to have just one word to describe the case when an author claims that something is true (presents it as being true); we shall say that such a claim is *asserted* and we shall call it an *assertion*. (For a fuller explanation, see Appendix, p. 173.)

Suppose that police have evidence leading them to the conclusion that,

Either Jones killed Brown, or Smith did   (J or S)

For present purposes, the important thing to notice is that the police are *not* asserting that Jones did it, *nor* are they asserting that Smith did it: they are asserting the whole 'disjunction' (as logicians call it) 'J or S'. So in identifying reasons and conclusions, disjunctions must not be broken up into their parts. (Of course, if Smith produces a cast-iron alibi, this, together with the police conclusion 'J or S', yields an argument with the *asserted* conclusion, 'Jones killed Brown' – but that is a further stage in the argument.)

Disjunctions don't often create problems in argument analysis, but hypotheticals do. Remember that a hypothetical is a sentence of the form 'if . . . then . . .'. Clearly, when someone says,

† If [the money supply is increasing in Britain], then {the rate of inflation in Britain will increase}

they are *neither* asserting that the money supply is increasing in Britain *nor* asserting that the rate of inflation in Britain will increase. They are asserting the whole hypothetical, 'If [A] then {B}'. Such hypotheticals are very common and very important in reasoning. Partly because of this the 'parts' of a hypothetical have special names, the [A] part, the part governed by 'if', is called the 'antecedent' and the {B} part the 'consequent'. (In the hypothetical 'B, if A' the B part is still the 'consequent' etc.) There are two points we need to make about hypotheticals here.

Firstly, a hypothetical may occur as either a reason or a conclusion in the course of a piece of reasoning (e.g. † above could). In that case the hypothetical *should not be broken up* into antecedent and consequent. What is functioning as a reason, or conclusion – what is being asserted – is the whole hypothetical. Here is an example where the three reasons and the conclusion are all hypotheticals.

> If every event has a cause then all my actions are caused. If all my actions are caused, I am not free to do what I choose. In that case I am not responsible for my actions. So if every event has a cause, I am not responsible for my actions.

Secondly, there are numerous phrases which signal the presence of a hypothetical statement: we mention some of them now (and call them 'hypothetical indicators'),

> *Hypothetical indicators*
> if . . . then . . .
> suppose . . . then . . .
> unless . . . then . . .
> . . . provided that . . .
> . . . on the condition that . . .

As with inference indicators, these phrases are markers which have to be used with understanding.

Much more could be said about the internal logical structure of sentences but we have said all we need for the present. Further explanation is provided in the Appendix and there are many excellent logic texts which develop the subject in various ways, but more detail is unnecessary for our purposes at this stage.

This completes our outline of the method for extracting an argument from its context; we now move on to the method for evaluating it.

III Tests for a good argument

Once it is clear what argument we are considering then we are in a position to test whether it establishes its conclusion. Remember that we are still restricting our attention to those arguments in which the reasons are presented as being true.

In real arguments the first thing people normally challenge is the truth of the premises. If the premises of an argument are not true (or at least *one* must be true in the case of independent reasons) then they cannot establish their conclusion, so the argument loses much of its interest. (Although in theoretical arguments – or in contexts where you don't know if the premisses are true – it may still be interesting to ask, 'If the premisses *were* true would they establish the conclusion?') So the first condition an argument must satisfy if it is to establish its conclusion is,

> I All its premisses must be true – except that where independent reasons are given for some conclusion at least *one* must be true.

Now let us suppose that the argument we are considering has true premisses, so that it satisfies condition I. At this point in real arguments, people who think the argument fails to establish its conclusion will say things like, 'the conclusion is *not justified*' or 'the argument is *not sound*' or 'the conclusion *does not follow* from the premisses'. It is easy to think of an argument which has true premisses but whose conclusion does not follow, for example,

(1) All women are mortal

and (2) The American President is mortal $\underbrace{1+2}_{3}$

therefore

(3) The American President is a woman.

(Ask yourself why the conclusion does *not* follow in this example. Does the conclusion follow in 'All *men* are mortal and the American President is mortal so the American President is a man?')

So the second condition an argument must satisfy if it is to establish its conclusion is,

> II The conclusion must *follow* from the premisses

and we must now explain how one decides whether this is the case.

The intuitive idea is this: a conclusion *follows from* its premisses if and only if the truth of the premisses *guarantees* the truth of the conclusion, so the test to apply is,

> Could the premisses be true and the conclusion false?

If the answer to the question is 'Yes' the conclusion does *not* follow from its premisses. If the answer is 'No' then the truth of the premisses guarantees the truth of the conclusion, the conclusion *follows from* its premisses – and if you accept the premisses you must accept the conclusion.

An illustrative example

To illustrate how the test works consider an example. Let A, B and C be politicians or policies of your choice and ask whether the conclusion follows in this argument;

(1) Most electors prefer A to B

and (2) Most electors prefer B to C

therefore

(3) Most electors prefer A to C.

Could the premisses be true and the conclusion false? Can we describe circumstances in which this is the case? Yes, with a little ingenuity we can. If we number the first preference of each elector 1, the second 2 and the third 3, the following table shows how each third of the electorate might vote:

	$\frac{1}{3}$	$\frac{1}{3}$	$\frac{1}{3}$
1	A	C	B
2	B	A	C
3	C	B	A

In this case,

> 66% of the electorate prefers A to B
>
> and 66% of the electorate prefers B to C,
>
> *but* 66% of the electorate prefers *C to A.*

This demonstrates that the premisses could be true whilst the conclusion is false, so the conclusion does *not follow*. Incidentally this is a classic example from the theory of voting. Most people are surprised to discover that what seems a reasonable argument at first sight is so clearly unsound.

This example shows how our test is to be applied in one case. It is not so easy to explain how to apply it in all cases. Indeed we shall need to revise it in order to do this.

A revised test

Consider an orthodox scientific case for believing that the earth is not flat but is roughly spherical. If you apply our test *strictly*, you might say, 'I suppose all the reasons could be true and the conclusion false.' In that case you may well be launched into philosophy but you will make very little progress in science!

Consider the historical case for believing that Hitler died in Berlin in 1945 (see p. 193 for a statement of the case). If you apply our test strictly you might again say, 'I suppose the reasons could all be true and the conclusion false.' In that case you will learn very little history.

Consider the case for believing that certain things *will* happen, that President Reagan will not have a third term as President or that the sun will continue to rise; consider the case for believing that someone writhing on the ground with a terrible injury is in pain. In these cases too, if you apply the standard test strictly you might say, 'I suppose all the reasons could be true and the conclusion false.' In that case you will make very little progress in learning what we can about the future and about 'other minds'.

Such scepticism is quite remote from *normal* – and *appropriate* – standards of argument. For this reason we shall revise our test so that it makes explicit reference to these standards: we shall revise it to read,

> Could the premises be true and the conclusion false judging by appropriate standards of evidence or appropriate standards of what is possible?

Furthermore, we shall use the Assertibility Question in order to decide the appropriate standards:

AQ: What argument or evidence would justify me in asserting the conclusion? (What would I have to know or believe to be justified in accepting it?)

Obviously, the kind of answer given is different in different contexts: claims about the past, or about the future, or about causal connections, or about other people's intentions, or about mathematics (etc.), all these have different standards of proof. The considerations which establish an historical claim conclusively (e.g. Hitler died in Berlin in 1945) will in general be different in kind from those required to justify a claim about the future (e.g. Prince Charles will become king if he outlives his mother), and both will differ again from the considerations appropriate to a causal claim (e.g. increased money supply causes inflation), or a claim about intentions (e.g. the Russians intend to attack the USA with nuclear weapons – see Chapter 4). Besides differences of this sort, there are different views about what can be known and how things can be known. There is no concealing all these differences. They are best brought out into the open and that is what our method aims to achieve. Only in this way can disagreements be resolved and the truth revealed.

It is worth returning for a moment to some of the remarks made at the beginning of Chapter 1. When you use the method of this chapter – the revised test and the Assertibility Question – you have to make a judgement about 'appropriate standards'. That judgement will be *yours*; it is a judgement which requires justification and which is open to criticism. Set too severe a standard and it will seem that nothing can be known with certainty; set too unimaginative a standard and you will be led easily into error. But the method can be employed by *anyone*, at their level of understanding (cf. principle * p. 23); given an understanding of the language and imagination it is surprising how far you can get. In effect the method requires you to enter into the realm of philosophy, in particular the 'theory of knowledge', though you need no expertise in formal philosophy. We shall show how the method works out in a number of instructive examples in the rest of the book. Much of our discussion will be about choosing 'appropriate standards': these are not established, objective facts, nor are they arbitrary, they require a good deal of argument. The concluding chapter will then attempt to provide a philosophical justification for the method outlined here and applied in the intervening chapters.

3 · A first example – from Thomas Malthus

> If the present world population doubles itself every twenty-five years, in 150 years' time there will be standing room only since the number of people will be greater than the number of square metres on the land surface of the Earth.

In this chapter we show how to analyse and evaluate a very famous argument due to Thomas Malthus (1766–1834) and we apply and develop the method of Chapter 2 in the process. Malthus's father was a friend of David Hume and of Jean-Jacques Rousseau, both of whom visited his house together when Thomas was only three weeks old. It was under the influence of Rousseau's *Emile* that his father had Thomas privately educated until he became an undergraduate at Jesus College, Cambridge, at the age of eighteen, in 1784. He graduated well in mathematics in 1788, and he took Holy Orders in the same year. His *Essay on the Principle of Population as it affects the Future Improvement of Society with Remarks on the Speculations of Mr. Godwin, M. Condorcet and other Writers* was first published in 1798. There was much discussion at that time – in the wake of the French Revolution – about the possibility of establishing a society based on social and economic equality. Malthus's *Essay* originated as a polemic against such utopian speculations. His argument was not new,

> The most important argument that I shall adduce is certainly not new. The principles on which it depends have been explained in part by Hume, and more at large by Dr. Adam Smith.

We now present Malthus's basic argument. Our extract consists of most of Chapter 1 of the *Essay* and is the part which Malthus explicitly described in his text as 'an outline of the principal argument of the essay'.

I Thomas Malthus, *An Essay on the Principle of Population,* Chapter 1

(Successive paragraphs are labelled to enable easy reference to them later.)

(a) In entering upon the argument I must premise that I put out of the question, at present, all mere conjectures, that is, all suppositions, the probable realization of which cannot be inferred upon any just philosophical grounds. A writer may tell me that he thinks man will ultimately become an ostrich. I cannot properly contradict him. But before he can expect to bring any reasonable person over to his opinion, he ought to shew that the necks of mankind have been gradually elongating, that the lips have grown harder and more prominent, that the legs and feet are daily altering their shape, and that the hair is beginning to change into stubs of feathers. And till the probability of so wonderful a conversion can be shewn, it is surely lost time and lost eloquence to expatiate on the happiness of man in such a state; to describe his powers, both of running and flying, to paint him in a condition where all narrow luxuries would be contemned, where he would be employed only in collecting the necessaries of life, and where, consequently, each man's share of labour would be light, and his portion of leisure ample.

(b)   I think I may fairly make two postulata.

First, That food is necessary to the existence of man.

Secondly, That the passion between the sexes is necessary and will remain nearly in its present state.

(c)   These two laws, ever since we have had any knowledge of mankind, appear to have been fixed laws of our nature, and, as we have not hitherto seen any alteration in them, we have no right to conclude that they will ever cease to be what they now are, without an immediate act of power in that Being who first arranged the system of the universe, and for the advantage of his creatures, still executes, according to fixed laws, all its various operations.

(d)   I do not know that any writer has supposed that on this earth man will ultimately be able to live without food. But Mr. Godwin has conjectured that the passion between the sexes may in time be extinguished. As, however, he calls this part of his work a deviation into the land of conjecture, I will not dwell longer upon it at present than to say that the best arguments for the perfectibility of man are drawn from contemplation of the great progress that he has already made from the savage state and the difficulty of saying where he is to stop. But towards the extinction of the passion between the sexes, no progress whatever has hitherto been made. It appears to exist in as much force at present as it did two thousand or four thousand years ago. There are individual exceptions now as there always have been. But, as these exceptions do not appear to increase in number, it would surely be a very unphilosophical mode of arguing, to infer merely from the existence of an exception, that the exception would, in time, become the rule, and the rule the exception.

(e) Assuming then, my postulata as granted, I say that the power of population is indefinitely greater than the power in the earth to produce subsistence for man.

(f) Population, when unchecked, increases in a geometrical ratio. Subsistence increases only in an arithmetical ratio. A slight acquaintance with numbers will show the immensity of the first power in comparison of the second.

(g) By that law of our nature which makes food necessary to the life of man, the effects of these two unequal powers must be kept equal.

(h) This implies a strong and constantly operating check on population from the difficulty of subsistence. This difficulty must fall somewhere and must necessarily be severely felt by a large portion of mankind.

(j) Through the animal and vegetable kingdoms, nature has scattered the seeds of life abroad with the most profuse and liberal hand. She has been comparatively sparing in the room and the nourishment necessary to rear them. The germs of existence contained in this spot of earth, with ample food and ample room to expand in, would fill millions of worlds in the course of a few thousand years. Necessity, that imperious all pervading law of nature, restrains them within the prescribed bounds. The race of plants and the race of animals shrink under this great restrictive law. And the race of man cannot, by any efforts of reason, escape from it. Among plants and animals its effects are waste of seed, sickness, and premature death. Among mankind, misery and vice. The former, misery, is an absolutely necessary consequence of it. Vice is a highly probable consequence, and we therefore see it abundantly prevail, but it ought not, perhaps, to be called an absolutely necessary consequence. The ordeal of virtue is to resist all temptation to evil.

(k)   This natural inequality of the two powers of population and of production in the earth and that great law of our nature which must constantly keep their effects equal form the great difficulty that to me appears insurmountable in the way to the perfectibility of society. All other arguments are of slight and subordinate consideration in comparison of this. I see no way by which man can escape from the weight of this law which pervades all animated nature. No fancied equality, no agrarian regulations in their utmost extent, could remove the pressure of it even for a single century. And it appears, therefore, to be decisive against the possible existence of a society, all the members of which should live in ease, happiness, and comparative leisure, and feel no anxiety about providing the means of subsistence for themselves and families.

(m)   Consequently, if the premises are just, the argument is conclusive against the perfectibility of the mass of mankind.

(n)   I have thus sketched the general outline of the argument, but I will examine it more particularly and I think it will be found that experience, the true source and foundation of all knowledge, invariably confirms its truth.

Our immediate interest is in getting clear exactly what Malthus's argument is and in showing the reader how far it is possible to get by reading carefully and thinking things through. Some readers may feel that they can answer the questions below without recourse to the method described in Chapter 2, but we hope that others will find that it enables them to answer questions which would otherwise defeat them. In either case it will help the reader to assess the utility of the method if he or she writes careful answers to the following questions before reading the answers revealed in sections II and III below.

Questions on Malthus's argument

(1) What is Malthus's main conclusion?
(2) What is his argument for this conclusion?
(3) Do his postulates function as basic reasons in his argument?
(4) What would show the following:

      (i) 'Subsistence increases only in an arithmetical ratio' is *true*;

     (ii) 'Population, when unchecked, increases in a geometrical ratio' is *true*; and

    (iii) 'Food is necessary to the existence of man' is *false*?

(5) Does Malthus's argument establish its conclusions?

II Extracting the argument from Malthus's text

To extract the argument from Thomas Malthus's text we follow the steps described in Chapter 2. We first circle all the explicit argument indicators. The obvious ones are 'First' (b), 'Secondly' (b), 'This implies' (h), 'therefore' (j) and again in (k) and 'consequently' (m). The reader may fail to notice that 'By' (g) is functioning as a reason indicator or may judge that 'Assuming then my postulata as granted, I say that' is a conclusion indicator. Neither would affect the operation of our method. At this stage we locate argument indicators in order to help us to find arguments, but subsequent, closer, attention may well reveal less common inference indicators which were overlooked at first reading.

We next bracket any clearly indicated reasons and underline clearly indicated conclusions using inference indicators to speed our judgement. Again, this is an intermediate stage in reaching our final judgement. Some reasons and conclusions will be clear – others less so. For example it may be unclear at this stage what reason 'This implies' in (h) refers to, but we hope that closer scrutiny of the argument will settle it shortly.

The next step is to identify what you take to be the main conclusion and to mark it. The reader may think there are several possible candidates but in fact Malthus is quite explicit. He says, in (m),

> Consequently, if the premises are just, the argument is conclusive against the perfectibility of the mass of mankind.

The only query concerns what he means by the 'perfectibility of the mass of mankind', but it is clear from the context that this is what is expanded in the previous sentence, so we take his main conclusion to be,

>   against the possible existence of a society, all the members of which
> C should live in ease, happiness and comparative leisure, and feel no anxiety about providing the means of subsistence for themselves and families.

The next step is to trace Malthus's reasoning for this conclusion and we begin by asking 'What immediate reasons are presented in the text for accepting C?' What is it that,

appears therefore to be decisive against the possible existence of
a society, all the members of which should live in ease, happiness
[etc.]?

Looking back through the preceding sentences we see that,

No fancied equality, . . . [etc.] . . . could remove the pressure

and that,

no . . . man . . . can escape . . . this law

and that,

All other arguments are slight in comparison with them

and it is clear that the basic argument is,

This natural inequality of the two powers of population and of production in the earth and that great law of nature which must constantly keep their effects equal form the great difficulty that appears
to me insurmountable in the way to the perfectibility of society.

Whether this is a compelling argument is a question we shall come to
shortly but his language makes it clear that this *is* Malthus's argument and
that is the question we are interested in at present.

In attempting to extract his full reasoning we next ask 'What immediate
reasons are presented by Malthus for believing in the "Natural inequality
of the two powers of population and of production in the earth"?' If one
searches back through the text his language makes it clear that his reasons
are,

Population, when unchecked, increases in a geometrical ratio. Subsistence increases only in an arithmetical ratio.   (paragraph (f))

The 'great law of nature' Malthus has in mind is clearly,

that law of our nature which makes food necessary to the life of
man   (paragraph (g))

which is also his first postulate. Thus the reasoning we have so far is,

(1) Population, when unchecked, increases in a geometrical ratio
and (2) Subsistence increases only in an arithmetical ratio
therefore
(3) There is a natural inequality of the two powers of population and of
production in the earth.

(3) is true *and*

    (4) It is a law of our nature that food is necessary to the life of man

therefore

    C Society is not perfectible

and the argument structure is diagrammed as follows,

$$\underbrace{1+2}_{}$$
$$\downarrow$$
$$\underbrace{3+4}_{}$$
$$\downarrow$$
$$C$$

Before asking for the further reasons Malthus gives for (1), (2) and (4) we note that he clearly amplifies the inference from (3) and (4) to C. His language after paragraph (f) suggests that we should insert the following steps,

    (3) There is a natural inequality of the two powers of population and of production in the earth

and (4) It is a law of our nature that food is necessary to the life of man

therefore

    (5) The effects of these two unequal powers must be kept equal

therefore

    (6) There must be a strong and constantly operating check on population from the difficulty of subsistence

therefore

    (7) This difficulty must fall somewhere and must necessarily be severely felt by a large portion of mankind. Its effects are necessarily misery and probably vice

therefore

    C There cannot be a society all the members of which live in ease, happiness and comparative leisure [etc.].

(In short, this elaboration of the argument is justified as follows. In paragraph (g) the word 'By' is clearly being used as a reason indicator; this usage is common in mathematics, as in 'By the previous theorem'. It is now clear what the phrase 'This implies' in paragraph (h) refers to. It seems natural to insert 'therefore' between the first and second sentence in paragraph (h) and the inferences to and from (5) are already summarised in the basic argument in paragraph (k) but are easier to see in their expanded form around paragraph (g).)

Let us return now to seeking Malthus's reasons for the basic reasons we have so far. We begin by asking 'What immediate reasons are presented in the text for accepting that population, when unchecked, increases in a geometrical ratio?' His language may suggest that Malthus derives this claim from his second postulate. The second postulate is

> That the passion between the sexes is necessary, and will remain nearly in its present state,

and Malthus says, in paragraph (e),

> Assuming then, my postulata as granted, I say that the power of population is indefinitely greater than the power in the earth to produce subsistence for man.

The case is difficult to decide: Malthus does not explicitly derive this basic reason from his second postulate, nor is it quite clear from the context that this is what he intends. We leave the question open for the moment and we shall return to it in the next section.

Turning to the claim,

> Subsistence increases only in an arithmetical ratio

there appear to be no reasons given for this in our extract so we must take it as a basic reason.

Moving on to his first postulate

> That food is necessary to the existence of man

one might think that it is too obvious to need justification and since Malthus calls it a 'postulate' one might expect him to take the same view. On the other hand he may be giving a reason for it in paragraph (c) where he says,

> These two laws, ever since we have had any knowledge of mankind, appear to have been fixed laws of our nature, and, as we have not hitherto seen any alteration in them, we have no right to conclude that they will ever cease to be what they now are [etc.].

The reasoning is not explicit, context does not make it obvious so as before we leave the question open until the next section. So the argument we have extracted from Malthus's text is the one given above; its structure is displayed in the following diagram:

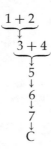

The passage, marked up according to the method of Chapter 2 in the process of extracting the argument, will look somewhat as follows:

> In entering upon the argument I must premise that I put out of the question, at present, all mere conjectures, that is, all suppositions, the probable realization of which cannot be inferred upon any just philosophical grounds. A writer may tell me that he thinks man will ultimately become an ostrich. I cannot properly contradict him. But before he can expect to bring any reasonable person over to his opinion, he ought to shew that the necks of mankind have been gradually elongating, that the lips have grown harder and more prominent, that the legs and feet are daily altering their shape and that the hair is beginning to change into stubs of feathers. And till the probability of so wonderful a conversion can be shewn, it is surely lost time and lost eloquence to expatiate on the happiness of man in such a state; to describe his powers, both of running and flying, to paint him in a condition where all narrow luxuries would be contemned, where he would be employed only in collecting the necessaries of life, and where, consequently, each man's share of labour would be light, and his portion of leisure ample.
>
> I think I may fairly make two postulata.
>
> 4 ⌐First,⌐ that ⟨food is necessary to the existence of man.⟩
>
> ⌐Secondly,⌐ that ⟨the passion between the sexes is necessary and will remain nearly in its present state.⟩
>
> These two laws, ever since we have had any knowledge of mankind, appear to have been fixed laws of our nature, and, as we have not hitherto seen any alteration in them, we have no right to

conclude that they will ever cease to be what they now are, without an immediate act of power in that Being who first arranged the system of the universe, and for the advantage of his creatures, still executes, according to fixed laws, all its various operations.

I do not know that any writer has supposed that on this earth man will ultimately be able to live without food. But Mr. Godwin has conjectured that the passion between the sexes may in time be extinguished. As, however, he calls this part of his work a deviation into the land of conjecture, I will not dwell longer upon it at present than to say that the best arguments for the perfectibility of man are drawn from a contemplation of the great progress that he has already made from the savage state and the difficulty of saying where he is to stop. But towards the extinction of the passion between the sexes, no progress whatever has hitherto been made. It appears to exist in as much force at present as it did two thousand or four thousand years ago. There are individual exceptions now as there always have been. But, as these exceptions do not appear to increase in number, it would surely be a very unphilosophical mode of arguing, to infer merely from the existence of an exception, that the exception would, in time, become the rule, and the rule the exception.

Assuming then, my postulata as granted, I say that the power of population is indefinitely greater than the power in the earth to produce subsistence for man.

1 ⟨Population, when unchecked, increases in a geometrical ratio.⟩

$\frac{1+2}{3}$ 2 ⟨Subsistence increases only in an arithmetical ratio.⟩ A slight acquaintance with numbers will shew the immensity of the first power in comparison of the second.

4 ⟨By⟩ ⟨that law of our nature which makes food necessary to the life of man,⟩ ⟨the effects of these two unequal powers must be kept
5 equal.⟩

$\frac{1+2}{\frac{3+4}{5}}$ 6 ⟨This implies⟩ ⟨a strong and constantly operating check on
7 population from the difficulty of subsistence.⟩ ⟨therefore⟩ ⟨this difficulty must fall somewhere and must necessarily be severely felt by a large portion of mankind.⟩

5
↓
6
↓
7
↓
C

Through the animal and vegetable kingdoms, nature has scattered the seeds of life abroad with the most profuse and liberal hand. She has been comparatively sparing in the room and the nourishment necessary to rear them. The germs of existence contained in this spot of earth, with ample food and ample room to expand in, would fill millions of worlds in the course of a few thousand years. Necessity, that imperious all pervading law of nature, restrains them within the prescribed bounds. The race of plants and the race of animals shrink under this great restrictive law. And the race of man cannot, by any efforts of reason, escape from it. Among plants and animals its effects are waste of seed, sickness, and premature death. Among mankind, misery and vice. The former, misery, is an absolutely necessary consequence of it. Vice is a highly probable consequence, and we therefore see it abundantly prevail, but it ought not, perhaps, to be called an absolutely necessary consequence. The ordeal of virtue is to resist all temptation to evil.

3
4

3 + 4
C

⟨This natural inequality of the two powers of population and of production in the earth⟩ and ⟨that great law of our nature⟩ which must constantly keep their effects equal form the great difficulty that to me appears insurmountable in the way to the perfectibility of society. All other arguments are of slight and subordinate consideration in comparison of this. I see no way by which man can escape from the weight of this law which pervades all animated nature. No fancied equality, no agrarian regulations in their utmost extent, could remove the pressure of it even for a single century. And it appears, therefore, to be decisive against the possible

C existence of a society, all the members of which should, live in ease, happiness, and comparative leisure, and feel no anxiety about providing the means of subsistence for themselves and families.

Consequently, if the premises are just, the argument is conclusive against the perfectibility of the mass of mankind.

I have thus sketched the general outline of the argument, but I will examine it more particularly and I think it will be found that experience, the true source and foundation of all knowledge, invariably confirms its truth.

III 'Tests for a good argument' applied to Malthus

Now that we are as clear as we can be about Malthus's argument we can ask whether it establishes its conclusion. If the argument is to do this its premisses must be *true* and its conclusion must *follow* from them. Since the focus of our interest in this book is on the method of analysis rather than on the substance of the arguments we do not usually make judgements about whether an argument's premisses or conclusion *are* true or false. However, in order to apply the test, 'Could the premisses be true and the conclusion false judging by appropriate standards (etc.)?' we have to understand them, i.e. we have to have at least some idea what *would* show them true or false (since we use the Assertibility Question to decide 'appropriate' standards).

In the case of Malthus's argument we shall spend some time over the meaning of his three premisses: we shall do this partly because two are semi-technical and need explanation, but mainly because it will show in our first example how the principle * (p. 23) and the Assertibility Question work in some instructive cases. We look first at the easiest example,

Subsistence increases only in an arithmetical ratio.

'Subsistence' refers to the basic necessities of human life – food, warmth, clothing and shelter – the most important being food. To say that it 'increases in an arithmetical ratio' is to say that starting with some initial quantity (possibly zero) a constant quantity is *added* in each successive period. For example, suppose that in its first year of cultivation a piece of land yields ten sacks of corn and that in its second year it produces eleven, in the third twelve, and so on, each year's output being the previous year's output *plus one additional sack*: this land would be increasing its annual output of corn 'in an arithmetical ratio'. A graph of such an 'arithmetical progression' (as it is called) is a straight line like the one in the diagram below – which is the graph of our example.

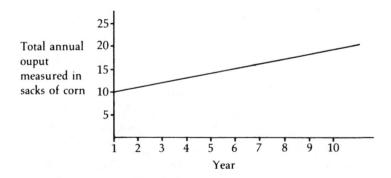

The steepness of the slope reflects the size of the annual increment.

Clearly then, in order to decide whether 'subsistence increases only in an arithmetical ratio' one must look at the historical record to see how food production (etc.) has increased over time – with new land being taken in hand, new production methods being employed, new resources being harnessed, and so on. One must pay careful attention to periods when production has increased very rapidly because these threaten the claim. Not only should one look at the historical record and at the trends thus revealed but one should also attempt to 'fit' these into our general pattern of beliefs by showing that they imply and are implied by other things we know and believe, i.e. one should try to explain them and show how they explain other things. The historical record may be hard to read but it could bear out Malthus's claim. It could also refute it; for example it might show that production increases in line with population even when population increases geometrically. One can even think of a reason why this might be so; each new person is a new pair of hands which can in due course be put to work to produce more food, so why should not twice as many people produce twice as much food? Though this was a reasonable thought in Malthus's day, economic theory taught, and still teaches, that diminishing marginal returns are bound to set in sooner or later and this is said to explain why twice as many people will not in general produce twice as much food.

In summary, the claim that 'subsistence increases only in an arithmetical ratio' is an empirical claim; it is a claim about the way the world is which must be supported by the historical evidence and which must fit – must be firmly embedded in our system of knowledge – before we can claim to know that it is true. But if both these conditions *are* satisfied then we can legitimately claim that it is true.

We turn now to the premiss,

Population, when unchecked, increases in a geometrical ratio.

To say that population 'increases in a geometrical ratio' is to say that, starting with some initial population, that population is *multiplied* by a constant factor in each successive period. For example a population might *double* every twenty-five years, so starting with 100 people, the population after successive periods of twenty-five years increases as follows, 100, 200, 400, 800, 1600, etc. and a graph of the increase looks like this,

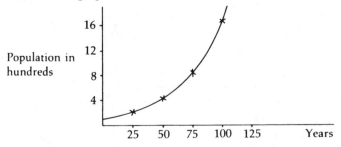

41

Now, this premiss says that population 'when *unchecked*' increases geometrically, but what does 'unchecked' mean? Clearly starvation is a major check that Malthus has in mind. Presumably he also means enemies of various kinds including disease and war in the case of human beings. Human beings impose other checks on population growth too, ranging from religious taboos through to contraception, abortion and infanticide.

Clearly Malthus's premiss is meant to be a claim about human population trends in the real world – as they have been and will continue. Evidence about animal and plant populations could be relevant but of course human beings might be very different, so surely in order to judge whether population when unchecked does or does not increase geometrically we have to study the historical record – again. However, we cannot simply inspect population figures, because these will show how populations have grown *when checked* in various ways. We could either search for populations which have grown unchecked – which have grown without constraints of fertile land, without enemies, without disease, etc. – to see if they have grown geometrically or, since such societies are likely to be rare, we could look at societies which have various checks operating, but we could look at their *birth rates*. If Malthus is right these will show that human populations *tend* to increase geometrically but it will also be true that starvation, disease and generally early death keep population in line with subsistence. As with the previous case, if Malthus's second premiss is correct it will also 'fit' with many other things we know about population and related matters.

This is perhaps an appropriate moment to return to a question left unanswered in the previous section and to ask whether Malthus gives a further reason for accepting this premiss in the form of his second postulate,

> That the passion between the sexes is necessary and will remain nearly in its present state.

Although the text may suggest that he takes this to be a reason for believing in geometric population growth, his language is not explicit and context doesn't make it quite clear so we have to ask whether it is a *good* reason. The question is hard to answer because it is not clear what Malthus means by 'passion between the sexes'. Presumably, the best one can say is that he means there is and always has been a fairly constant level of sexual activity among human beings. But what evidence could he have for this except birth rates, which are precisely what he needs in order to establish (independently of any claim about levels of sexual activity) his claim that population, when unchecked, increases geometrically? It is hard to see how his second postulate could be a further reason for his belief in geometric population growth so we omit it from further consideration.

How to deal with an obvious truth

We come finally to Malthus's first postulate,

> That food is necessary to the existence of man.

The reader may wonder why we delay over this assertion at all since it is easy to understand and it is so obviously true. However, it is precisely for these reasons that it raises some questions about the methods we are expounding so we take this opportunity to deal with them.

'If you understand Malthus's first postulate you must be able to give at least some account of how you could decide whether it was true or false' (the principle *, see p. 23) but the evidence for it is so overwhelming – it is so obviously true – that it is hard to imagine that anything could show it to be false. Of course it is easy to say what shows it to be true:

 (i) all known human beings have needed food and
 (ii) we have looked for and found no exceptions and
 (iii) we know a good deal about human bodies and what we know implies or is implied by Malthus's postulate, i.e. it 'fits' with many other beliefs.

This is not only what *does* show the postulate to be true, it is also what *would* show it to be true if we did not know whether it was (that is what it means; that is the sort of claim it is). It is precisely because we know that conditions (i)–(iii) are satisfied that we know Malthus's postulate is true and it is precisely because we know they are true that we have difficulty in saying what could show it *false*. But the philosophical principle which underlies our work (p. 23) does not require us to say what, *given that we know (i)–(iii)*, could none the less show Malthus's claim false (since nothing could); what the principle asks us to do, *on the assumption that we do not know whether it is true or false*, is to spell out what would show it true or false. If conditions (i)–(iii) were not all satisfied we should not be entitled to believe this postulate; if there were human beings who could stay alive without food or if we knew other things which implied that food was not necessary then it would be false.

To summarise, Malthus's first postulate could be false, we can say what would show it to be false, but given the world as we know it, it cannot be false; to put it another way, the truth of (i)–(iii) is sufficient to justify accepting Malthus's postulate. Discounting his remarks about God Malthus says something similar to what is required in paragraph (c),

> These two laws, ever since we have had any knowledge of mankind, appear to have been fixed laws of our nature, and, as we have not hitherto seen any alteration in them, we have no right to conclude that they will ever cease to be what they now are

and, by the Assertibility Principle we could reasonably construe this remark as his reason for accepting his first postulate – however, nothing turns on this since it is so obviously true.

Back to the soundness of the argument

Although one premiss is obviously true what are we to say of the other two? On population, whilst it is clear that human beings have a much greater 'power of population' than they actually realise (in the sense that they *could* have far more children than they do) it is not clear that this matters. What matters for Malthus's argument is what human beings *do*. His text seems to suggest that Malthus believes that the mathematics of geometric and arithmetic progressions forces his conclusion (see paragraph (f)) and provided the factor by which population tends to multiply is greater than 1 he is right – eventually – but notice that if every human being marries just once and every married couple has just two children, the population remains constant and the factor by which it *'multiplies'* in successive periods is 1. Since many subgroups within the world's population are already nearly stable in this way it is possible that more and perhaps even all should be – eventually. Many actual populations impose checks on themselves already, ranging from religious taboos, abortion and infanticide, to – in modern times – effective contraception. Whether these count as checks for Malthus is unclear. If they *don't* then his first premiss,

> Population when unchecked increases in a geometrical ratio

is false for many populations and could be false for all. If they *do* count as checks it could well be true that populations, *when unchecked,* increase in a geometrical ratio but this would not matter and would lend no weight whatever to the rest of Malthus's argument if it so happened that actual populations controlled their own numbers at levels which could be provided for.

On his other basic claim that

> Subsistence increases only in an arithmetical ratio,

Malthus can be and has been severely criticised. The criticism in short is that science and technology enables output to grow in leaps and bounds. The point was made forcefully by Marx and Engels in their many attacks on Malthus's views. Engels puts it thus in his *Outlines of a Critique of Political Economy*, written in 1844; he asks

> has it been proved that the productivity of land increases in an arith-metical progression? The extent of land is limited – that is perfectly true. But the labour power to be employed on this area increases along with population; and even if we assume that the increase in

yield due to this increase does not always rise in proportion to the labour, there still remains a third element – which the economists, however, never consider as important – namely, science, the progress of which is just as unceasing and at least as rapid as that of populations. What progress does the agriculture of this century owe to chemistry alone... But science increases at least as fast as population. The latter increases in proportion to the size of the previous generation. Science advances in proportion to the knowledge bequeathed to it by the previous generation, and thus under the most ordinary conditions it also grows in geometrical progression – and what is impossible for science?

If we move now from considering the truth of Malthus's basic premisses to looking at his inferences from them, we find that we already have good reason to reject some of them.

Consider the initial inference,

(1) Population, when unchecked, increases in a geometrical ratio

and (2) Subsistence increases in only an arithmetical ratio

therefore

(3) There is a natural inequality of the two powers of population and of production in the earth.

Clearly it *could* be true that population *when unchecked,* increases in a geometrical ratio, whilst actual populations impose checks on themselves including religious taboos, abortion, infanticides and, in modern times, effective contraception – which keeps population growth within the rate of increase of subsistence. In that case Malthus's premisses (1) and (2) could both be true whilst his conclusion (3) was false. (This interprets the reference to 'powers of population' to mean not the theoretical number of children women could physically bear but how actual populations tend to grow – as revealed by their birth rates – since this is clearly what matters for Malthus's argument.) There is a problem about where to locate Malthus's mistake here: if contraception (for example) counts as a check then both Malthus's premisses could well be true, but in that case his conclusion (3) does not follow, because as we have just pointed out, people may impose checks on themselves for all sorts of reasons having nothing whatever to do with the 'difficulty of subsistence'. If on the other hand contraception does not count as a check we know now that Malthus's premiss (1) is false for many populations in the world.

Malthus makes a further inference to,

(6) There must be a strong and constantly operating check on populations from the difficulty of subsistence.

If we grant that population grows geometrically and subsistence grows arithmetically it does indeed *follow* that population growth will *eventually* be checked by insufficient food (etc.) if no other check intervenes first. But it does *not* follow that this check is operating *now*, or *constantly*, or even that it must *eventually* come into play – because some other check may intervene first. In terms of our graphs the picture might look like this,

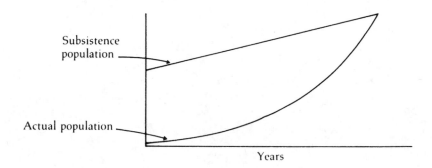

where the graph represents the fact that the Earth can support a population well beyond what it does for some time before the pressure Malthus sees as *constantly* operating arises at all.

As Engels puts it,

> Malthus . . . asserts that population constantly exerts pressure on the means of subsistence; that as production is increased, population increases in the same proportion; and that the inherent tendency of population to multiply beyond the available means of subsistence is the cause of all poverty and vice. For if there are too many people, then in one way or another they must be eliminated; they must die, either by violence or through starvation. When this has happened, however, a gap appears once more, and this is immediately filled by other propagators of population, so that the old poverty begins anew. Moreover, this is the case under all conditions . . . The savages of New Holland, who live *one* to the square mile, suffer just as much from overpopulation as England. In short, if we want to be logical, we have to recognise *that the earth was already overpopulated when only one man existed.*

This *reductio ad absurdum* is surely refutation enough of Malthus's claim if more were needed than has already been said.

In short Malthus's argument looks highly questionable at many points; its premises are far from secure and some of its inferences are downright fallacious. What is fascinating is why such a poor argument should have persuaded so many people, should have been of such historic importance and should still be so widely believed. We give the last, provocative, word on this subject to Engels again,

> Now the consequence of this theory is that since it is precisely the poor who constitute this surplus population, nothing ought to be done for them, except to make it as easy as possible for them to starve to death; [and] to convince them that this state of affairs cannot be altered

and indeed it is true that Malthus opposed the provision of poor relief on precisely these grounds. In short Malthus's arguments have always been welcome in the battle of the rich against the poor! They are used even today to explain why nothing can or should be done to help the starving in the Third World. Malthus's conclusion is sometimes called The Dismal Theorem. Kenneth Boulding, the economist, extended the logic of its argument to a corollary which he christened 'The Utterly Dismal Theorem' (see his Foreword to Malthus's *Population: The First Essay*). His argument is this:

> Since equilibrium between resources and population can be maintained only by misery and/or vice and since population tends to rise to the limit of available subsistence, any improvements leading to an increase in the production of food must increase the equilibrium population, and hence presumably, increase the sum of human misery and vice.

We can hardly leave this subject without also noting that Malthus always strongly opposed contraception. Such is the logic of man!

4 · Reasoning about nuclear deterrence

> The splitting of the atom has changed everything save our
> modes of thinking, and thus we drift towards unparalleled catas-
> trophe.   Albert Einstein

The arguments we consider in this chapter are about nuclear deterrence.
This is a subject in which reasoning plays an enormously important part.
Deciding which is the best policy is not simply a matter of discovering the
facts about the weapons systems available to the two sides because it is hard
to tell what these facts imply about intentions under deterrence, nor is it
simply a matter of resolving to *defend* oneself since the difference between
defensive and aggressive acts is obscure under deterrence. The importance of
the arguments cannot be disputed, so how should we resolve them?

This chapter attempts to contribute to the debate not directly, but by
explaining a *method of analysing arguments* using two specimen texts from
the very extensive literature on the subject. The texts we have chosen are
quite typical: there are certainly many other pieces expressing similar arguments and no doubt many of these would have served our purpose equally
well; however, our focus of interest is not on these particular texts (typical
or not) but in the *method* of assessing them. We succeed in our objective
if the reader grasps the method of analysis explained by reference to these
examples and is then able to apply it to other pieces of reasoning.

We begin with the text of a letter written in August 1982 by Mr Caspar
Weinberger, US Defence Secretary, to the editors of newspapers in NATO
countries and published widely throughout Europe. It is an important docu-
ment in the history of this debate and a powerful piece of argument.

The American Government appears to have been increasingly worried by
the growth of the European peace movement in the face of proposals to deploy
Cruise and Pershing missiles in Europe and this prompted Mr Weinberger's
letter. The letter does not merely *state* American Government policy, nor
does it simply *threaten* the Russian Government (although, government
pronouncements being what they are, it is partly doing both of these things),
it also *argues* the case, and that is what we are interested in, its reasoning.

The reader who has mastered the method outlined in Chapter 2 should
now apply it to the unmarked copy of Weinberger's letter which is provided
below and should attempt to answer the exercises which immediately follow

it. Readers should then compare their answers with those contained below on pp. 52f.

I Weinberger defends US policy on nuclear warfare

The following is the text of a letter from Mr Weinberger, US Defence Secretary, to the editors of newspapers in NATO countries.

(a) I am increasingly concerned with news accounts that portray this Administration as planning to wage protracted nuclear war, or seeking to acquire a nuclear 'war-fighting' capability. This is completely inaccurate, and these stories misrepresent the Administration's policies to the American public and to our Allies and adversaries abroad.

(b)   It is the first and foremost goal of this Administration to take every step to ensure that nuclear weapons are never used again, for we do not believe there could be any 'winners' in a nuclear war. Our entire strategy aims to deter war of all kinds, but most particularly to deter nuclear war. To accomplish this objective, our forces must be able to respond in a measured and prudent manner to the threat posed by the Soviet Union. That will require the improvements in our strategic forces that the President has proposed. But it does not mean that we endorse the concept of protracted nuclear war or nuclear 'war-fighting'. It is the Soviet Union that appears to be building forces for a 'protracted' conflict (the doctrine of Zatyazhnaya Voyna).

(c)   The policy of deterrence is difficult for some to grasp because it is based on a paradox. But this is quite simple: to make the cost of a nuclear war much higher than any possible 'benefit' to the country starting it. If the Soviets know in advance that a nuclear attack on the United States could and would bring swift nuclear retaliation, they would never attack in the first place. They would be 'deterred' from ever beginning a nuclear war.

(d)   There is nothing new about our policy. Since the age of nuclear weapons began, the United States has sought to prevent nuclear war through a policy of deterrence. This policy has been approved, through the political processes of the democratic nations it protects, since at least 1950. More important, it works. It has worked in

49

the face of international tensions involving the great powers and it worked in the face of war itself.

(e) But for deterrence to continue to be successful in the future we must take steps to offset the Soviet military build-up. If we do not modernise our arsenal now, as the Soviets have been doing for more than 20 years, we will, within a few years, no longer have the ability to retaliate. The Soviet Union would then be in a position to threaten or actually to attack us with the knowledge that we would be incapable of responding. We have seen in Poland, in Afghanistan, in Eastern Europe, and elsewhere that the Soviet Union does not hesitate to take advantage of a weaker adversary. We cannot allow the Soviet Union to think it could begin a nuclear war with us and win.

(f) This is not just idle speculation. The Soviet Union has engaged in a frenzied military build-up, in spite of their economic difficulties. They have continued to build greater numbers of nuclear weapons far beyond those necessary for deterrence. They now have over 5,000 nuclear warheads on ICBMs, compared to about 2,000 five years ago. They have modified the design of these weapons and their launchers so that many of their land-based missiles are now more accurate, more survivable, and more powerful than our own.

(g) They have also developed a refiring capability that will allow them to reload their delivery systems several times. They have elaborate plans for civil defence and air defence against any retaliation we might attempt. And finally, their writings and military doctrine emphasise a nuclear war-fighting scenario. Whatever they claim their intentions to be, the fact remains that they are designing their weapons in such a way and in sufficient numbers to indicate to us that they think they could begin, and win, a nuclear war.

(h) In the face of all this, it is my responsibility and duty as Secretary of Defence to make every effort to modernise our nuclear forces in such a way that the United States retains the capability to deter the Soviet Union from ever beginning a nuclear war. We must take the steps necessary to match the Soviet Union's greatly improved nuclear capability.

(j)   That is exactly why we must have a capability for a survivable and endurable response – to demonstrate that our strategic forces *could* survive Soviet strikes over an extended period. Thus we believe we could deter any attack. Otherwise we would be tempting them to employ nuclear weapons or try to blackmail us. In short, we cannot afford to place ourselves in a position where the survivability of our deterrent would force the President to choose between using our strategic forces before they were destroyed or surrendering.

(k)   Those who object to a policy that would strengthen our deterrent, then, would force us into a more dangerous, hair-triggered posture. Forces that must be used in the very first instant of any enemy attack are not the tools of a prudent strategy. A posture that encourages Soviet nuclear adventurism is not the basis of an effective deterrent. Our entire strategic programme, including the development of a response capability that has been so maligned in the press recently, has been developed with the express intention of assuring that nuclear war will never be fought.

(m)   I know this doctrine of deterrence is a difficult paradox to understand. It is an uncomfortable way to keep the peace. We understand deterrence and accept the fact that we must do much more in order to continue to keep the peace. It is my fervent hope that all can understand and accept this so that we can avoid the sort of sensationalist treatment of every mention of the word 'nuclear' that only serves to distort our policy and to frighten people all over the world. Our policy is peace, and we deeply believe that the best and surest road to peace is to secure and maintain an effective and credible deterrent.

(n)   The purpose of US policy remains to prevent aggression through an effective policy of deterrence, the very goal which prompted the formation of the North Atlantic Alliance, an alliance which is as vital today as it was the day it was formed.

Questions

(1) What are Weinberger's main conclusions in this piece?
(2) Outline the basic argument for each of these.
(3) Are there any serious weaknesses in his arguments?

(4) What would show the following,

    (i) 'Whatever they claim their intentions to be, the fact remains that the Americans are designing their weapons in such a way and in sufficient numbers to indicate to the Soviet Union that they think they could begin and win a nuclear war' is *true*,

    (ii) 'The USA does not hesitate to take advantage of a weaker adversary' is *true*, and

    (iii) 'The USSR wants peace' is *true*?

(5) Does Weinberger contradict himself?

II Extracting the arguments from Weinberger's text

To extract the argument from Weinberger's text we again follow the steps described in Chapter 2. We first circle all the explicit argument indicators. These appear to be 'for' (b), 'because' (c), 'finally' (g), 'That is exactly why' (j), and 'then' (k). The word 'since' in (d) is not an argument indicator; it has only a temporal connotation. 'Thus' in (j) appears to mean 'in that way' and is not therefore a conclusion indicator.

We next bracket any clearly indicated reasons and underline clearly indicated conclusions using inference indicators to help us. The obvious conclusions are,

    (j) We must have a capability for a survivable and endurable response

and (k) Those who object to a policy that would strengthen our deterrent, would force us into a more dangerous, hair-triggered posture.

It is not so obvious whether 'because' in (c) signals a conclusion or an explanation. (Cf. p. 18.) If anything turns on it we shall have to return to it.

Although there is no explicit conclusion indicator, context strongly suggests that paragraphs (f) and (g) give a conjunction of reasons for the conclusion,

    (g) Whatever they claim their intentions to be, the fact remains that they are designing their weapons in such a way and in sufficient numbers to indicate to us that they think they could begin, and win, a nuclear war.

The reader may think that there are other conclusions (and indeed there are) but one must be careful not to confuse conclusions with other, *unsupported*, assertions: for example 'Our policy is peace' in paragraph (m) is not a conclusion, though people often take it to be one. We return to this briefly later.

The next step is to identify the main conclusion and to mark it. We take it to be,

C we must have a capability for a survivable and endurable response.

If we now attempt to trace Weinberger's reasoning for this conclusion it turns out to be surprisingly difficult. We begin by asking 'What immediate reasons are presented in the text for accepting C?' But what reasons does the phrase 'That is exactly why' point to? Part of the answer must surely be the previous sentence, but it is not clear whether anything else is intended.

It might seem natural to read the paragraph leading to this main conclusion as a 'chain of reasons' as follows,

> [For these reasons] we must make every effort to modernise our nuclear forces in such a way that the United States retains the capability to deter the Soviet Union from ever beginning a nuclear war. [Therefore] we must take the steps necessary to match the Soviet Union's greatly improved nuclear capability. [Therefore] we must have a capability for a survivable and endurable response.

However, there are several reasons for not being too quick to attribute this reasoning to Weinberger. Firstly, he does not explicitly indicate this intention with the appropriate inference indicators. Secondly, though the context is suggestive it does not clearly show this to be Weinberger's intention. Thirdly, it is a poor argument as it stands: (i) it does not follow from the fact that the USA needs to 'modernise' its nuclear forces that it needs to 'match' the Soviet Union's nuclear capability – less than matching power, or different forces differently deployed, might be sufficient to deter – and (ii) the inference from 'we must match them' to 'we must have a capability for a survivable and endurable response' assumes that the Soviet Union has such a capability and this needs to be spelt out/added as a premiss to make the argument compelling.

One *could* respond to these points by searching his text to see if Weinberger supplies what is necessary to supplement this line of reasoning. Alternatively one can use the Assertibility Question directly from the beginning (i.e. without the 'natural' guess we made above) and we now demonstrate this more systematic method.

As we have already said, the inference indicator 'That is exactly why' must point to the previous sentence,

(1) We must take the steps necessary to match the Soviet Union's greatly improved nuclear capability

so we ask the Assertibility Question in the form 'What must be added to (1) to justify C?' As we have already seen the obvious answer is,

(2) The Soviet Union has a capability for a survivable and endurable response.

53

Weinberger does not assert this very sentence but he clearly believes it. He says,

> (b) It is the Soviet Union that appears to be building forces for a 'protracted' conflict

and he gives a whole string of reasons for believing it. These are in paragraphs (f) and (g); they are,

> (3) [The Soviets] have continued to build greater numbers of nuclear weapons far beyond those necessary for deterrence.
>
> (4) many of their land-based missiles are now more accurate, more survivable, and more powerful than our own.
>
> (5) They have developed a refiring capability
>
> (6) They have elaborate plans for civil defence ... against any retaliation
>
> (7) Their writings and military doctrine emphasise a nuclear war-fighting scenario.

Ask the Assertibility Question, 'What would show that the Soviet Union had a survivable and endurable response capability?', and these are just the sorts of reasons one would have to give, so we shall construe Weinberger as intending this line of reasoning. We can summarise it in the following argument diagram,

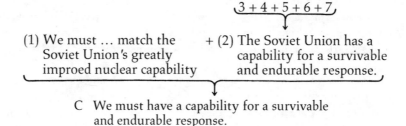

Since no further reasons are presented by Weinberger for believing the claims (3) to (7), these are basic reasons. We must next ask, 'What immediate reasons are presented for accepting (1)?' As we saw earlier, the preceding sentence,

> [We must] make every effort to modernise our nuclear forces in such a way that the United States retains the capability to deter the Soviet Union from ever beginning a nuclear war

is a natural candidate. It is true that there is no explicit argument indicator, but context suggests that this inference is intended and it reads naturally to insert 'for this reason' or 'therefore' between the two sentences. The problem is that the resulting inference is a poor one since, as we mentioned earlier, something other than 'matching' power might be a sufficient deterrent. The way to proceed is to ask the Assertibility Question, in short, 'What would justify me in asserting (1)?' The obvious way to justify such a claim is to refer to one's objective and to the fact that some course of action is the only or the best way to achieve that objective. Clearly then in this case we need something like,

(8) The United States wishes to/must (retain the capability to) deter the Soviet Union from beginning a nuclear war

8 + 9a
⎵
1

and

(9a) If the US is to do this it must match the USSR's greatly improved nuclear capability

therefore

(1) We must . . . match the Soviet Union's greatly improved nuclear capability.

In fact Weinberger says something very like (8) in several places,

(b) It is the foremost goal of this Administration to take every step to ensure that nuclear weapons are never used again,

(b) Our entire strategy aims to deter war of all kinds, but most particularly to deter nuclear war.

(h) [we must] make every effort to modernise our nuclear forces in such a way that the United States retains the capability to deter the Soviet Union from ever beginning a nuclear war.

(k) Our entire strategic programme, including the development of a response capability . . . has been developed with the express intention of assuring that nuclear war will never be fought.

(n) The purpose of US policy remains to prevent aggression through an effective policy of deterrence.

The nearest he gets to the other premiss we need is,

(b) To accomplish this objective, our forces must be able to respond in a measured and prudent manner to the threat posed by the Soviet Union

or

(e) for deterrence to continue to be successful in the future we must take steps to offset the Soviet military build-up.

55

Neither of these is quite as strong as we need but we can find nothing better in the text, so we must take one (or both *independently*) as Weinberger's other premiss at this stage and continue to trace back his reasoning. For the sake of brevity we shall trace out the reasoning only for the second alternative, so the immediate reasons we attribute to Weinberger at this point are,

> (8) The United States must (retain the capability to) deter the Soviet Union from beginning a nuclear war

and (9) For deterrence to continue to be successful in future we [the US] must take steps to offset the Soviet military build-up

$$\underbrace{8+9}_{1}$$

therefore

> (1) we must . . . match the Soviet Union's greatly improved nuclear capability.

We now repeat the process of searching for reasons for both (8) and (9). Without going through the details of our method (argument indicators, context, then Assertibility Question) it is clear that what would justify (8) is something like this,

> (10) The United States wants (to ensure that there is) peace

and

> (11) The Soviet Union threatens war

$$\underbrace{10+11}_{8}$$

so (8) The United States must (retain the capability to) deter the Soviet Union from beginning fighting a nuclear war.

There is ample evidence in the text that Weinberger is committed to the truth of both (10) and (11), so we turn now to,

> (9) for deterrence to continue to be successful in the future we must take steps to offset the Soviet military build-up.

There are no explicit argument indicators to signal the case Weinberger intends for this claim, so we ask the Assertibility Question, 'What would justify it?' The obvious way to justify such a claim is to show that something very undesirable will happen if we do *not* 'take steps to offset the Soviet military build-up', so Weinberger's intended argument is clearly,

> (12) If we do not modernise our arsenal now, as the Soviets have been doing for more than 20 years, we will, within a few years, no longer have the ability to retaliate

and

    (13) The Soviet Union would then be in a position to threaten or actually to attack us with the knowledge that we would be incapable of responding

and

    (14) The Soviet Union does not hesitate to take advantage of a weaker adversary

$$\underbrace{12 + 13 + 14}_{9}$$

therefore

    (9) for deterrence to continue to be successful in future we must take steps to offset the Soviet military build-up.

Further reasons for believing (12) are presumably contained in paragraphs (f) and (g) and the case for (14) is what,

    (15) We have seen in Poland, in Afghanistan, in Eastern Europe and elsewhere

but we have probably gone as far as we need in extracting from Weinberger's text the best argument we can for what we took to be his main conclusion.

    The summary argument diagram is this,

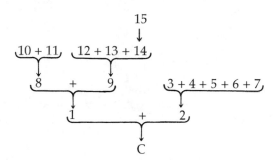

Notice that there are certainly other conclusions and other arguments in Weinberger's text. Here are some examples. Firstly, context strongly suggests that paragraphs (f) and (g) are presenting a conjunction of reasons for the conclusion,

    (g) Whatever they claim their intention to be, the fact remains that they are designing their weapons in such a way and in sufficient numbers to indicate to us that they think they could begin, and win, a nuclear war.

Secondly, the argument we have elicited from Weinberger's text suggests that, despite the absence of any argument indicators, we should construe his paragraph (b) as an initial statement of a similar argument;

> R_1 Our entire strategy aims to deter war of all kinds but most particularly to deter nuclear war

and R_2 To accomplish this objective, our forces must be able to respond in a measured and prudent manner to the threat posed by the Soviet Union

$$R_1 + R_2 \atop \downarrow \atop C_1$$

therefore

> C_1 [We must have] the improvements in our strategic forces that the President has proposed.

Thirdly, Weinberger clearly believes that,

> we must have a capability for a survivable and endurable response $\boxed{\text{because}}$ we want to demonstrate that our strategic forces *could* survive Soviet strikes over an extended period

and this is a line of argument we have not traced out at all though we could easily do so by successive applications of the Assertibility Question.

In short there is no reason why there should not be several lines of argument discernible in a text like this and there is no reason why they should not cross and criss-cross each other.

One last point. It is surprising how often people think that 'Our policy is peace', in paragraph (m), is Weinberger's main conclusion. But this is not argued for at all, so it can't be a conclusion: conclusions have to be argued for and reasons have to be given for them. A bald statement of belief or policy (of which there are several in Weinberger's text) is one thing; an argument presenting a case for such a belief or policy is quite another. Of course it is not always easy to decide which you have. For example Weinberger clearly asserts that deterrence works (in paragraph (d)), but whether it is to be taken as a conclusion depends on whether the reader judges that Weinberger gives any reason for accepting it.

Weinberger's letter marked up according to the method of Chapter 2 looks as follows:

> I am increasingly concerned with news accounts that portray this Administration as planning to wage protracted nuclear war, or seeking to acquire a nuclear 'war-fighting' capability. This is completely inaccurate, and these stories misrepresent the Administration's policies to the American public and to our Allies and adversaries abroad.

It is the first and foremost goal of this Administration to take every step to ensure that nuclear weapons are never used again, for we do not believe there could be any 'winners' in a nuclear war.

R 1 ⟨Our entire strategy aims to deter war of all kinds, but most particularly to deter nuclear war.⟩ ⟨To accomplish this objective,

R 2 our forces must be able to respond in a measured and prudent manner to the threat posed by the Soviet Union.⟩ That will require

C 1 the improvements in our strategic forces that the President has proposed. But it does not mean that we endorse the concept of protracted nuclear war or nuclear 'war-fighting'. It is the Soviet Union that appears to be building forces for a 'protracted' conflict (the doctrine of Zatyazhnaya Voyna).

$R_1 + R_2$ over C_1

The policy of deterrence is difficult for some to grasp because it is based on a paradox. But this is quite simple: to make the cost of a nuclear war much higher than any possible 'benefit' to the country starting it. If the Soviets know in advance that a nuclear attack on the United States could and would bring swift nuclear retaliation, they would never attack in the first place. They would be 'deterred' from ever beginning a nuclear war.

There is nothing new about our policy. Since the age of nuclear weapons began, the United States has sought to prevent nuclear war through a policy of deterrence. This policy has been approved, through the political processes of the democratic nations it protects, since at least 1950. More important, it works. It has worked in the face of international tensions involving the great powers and it worked in the face of war itself.

9   But ⟨for deterrence to continue to be successful in the future we must take steps to offset the Soviet military build-up.⟩ ⟨If we do not modernise our arsenal now, as the Soviets have been doing for

12 more than 20 years, we will, within a few years, no longer have the ability to retaliate.⟩ ⟨The Soviet Union would then be in a position

13 to threaten or actually to attack us with the knowledge that we would be incapable of responding.⟩ ⟨We have seen in Poland, in

15 Afghanistan, in Eastern Europe, and elsewhere⟩ that ⟨the Soviet

14 Union does not hesitate to take advantage of a weaker adversary.⟩

$\frac{15}{12 + 13 + 14}$ over 9

We cannot allow the Soviet Union to think it could begin a nuclear war with us and win.

This is not just idle speculation. The Soviet Union has engaged in a frenzied military build-up, in spite of their economic difficulties. ⟨They have continued to build greater numbers of nuclear weapons

3 far beyond those necessary for deterrence.⟩ They now have over 5,000 nuclear warheads in ICBMs, compared to about 2,000 five years ago. ⟨They have modified the design of these weapons and

4 their launchers so that many of their land-based missiles are now more accurate, more survivable, and more powerful than our own.⟩

5 ⟨They have also developed a refiring capability that will allow them to reload their delivery systems several times.⟩ ⟨They have

6 elaborate plans for civil defence and air defence against any retalia-

7 tion we might attempt.⟩ And ⟨finally⟩, ⟨their writings and military doctrine emphasise a nuclear war-fighting scenario.⟩ Whatever they claim their intentions to be, the fact remains that they are designing their weapons in such a way and in sufficient numbers to indicate to us that they think they could begin, and win, a nuclear war.

$$\underbrace{3+4+5+6+7}_{\downarrow}$$

(2) The Soviet Union has a capability for a survivable and endurable response.

In the face of all this, it is my responsibility and duty as Secretary of Defence to ⟨make every effort to modernise our nuclear forces in

8 such a way that the United States retains the capability to deter the Soviet Union from ever beginning a nuclear war.⟩ ⟨We must take

1 the steps necessary to match the Soviet Union's greatly improved nuclear capability.⟩

$$\underbrace{1+2}_{\downarrow}\ \text{C}$$
$$\text{C}$$

⟨That is exactly why⟩ we must have a capability for a survivable and endurable response – to demonstrate that our strategic forces *could* survive Soviet strikes over an extended period. Thus we believe we could deter any attack. Otherwise we would be tempting them to employ nuclear weapons or try to blackmail us. In short, we cannot afford to place ourselves in a position where the survivability of our deterrent would force the President to choose between using our strategic forces before they were destroyed or surrendering.

Those who object to a policy that would strengthen our deterrent, ⟨then,⟩ would force us into a more dangerous, hair-triggered posture.

Forces that must be used in the very first instant of any enemy attack are not the tools of a prudent strategy. A posture that encourages Soviet nuclear adventurism is not the basis of an effective deterrent. Our entire strategic programme, including the development of a response capability that has been so maligned in the press recently, has been developed with the express intention of assuring that nuclear war will never be fought.

I know this doctrine of deterrence is a difficult paradox to understand. It is an uncomfortable way to keep the peace. We understand deterrence and accept the fact that we must do much more in order to continue to keep the peace. It is my fervent hope that all can understand and accept this so that we can avoid the sort of sensationalist treatment of every mention of the word 'nuclear' that only serves
10 to distort our policy and to frighten people all over the world. (Our policy is peace,) and we deeply believe that the best and surest road to peace is to secure and maintain an effective and credible deterrent.

The purpose of US policy remains to prevent aggression through an effective policy of deterrence, the very goal which prompted the formation of the North Atlantic Alliance, an alliance which is as vital today as it was the day it was formed.

III 'Tests for a good argument' applied to Weinberger's letter

Now that we are reasonably clear about Weinberger's arguments we can ask whether they establish their conclusions. We have already addressed the question in part – where we used the Assertibility Question to extract the best possible reasoning from the text – but we need a good deal more work to complete the answer.

We look initially at Weinberger's main argument as elicited in the previous section and we proceed step by step from basic reasons to main conclusion. A thoroughgoing critique of the argument would require us to check the factual claims on which it is based at some points, for example claims about missile numbers, etc., but our main interest is in a method of analysis and in showing how far you can get by 'thinking things through', so we shall assume these claims to be true for our purposes. Other basic reasons will also be assumed to be true unless thought alone gives us reason to doubt them: subsequent analysis may force us to revise this assumption, if, for example, it leads to inconsistency, but that will generally be our starting point.

We look first then at the argument,

(10) The United States wants (to ensure that there is) peace

and

(11) The Soviet Union threatens war

so (8) The United States must (retain the capability to) deter the Soviet Union from beginning/fighting a nuclear war.

If the premisses are true it is hard to see how the conclusion could be false judging by appropriate standards etc. (and given the obvious assumption that the USA does not want to be attacked or dominated by the USSR). Of course the interesting question in this case is, 'What would show the premisses to be true?', and we shall have to return to this question shortly.

Let us now look at the reasoning,

(12) If we do not modernise our arsenal now, as the Soviets have been doing for more than 20 years, we will, within a few years, no longer have the ability to retaliate

and

(13) The Soviet Union would then be in a position to threaten or actually attack us with the knowledge that we would be incapable of responding

and

(14) The Soviet Union does not hesitate to take advantage of a weaker adversary

so (9) For deterrence to continue to be successful in the future we must take steps to offset the Soviet military build-up.

We used the Assertibility Question earlier to elicit this reasoning so since we thought it a good argument then we must do so now. If the premisses are true it is hard to see how the conclusion could be false. Again there are questions about the premisses. It is hard to believe that the USA has not been modernising its arsenal during the past twenty years, but perhaps the record shows that the USSR has leapt ahead. That's a matter we can't go into, but clearly information comparing the two arsenals is what is relevant to this claim.

There is also a question mark over the claim that,

(14) The Soviet Union does not hesitate to take advantage of a weaker adversary

if the case for this is what

(15) We have seen in Poland, in Afghanistan, in Eastern Europe, and elsewhere

It is hard to say what would show (14) to be true or false because of an obvious 'openness' about phrases like 'take advantage of' and 'weaker adversary'. No doubt one could argue endlessly about whether the Soviet Union had 'taken advantage of' China, Yugoslavia, South Africa, and many other countries. No doubt some would argue that the USA does much the same, saying, 'Look at Vietnam, Central America, and the Middle East.' On the face of it (14) is rather vague and poorly supported.

Let us now look at the step in the argument which draws together the two previous threads we have considered:

(8) The United States must (retain the capability to) deter the Soviet Union from beginning nuclear war

and (9) For deterrence to continue to be successful in future we [the USA] must take steps to offset the Soviet military build-up

therefore

(1) We must . . . match the Soviet Union's greatly improved nuclear capability.

This is undoubtedly a weak link in the chain: in short it doesn't follow from the fact that the USA needs to 'offset' the Soviet military build-up that it needs to 'match' it. Deterrence continues to be effective if one can make the 'cost' of a nuclear attack too high (cf. paragraph (c)), and this is possible without matching forces. The British and French independent nuclear deterrents are tiny compared with the Soviet Union's nuclear arsenal, but are believed by both governments to be devastating enough to deter the Soviet Union from attacking either country. Whether these governments are right or not, it seems clear that both premises in this inference could be true and its conclusion false, judging by appropriate standards. As we mentioned in the previous section there may be an independent line of reasoning to this conclusion based on the claim that,

(b) To accomplish this objective [deterrence] our forces must be able to respond in a measured and prudent manner to the threat posed by the Soviet Union.

But, again, this claim is not strong enough and it needs a good deal of further argument to justify the need for 'matching' forces.

Let us look now at the argument Weinberger uses to show what forces the Soviet Union has (and which must therefore be 'matched'). The argument appears to be that,

(3) [The Soviets] have continued to build greater numbers of nuclear weapons far beyond those necessary for deterrence

(4) many of their land-based missiles are now more accurate, more survivable, and more powerful than our own.

(5) They have developed a refiring capability

(6) They have elaborate plans for civil defence ... against any retaliation

(7) Their writings and military doctrine emphasise a nuclear war-fighting scenario

therefore

(2) The Soviet Union has a capability for a survivable and endurable response.

We have already granted that this is a good argument so, by the same token, similar reasoning would show that,

The United States has a capability for a survivable and endurable response.

But, of course, the Soviet Union argues that similar reasoning *does* apply to the United States: that they too have far more nuclear weapons than are necessary for deterrence; that many of their submarine-based missiles are more survivable and more powerful than the Russians'; that they too have elaborate civil defence plans and that their writings and military doctrine also emphasise a nuclear war-fighting scenario (though the Americans call it 'flexible response') etc. To settle whether similar reasoning does apply to the USA we should have to look in detail at the facts and figures; the important point to note for our purposes is that the criteria would have to be similar, the reasoning would have to be comparable in both cases.

Of course, Weinberger also appears to use this line of reasoning about Soviet capabilities to reach a conclusion about their intentions;

(g) Whatever they claim their intentions to be, the fact remains that they are designing their weapons in such a way and in sufficient numbers to indicate to us that they think they could begin and win a nuclear war.

But it is not difficult to see that if the reasoning in paragraphs (f) and (g) shows that the Soviet Union has aggressive intentions a similar argument would show the same for the United States. Here we reach a very intractable problem: if we use the Assertibility Question and ask 'What would show that the Soviet Union/United States had aggressive intentions?' the answer presumably lies in what they say and do, with the latter being more revealing. We do read people's and governments' intentions all the time – we have to – so we can't pretend that we have no idea how to answer the question. The process is complicated and liable to error, but we have to try because intentions, rather than mere capabilities, appear to be crucial to the whole argument. It is crucial to Weinberger's argument that the Soviet Union poses a *threat* to the United States. The United States has the capability to annihilate Britain but Britain does not defend herself against the USA because she does not believe the USA threatens her. But the problem here is so intractable precisely because under deterrence it appears that one *does* much the same whether one's intentions are aggressive or defensive (and certainly that is how it looks to one's opponents). So the problem is that one needs to be able to read the intentions of one's 'opponents' but deterrence makes it very difficult or perhaps impossible!

We can make no progress with that line of reasoning in Weinberger's text so we turn finally to the last step we attributed to him,

> (1) We must take the steps necessary to match the Soviet Union's greatly improved nuclear capability

and (2) The Soviet Union has a capability for a survivable response)

therefore

> C We must have a capability for a survivable and endurable response.

In attributing this inference to Weinberger we already granted that the conclusion follows, so we need not delay over that. However, we cannot leave his argument without pointing out that Weinberger's main conclusion appears to flatly contradict his initial 'insistence' that

> (a) we are not seeking to acquire a nuclear war-fighting *capability* [our italics].

As we pointed out in the previous paragraph, 'capability' and 'intention' are two different things, but in his initial claim and in his main conclusion he is referring to '*capability*' and what could be the difference between a 'war-fighting capability' and a 'capability for a survivable and endurable response'?

IV From a speech by Enoch Powell

We conclude this chapter with a brief extract from a speech delivered by the former spokesman for defence, Enoch Powell, in Bristol on 29 October 1982. In the speech Powell strongly argued the case for unilateral nuclear disarmament for Britain. For ease of subsequent reference we mark our extract straightaway.

(9) There are some who believe that if America and Russia had not both possessed nuclear weapons, Russia would have invaded Western Europe at some time in the last 30 years or so. There can in the nature of things be no absolute disproof of this belief; but the structure of assumptions on which it rests is exceedingly rickety.

(7) It assumes first that Russia wishes anyhow to conquer Western Europe, and to do so by force of arms. (I remark – only in parentheses, because it does not affect the general argument – that I do not happen to believe this.) The second assumption is that Russia

(8) would assume that the United States would respond to an attack on Western Europe by exerting against Russia the full might of its atomic arsenal, that being the only way to minimise the probability or scale of reprisals.

The last assumption, which is of course the assumption crucial to the whole case, is of a subtle nature. It cannot be met by retorting that America would not regard even the conquest of Western Europe by Russia as justifying a nuclear exchange, with all its possible or likely consequences for the American homeland. That may well be so; but the assumption is an assumption about an assumption: could Russia be sure enough that America would not think that 'Europe is worth a mess'? This is a question which cannot be answered in the abstract. The answer is that everything depends on the scale, nature, circumstances and perceived limits of a Russian

(5) attack. If there were unsureness on the part of Russia, she would, if her intention were to conquer Europe, proceed piecemeal, by creating limited and local *casus belli* as Germany did in 1938–39; so that at each stage the stakes were plainly so low as not conceivably to be regarded by the United States as justifying even semi-suicide.

[My conclusion is that] the mutually countervailing nuclear

C armament of Russia and the United States has not been the reason why Russia has not advanced beyond the limits established at the end of the 1940s. If I were asked – what is not germane to my present subject – what then I believe the reason to have been, I would offer two which are not necessarily alternative to one

(4) another: first, Russia does not want to occupy Western Europe;

second, Russia's assumption is that to do so or attempt to do so would almost certainly involve her in a long and exacting war, which, even if she could not lose it in the sense that Napoleon, Wilhelm II and Hitler lost, she would, on historical precedent, be in danger of not winning; and Russia does not desire such a war.

The main conclusion is easy to find, but if we ask 'What immediate reasons are presented in the text for accepting C?' the answer is hard to find. This is partly because there are no explicit argument indicators, partly because Powell's language is rhetorical and complex and partly because his conclusion, C, is itself complex: it says that something (which happened) was *not the reason for* something else (which happened). However, if you understand Powell's conclusion, you must be able to give some account of how you could decide whether it was true or false so the way to proceed is to use the Assertibility Question, 'What would show that C was true?',

C the mutual countervailing nuclear armament of Russia and the United States has not been the reason why Russia has not advanced beyond the limits established at the end of the 1940s.

Given the context, what this surely *must* mean is that,

(1) Even if the USA had not possessed nuclear arms, still Russia would not have invaded Western Europe during the last thirty years or so.

And surely there are two quite *independent* ways of showing this to be true: one could show *either* that

(2) Even if the USA had not possessed nuclear arms, still Russia would not have *wanted* to advance into Western Europe (nor would she have felt the need to)

or that,

(3) Even if the USA had not possessed nuclear arms, Russia could not have invaded Western Europe (i.e. she would not have had the resources).

In saying this we are using our understanding of the meaning of C (and any knowledge we happen to have on the subject) to spell out how we would *have* to argue for C, what *would* be good arguments for it: if (1) is to be true surely either (2) or (3) must be and surely either would be sufficient to justify (1).

Having displayed what arguments we think would have to be produced to establish C we then look at the text to see if it contains them. The short answer is that it *doesn't* because Powell doesn't consider at all what *would have been the case* if the USA *had not had nuclear weapons.*

Powell certainly believes that Russia *does not* want to occupy Western Europe; he says so quite explicitly and he appears to present the following argument for believing it:

> (5) If there were unsureness on the part of Russia [about American reactions to an attack on Western Europe], she would, if her intention were to conquer Europe, proceed piecemeal, by creating limited *casus belli*

and (6) [Russia must be unsure about American reactions and has not created $\underbrace{5+6}_{4}$ local *casus belli*]

therefore

> (4) Russia does not want to [intend to] conquer Western Europe.

Powell does not assert (6) but it seems to be implicit (so we invoke the Principle of Charity): the argument is sound and establishes its conclusion if its premises are true. Powell's belief that Russia *does not* want to attack Europe also seems to be a reason for rejecting the argument he is attacking and which 'some believe', namely,

> (7) Russia wishes to conquer Western Europe, and to do so by force of arms

and (8) Russia [assumes] that the United States would respond to an attack on Western Europe by exerting against Russia the full might of its atomic arsenal

therefore

> (9) If America and Russia had not both possessed nuclear weapons, Russia would have invaded Western Europe at some time in the last thirty years or so.

This is indeed a poor argument but not for the reasons Powell appears to believe (including the falsity of (7)). It is a poor argument because both premises could be true and the conclusion false. Russia may want (now) to conquer Western Europe and may assume that the United States would respond to an attack with the full might of its atomic arsenal, but to show that the conclusion (9) is true one needs to show that *Russia would have wanted to* (and would have had the resources to) invade Western Europe if *the USA had not had nuclear weapons.* Perhaps we should be charitable and allow that this argument implicitly assumes that Russia *would have* wanted to (and been able to) conquer Western Europe if the USA had not had nuclear weapons. But then clearly Powell would have to rebut *that* assumption in order to fault the resulting argument and he doesn't address it at all.

Powell fails to do what is necessary either to establish his own conclusion *or* to fault the argument he criticises. In both cases the best one can say is that he appears to hold that Russia *does not want to* invade Western Europe, but this simply 'begs the question' (a very common fallacy) because in both cases to establish his case what needs to be shown is what Russia *would have wanted* if the United States had lacked nuclear weapons. It may be true that Russia *does* (or does not) want to invade Western Europe *because* the American nuclear forces are there. This is not the issue. The issue is 'What would she want if they were not there?'

Postscript
Those who dislike notation and diagrams should skip this postscript. Those who like such things and who want to draw out the connection between our approach and the method of semantic tableaux (see Appendix, pp. 181f.) will see that we could extend our diagramming technique to include the following,

(a)
$$
R \\
\downarrow \\
\widehat{C_1 + C_2}
$$
and (b)
$$
R \\
\downarrow \\
\widehat{C_1 \vee C_2}
$$

where (a) means 'R therefore C_1 *and* C_2', and (b) means 'R therefore C_1 *or* C_2'.

We could then summarise the arguments we think legitimate and necessary to establish Powell's conclusion C in the following diagram,

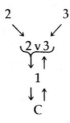

This reads, 'C therefore (1) therefore (2) or (3)', '(2) therefore (2) or (3) therefore (1) therefore C' etc.

5 · An example from John Stuart Mill

> My father never permitted anything which I learnt to degenerate
> into a mere exercise of memory. He strove to make the understand-
> ing not only go along with every step of the teaching, but if pos-
> sible, precede it. Anything which could be found out by thinking,
> I was never told, until I had exhausted my efforts to find out for
> myself.   J. S. Mill, *Autobiography*, Chapter 2

In this chapter we consider a classic 'nugget' of an argument due to John
Stuart Mill (1806–75). It comes from his *Principles of Political Economy*
which was first published in 1848 and which ran to seven editions in his own
lifetime.

James Mill, John Stuart Mill's father, and his friend Jeremy Bentham
founded and promulgated the philosophy of 'utilitarianism' which was based
on the doctrine that actions are good in so far as they 'promote the greatest
happiness of the greatest number'. James Mill was a highly educated man
in many spheres and he took sole charge of his son's education from the
beginning. He began to teach his son Greek at the age of three. They sat
at the same table at which his father worked and, since there were no such
things as English–Greek dictionaries,

> I was forced to have recourse to him for the meaning of every word
> which I did not know. This incessant interruption he, one of the most
> impatient of men, submitted to, and wrote under that interruption
> several volumes of his History and all else that he had to write in
> those years.   (*Autobiography*, Chapter 2)

Mill learned arithmetic in the same way and began Latin when he was
eight; his education included philosophy, logic, political economy and much
more. He describes it in detail in his *Autobiography* and it makes formidable
reading. His father was determined that Mill should take over the leadership
of the utilitarian movement and his education was necessary to and fitted
him well for that role, a role he took over in due course. J. S. Mill produced
many beautiful arguments in the course of his life and although the one we
have chosen is over one hundred years old it is still very much alive as you
can see in exercise 6, p. 194.

I   An argument from J. S. Mill's *Principles of Political Economy*

Before reaching our extract in the *Principles of Political Economy*, Mill argues the general case 'in favour of restricting to the narrowest compass the inter-vention of a public authority in the business of the community' (Book V, Chapter XI, §7). Having put the general case for keeping government 'off the backs of the people' he notes various exceptions to that case. One such exception is the following (sentences are labelled for ease of subsequent reference):

(a) To a fourth case of exception I must request particular attention, it being one to which as it appears to me the attention of political

(b) economists has not yet been sufficiently drawn. There are matters in which the interference of law is required, not to overrule the judg-ment of individuals respecting their own interest, but to give effect to that judgment: they being unable to give effect to it except by concert, which concert again cannot be effectual unless it receives

(c) validity and sanction from the law. For illustration, and without prejudging the particular point, I may advert to the question of

(d) diminishing the hours of labour. Let us suppose, what is at least supposable, whether it be the fact or not – that a general reduction of the hours of factory labour, say from ten to nine, would be for the advantage of the work-people: that they would receive as high

(e) wages, or nearly as high, for nine hours' labour as they receive for ten. If this would be the result, and if the operatives generally are

(f) convinced that it would, the limitation, some may say, will be adopted spontaneously. I answer, that it will not be adopted unless

(g) the body of operatives bind themselves to one another to abide by it. A workman who refused to work more than nine hours while there were others who worked ten, would either not be employed at all, or

(h) if employed, must submit to lose one-tenth of his wages. However convinced, therefore, he may be that it is in the interest of the class to work short time, it is contrary to his own interest to set the example, unless he is well assured that all or most others will follow

(j) it. But suppose a general agreement of the whole class: might not

(k) this be effectual without the sanction of law? Not unless enforced by

(m) opinion with a rigour practically equal to that of law. For however beneficial the observance of the regulation might be to the class collectively, the immediate interest of every individual would lie in violating it: and the more numerous those were who adhered to the

(n) rule, the more would individuals gain by departing from it. If nearly all restricted themselves to nine hours, those who chose to work for ten would gain all the advantages of the restriction, together with the profit from infringing it; they would get ten hours' wages for

(p) nine hours' work, and an hour's wages besides. I grant if a large majority adhered to the nine hours, there would be no harm done; the benefit would be, in the main, secured to the class, while those individuals who preferred to work harder and earn more, would

(q) have an opportunity of doing so. This certainly would be the state of things to be wished for; and assuming that a reduction of hours without any diminution of wages could take place without expelling the commodity from some of its markets – which is in every particular instance a question of fact, not of principle – the manner in which it would be most desirable that this effect should be brought about, would be by a quiet change in the general custom of the trade; short hours becoming, by spontaneous choice, the general practice, but those who chose to deviate from it having the

(r) fullest liberty to do so. Probably, however, so many would prefer the ten hours' work on the improved terms, that the limitation could not be maintained as a general practice: what some did from choice, others would soon be obliged to do from necessity, and those who had chosen long hours for the sake of increased wages, would be forced in the end to work long hours for no greater wages than

(s) before. Assuming then that it really would be the interest of each to work only nine hours if he could be assured that all others would do the same, there might be no means of attaining this object but by converting their supposed mutual agreement into an engagement

(t) under penalty, by consenting to have it enforced by law. I am not expressing any opinion in favour of such an enactment, which has never in this country been demanded, and which I certainly should not, in present circumstances, recommend: but it serves to exemplify the manner in which classes of persons may need the assistance of law, to give effect to their deliberate collective opinion of their own interest, by affording to every individual a guarantee that his competitors will pursue the same course, without which he cannot safely adopt it himself.

This is an ingenious piece of argument and it is just the sort of reasoning to which this book is addressed. It is not easy to say *what* the argument is or whether it is a *good* one but again we want to show how far you can get with careful thought. Again it will help the reader to assess the utility of our approach if he or she first writes careful answers to the following questions before reading sections II and III.

Questions

    (1) What is Mill's main conclusion?
    (2) What is his basic argument for it?
    (3) What would show the truth of,

> Assuming that it really would be in the interest of each to work only nine hours if he could be assured that all others would do the same, there might be no means of attaining this object but by converting their supposed mutual agreement into an engagement under penalty, by consenting to have it enforced by law?

    (4) Does Mill establish his conclusion?
    (5) Can you think of another example which resembles Mill's (which entails similar arguments)?

II Extracting the argument from Mill's text

To extract the argument from Mill's text we proceed as usual. We first read through the passage to get its sense and circle all the inference indicators as we go. These are 'therefore' (sentence (h)), 'For' (sentence (m)), and 'then' (sentence (s)). The reader might not notice at a first reading that 'then' in sentence (s) is functioning as a conclusion indicator but a closer reading should convince him or her that this is the case (and the next chapter will explain why this usage might mislead some readers). We next underline any clearly indicated reasons and conclusions using inference indicators to help us. This means we must underline the conclusions in sentences (h) and (s) and the reason in sentence (m): it is not quite clear what we should take as the 'scope' of 'For' in sentence (m); should it be,

> however beneficial the observance might be to the class collectively,
> the immediate interest of every individual would lie in violating it:

or should it continue to include,

> and the more numerous those were who adhered to the rule, the
> more would individuals gain by departing from it?

We leave it open at present and we can decide after further reflection on the argument – if anything turns on it.

The next step is to identify Mill's main conclusion. It is clear that Mill wants to establish that *there are cases* where the law must intervene in order to enable individuals to achieve *what they want* and he tries to do this by producing just such a case – as an 'illustration'. For this reason we must underline the general statement of this claim in both sentences (b) and (t) as his main conclusion; sentence (b) puts it like this,

> There are matters in which the interference of law is required, not to
> C overrule the judgment of individuals respecting their own interests,
> but to give effect to that judgment: they being unable to give effect to
> it except by concert, which concert again cannot be effectual unless
> it received validity and sanction from law.

If we next ask 'What immediate reason is presented in the text for accepting C?' the answer is clearly the conclusion of his 'illustration', from line (s),

> (1) Assuming . . . that it really would be the interest of each to work
> only nine hours if he could be assured that all others would do
> the same, there might be no means of attaining this object but by
> converting their supposed mutual agreement into an engagement
> under penalty, by consenting to have it enforced by law.

Most of the interest in this text focuses on the reasoning for (1); however, if we now ask, 'What immediate reasons are presented for (1)?' the question is surprisingly hard to answer and there are several reasons for this: it is partly because explicit argument indicators are lacking, partly because Mill uses long and logically complex sentences and partly because the conclusion (1) is itself complicated; it says something of the form 'Assuming W if X, there might be no means of attaining Y except by doing Z'. However, if you understand (1) you must be able to give some account of how you could decide whether it was true or false (see principle * p. 23), so the way to proceed here is to ask the Assertibility Question, in short, 'What would show (1) to be true?'

Surely the obvious way to show this is to consider the apparent alternatives and to show that these might not or will not achieve their objective. So

the question is, 'What are the alternatives to legal enforcement?' or, equivalently in the context, 'What scope is there for effective voluntary action?'
Mill appears to consider three broad possibilities. He considers what happens
firstly if an individual tries to act *alone* 'to set an example', and secondly if
individuals try to act *together* by 'general agreement', and thirdly if a 'large
majority' adheres to the nine hours by 'spontaneous choice'.

His argument against the effectiveness of the first possibility is clear from
the argument indicator and the context. It is this,

> (3) A workman who refused to work more than nine hours while there
> were others who worked ten, would either not be employed at all,
> or if employed, must submit to lose one-tenth of his wages

therefore

> (2) However convinced . . . he may be that it is in the interest of the
> class to work short time, it is contrary to his own interest to set an
> example, unless he is well assured that all or most others will follow
> it.

Mill's argument against the effectiveness of the second possibility seems
equally easy to find. He asks whether 'general agreement of the whole
class . . . might not be effectual without the sanction of law' and answers,

> (6) If nearly all restricted themselves to nine hours, those who chose
> to work for ten would gain all the advantages of the restriction,
> together with the profit from infringing it; they would get ten hours'
> wages for nine hours' work, and an hour's wages besides

therefore

> (5) however beneficial the observance of the regulation might be to the
> class collectively, the immediate interest of every individual would
> lie in violating it

therefore

> (4) [Even] a general agreement of the whole class might not . . . be
> effective . . . unless enforced by opinion with a rigour practically
> equal to that of the law.

His view of the third possibility appears to be that it would be the most
desirable state of things but that it would also probably be unstable; the
argument is,

> (8) Probably . . . so many would prefer the ten hours' work on the
> improved terms, that the limitation could not be maintained as a

75

general practice: what some did from choice, others would soon be obliged to do from necessity, and those who had chosen long hours for the sake of increased wages, would be forced in the end to work long hours for no greater wages than before

therefore

(7) [Majority choice might not be effective.]

Thus, in summary, Mill's argument appears to be represented by the following diagram,

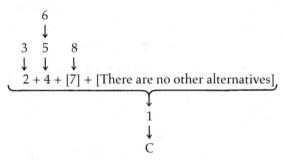

There are certainly other ways of representing this argument, but we have adopted this approach (using the Assertibility Question) because it seems to be the simplest way of extracting all that is *necessary* for understanding and evaluating the argument. The reasoning actually employs several 'suppositions' and we could analyse it quite differently using the techniques to be developed in the next chapter, but it is doubtful whether this would be worth the effort (whether it would generate any greater insight). It might be possible to try to apply the formalism of predicate logic (see pp. 184f.) to the analysis of this reasoning: that would certainly *not* be worth the effort if our objective is to spot as quickly and efficiently as possible any weaknesses we can in the argument. There is no doubt that our approach relies heavily on an understanding of the text – the approach outlined in Chapter 2 is skeletal and explicitly leaves room for judgement based on such understanding – but it is also intended to be relatively efficient.

The passage marked up according to the method of Chapter 2 looks as follows,

To a fourth case of exception I must request particular attention, it being one to which as it appears to me the attention of political economists has not yet been sufficiently drawn. There are matters in which the interference of law is required, not to overrule the
C judgment of individuals respecting their own interest, but to give effect to that judgment: they being unable to give effect to it except

by concert, which concert again cannot be effectual unless it receives validity and sanction from the law. For illustration, and without prejudging the particular point, I may advert to the question of diminishing the hours of labour. Let us suppose, what is at least supposable, whether it be the fact or not – that a general reduction of the hours of factory labour, say from ten to nine, would be for the advantage of the work-people: that they would receive as high wages, or nearly as high, for nine hours' labour as they receive for ten. If this would be the result, and if the operatives generally are convinced that it would, the limitation, some may say, will be adopted spontaneously. I answer, that it will not be adopted unless the body of operatives bind themselves to one another to abide by it.

3 ⟨A workman who refused to work more than nine hours while there were others who worked ten, would either not be employed at all, or if employed, must submit to lose one-tenth of his wages.⟩

2 ⟨However convinced, ⟨therefore⟩, he may be that it is in the interest of the class to work short time, it is contrary to his own interest to set the example, unless he is well assured that all or most others will follow it.⟩ But suppose ⟨a general agreement of the whole class: might not this be effectual without the sanction of law?⟩ Not unless enforced by opinion with a rigour practically equal to that of law.

5 ⟨For⟩ ⟨however beneficial the observance of the regulation might be to the class collectively, the immediate interest of every individual would lie in violating it:⟩ and the more numerous those were who adhered to the rule, the more would individuals gain by departing

6 from it. ⟨If nearly all restricted themselves to nine hours, those who chose to work for ten would gain all the advantages of the restriction, together with the profit from infringing it; they would get ten hours' wages for nine hours' work, and an hour's wages besides.⟩ I grant if a large majority adhered to the nine hours, there would be no harm done; the benefit would be, in the main, secured to the class, while those individuals who preferred to work harder and earn more, would have an opportunity of doing so. This certainly would be the state of things to be wished for; and assuming that a reduction of hours without any diminution of wages could take

place without expelling the commodity from some of its markets –
which is in every particular instance a question of fact, not of
principle – the manner in which it would be most desirable that this
effect should be brought about, would be by a quiet change in the
general custom of the trade; short hours becoming, by spontaneous
choice, the general practice, but those who chose to deviate from
it having the fullest liberty to do so. ⟨Probably, however, so many

8   would prefer the ten hours' work on the improved terms, that the
limitation could not be maintained as a general practice: what some
did from choice, others would soon be obliged to do from necessity, and those who had chosen long hours for the sake of increased
wages, would be forced in the end to work long hours for no greater

1   wages than before.⟩ ⟨Assuming (then) that it really would be the
interest of each to work only nine hours if he could be assured that
all others would do the same, there might be no means of attaining
this object but by converting their supposed mutual agreement into
an engagement under penalty, by consenting to have it enforced
by law.⟩ I am not expressing any opinion in favour of such an
enactment, which has never in this country been demanded, and
which I certainly should not, in present circumstances, recommend:

C   but it serves to exemplify the manner in which classes of persons
may need the assistance of law, to give effect to their deliberate
collective opinion of their own interest, by affording to every
individual a guarantee that his competitors will pursue the same
course, without which he cannot safely adopt it himself.

Margin notes:

8
↓
7 [Majority choice
might not be
effective.]

2 + 4 + [7]
+ [There are no
other alternatives.]
⎴
1

1
↓
C

III   'Test for a good argument' applied to Mill's text

Now that we are clear about Mill's argument we can ask whether it establishes
its conclusion. We have already seen that Mill's reasoning has the right
structure, i.e. he considers the apparent alternatives and argues that they
will not work, so now we have to look at the details of the reasoning.

The inference from (3) to (2),

> (2) it is contrary to [a worker's] own interest to set an example, unless
> he is well assured that all or most others will follow it

is hard to fault. There are many similar cases. If all or most car drivers refuse to pay an extra tax on car ownership which the government chooses to impose no doubt the government will have to think again, but if one car driver refuses to pay 'to set an example' he will probably not drive very far! No doubt the reader can think of other examples where something is in everyone's interest but if an individual tries to set an example he will simply lose out unless all or most others do the same.

Now let us look at the argument against the effectiveness of general agreement,

(6) If nearly all restricted themselves to nine hours, those who chose to work for ten would gain all the advantages of the restriction, together with the profit from infringing it. They would get ten hours' wages for nine hours' work, and an hour's wages besides

therefore

(5) however beneficial the observance of the regulation might be to the class collectively, the immediate interest of every individual would lie in violating it

therefore

(4) [Even] a general agreement of the whole class might not . . . be effective . . . unless enforced by opinion with a rigour practically equal to that of the law.

Assuming (6) to be true, could (5) be false judging by appropriate standards of what is possible? The answer to this question requires some thought: does it follow that 'the immediate interest of every individual would lie in violating' the nine-hour regulation? Surely this all depends on the value each person places on the extra hour's leisure as compared with the extra hour's income. Some people might value the extra leisure more than the extra income so it would *not* be in their interest to violate the nine-hour regulation. Hence, (5) does *not* follow from (6) unless one has some further assumption to the effect that everyone prefers more money to more leisure (and that may have been an appropriate assumption in Mill's day).

Of course, Mill's argument can be rescued by substituting for (5),

(5a) however beneficial the observance of the regulation might be to the class collectively the immediate interest of *some individuals might* lie in violating it.

and whether 'general agreement' could then be 'effective' in maintaining the nine-hour regulation would depend entirely upon *how many* people felt that it was in their own interest to violate it. Mill might have been aware of this line of thought because he grants in this context that,

> if a large majority adhered to the nine hours there would be no harm done (etc.)

and perhaps we should construe him as saying why general agreement might not work even in this case where he says,

(8) Probably . . . so many would prefer the ten hours' work on the improved terms, that the limitation could not be maintained as a general practice: what some did from choice, others would soon be obliged to do from necessity, and those who had chosen long hours for the sake of increased wages, would be forced in the end to work long hours for no greater wages than before.

Certainly, as Mill's argument stands, it appears to contain a slip, in the inference to 'the immediate interest of *every* individual would lie in violating the nine-hour regulation'. To be charitable to Mill we should probably reconstrue his reasoning as having the structure:

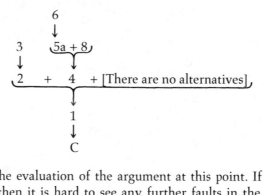

We leave the evaluation of the argument at this point. If 'there are no alternatives' then it is hard to see any further faults in the argument we have just diagrammed. We leave it to the reader to consider whether there are any other alternatives or any other faults. Exercise 6, p. 194, is a directly relevant exercise since it contains very similar reasoning.

Mill's argument is an example of a kind of argument which is quite important in economics and in some social and political theory. It is based on a widely held view about the sort of creatures human beings are – a 'model of man' as it is called by theorists – and it draws out some implications of that model for collective or social action. The model assumes that human beings have 'interests' – which are basically what each person happens to *prefer* or *want*. (Clearly on this view one person's interests might be quite different from another's; e.g. in Mill's example, one worker might want more money, another more leisure.) It also assumes that each of us, in so far as we are *rational*, pursues *only our own* self-interest. (So that, to take Mill's example again, a worker will not do something which is 'for the advantage of the work-people' out of a sense of group solidarity or loyalty; he will do it if and only if he conceives it to be in his *own* best interest.) In the language of the Utilitarians – and indeed of modern micro-economics – the 'rational economic man' tries to *maximise* his *own happiness* or '*utility*'.

It might be thought that if such 'rational economic men' belong to a group in which everyone has the same objective, this objective is bound to be realised. As Mancur Olson put it in his seminal work *The Logic of Collective Action,*

> if the members of some group have a common interest or objective and if they would all be better off if that objective were achieved, it has been thought to follow logically that the individuals in that group would, if they were rational and self-interested, act to achieve that objective.

But this does *not* follow. As Olson puts it:

> unless the number of individuals in the group is quite small, or unless there is coercion or some other device to make individuals act in their common interest, rational, self-interested individuals will not act to achieve their common or group interests.

Thomas Hobbes had a similar conception of human nature and he reached a similar conclusion. As he puts in in Chapter 18 of *Leviathan,*

> covenants being but words and breath, have no force to oblige, contain or constrain any man, but what [they have] from the public sword.

To conclude, Mill's insight was not new, nor does his argument exhaust the subject. In general, the pursuit of individual advantage may lead to what everyone recognises as an undesirable outcome. The problem is how to avoid that and coercion via the law may be the only way. The arguments in this area are tricky and fascinating; indeed its problems have generated a whole new branch of mathematics, called 'game-theory'. We can take the matter no further here except to remark that if freedom consists in doing what you want, you may have to submit to legal constraint to get it! (For a relevant exercise, see p. 194.)

6 · Arguments about God's existence

Does God exist? There are many fascinating arguments which relate to this subject and in this chapter we look at just two. We do this partly to give more examples which use our method of analysing and evaluating arguments, but also to see how the method copes with two distinctive kinds of argument – one *rhetorical* and one *philosophical*. We begin with a piece by Richard Dawkins called 'The more you understand evolution, the more you move towards atheism' and then we look at a piece by A. J. Ayer.

SECTION A: DAWKINS

I   Dawkins: 'The more you understand evolution, the more you move towards atheism'

Dr Richard Dawkins is Professor of Public Understanding of Science at Oxford University. He is famous worldwide for his work in biology, especially as he explains it in a number of very readable books including *The Selfish Gene, The Blind Watchmaker, River Out of Eden* and several others. The following piece is an edited version of a speech he made at the Edinburgh International Science Festival on 15 April 1992. It is reprinted from the *Independent* newspaper with the permission of Dr Dawkins (paragraphs are labelled for ease of subsequent reference).

(a) As a Darwinian, something strikes me when I look at religion. Religion shows a pattern of heredity which I think is similar to genetic heredity. The vast majority of people have an allegiance to one particular religion. There are hundreds of different religious sects, and every religious person is loyal to just one of these.

(b) Out of all the sects in the world, we notice an uncanny coincidence: the overwhelming majority just happen to choose the one their parents belonged to. Not the sect that has the best evidence in its favour, the best miracles, the best moral code, the best cathedral, the best stained-glass, the best music: when it comes to choosing from the smorgasbord of available religions, their potential virtues seem to count for nothing compared to the matter of heredity.

(c) This is an unmistakable fact; nobody could seriously deny it. Yet people with full knowledge of the arbitrary nature of this heredity, somehow manage to go on believing in their religion, often with such fanaticism that they are prepared to murder people who follow a different one.

(d) Truths about the cosmos are true all around the universe. They don't differ in Pakistan, Afghanistan, Poland or Norway. Yet we are apparently prepared to accept that the religion we adopt is a matter of an accident of geography.

(e) If you ask people why they are convinced of the truth of their religion, they don't appeal to heredity. Put like that it sounds too obviously stupid. Nor do they appeal to evidence. There isn't any, and nowadays the better educated admit it. No, they appeal to faith. Faith is the great cop-out, the great excuse to evade the need to think and evaluate evidence. Faith is belief in spite of, even perhaps because of, the lack of evidence. The worst thing is that the rest of us are supposed to respect it: to treat it with kid gloves.

(f) If a slaughterman doesn't comply with the law in respect of cruelty to animals, he is rightly prosecuted and punished. But if he complains that his cruel practices are necessitated by religious faith, we back off apologetically and allow him to get on with it. Any other position that someone takes up can expect to be defended with reasoned argument. But faith is immune. Faith is allowed not to justify itself by argument. Faith must be respected: and if you don't respect it, you are accused of violating basic human rights.

(g) Even those with no faith have been brainwashed into respecting the faith of others. When so-called Muslim community leaders go on the radio and advocate the killing of Salman Rushdie, they are clearly committing incitement to murder – a crime for which they would ordinarily be prosecuted and possibly imprisoned. But are they arrested? They are not, because our secular society respects their faith, and sympathizes with the deep hurt and insult to it.

(h) Well I don't. I will respect your views if you can justify them. But if you justify your views only by saying you have faith in them, I shall not respect them.

(j) I want to end by returning to science. It is often said . . . that although there is no positive evidence for the existence of a God, nor is there evidence against His existence. So it is best to keep an open mind and be agnostic.

(k) At first sight that seems an unassailable position, at least in the weak sense of Pascal's wager. But on second thoughts it seems a cop-out, because the same could be said of Father Christmas and tooth fairies. There may be fairies at the bottom of the garden. There is no evidence of it, but you can't *prove* that there aren't any, so shouldn't we be agnostic with respect to fairies?

(m) The trouble with the agnostic argument is that it can be applied to anything. There is an infinite number of hypothetical beliefs we could hold which we can't positively disprove. On the whole, people don't believe in most of them, such as fairies, unicorns, dragons, Father Christmas, and so on. But on the whole they do believe in a creator God, together with whatever particular baggage goes with the religion of their parents.

(n) I suspect the reason is that most people . . . nevertheless have a residue of feeling that Darwinian evolution isn't quite big enough to explain everything about life. All I can say as a biologist is that the feeling disappears progressively the more you read about and study what is known about life and evolution.

(p) I want to add one thing more. The more you understand the significance of evolution, the more you are pushed away from the agnostic position and towards atheism. Complex, statistically improbable things are by their nature more difficult to explain than simple, statistically probable things.

(q) The great beauty of Darwin's theory of evolution is that it explains how complex, difficult to understand things could have arisen step by plausible step, from simple, easy to understand beginnings. We start our explanation from almost infinitely simple beginnings: pure hydrogen and a huge amount of energy. Our scientific, Darwinian explanations carry us through a series of well-understood gradual steps to all the spectacular beauty and complexity of life.

(r) The alternative hypothesis, that it was all started by a supernatural creator, is not only superfluous; it is also highly improbable. It falls foul of the very argument that was originally put forward in its favour. This is because any god worthy of the name must have been a being of colossal intelligence, a supermind, an entity of enormous sophistication and complexity. In other words, an entity of extremely low statistical probability – a very improbable being.

(s) Even if the postulation of such an entity explained anything (and we don't need it to), it still wouldn't help because it raises a bigger mystery than it solves.

(t) Science offers us an explanation of how complexity (the difficult) arose out of simplicity (the easy). The hypothesis of God offers no worthwhile explanation for anything, for it simply postulates the difficult to explain and leaves it at that. We cannot prove that there is no God, but we can safely conclude that He is very, very improbable indeed.

As we have said of previous examples (cf. p. 32), our immediate interest is in getting clear exactly what Dawkins is arguing and in showing the reader how far you can get by following the method outlined in Chapter 2, but the reader will find it instructive to try to answer the following questions before going on. In effect, they are answered in the discussion below.

Questions

(1) What is Dawkins's main conclusion in this piece?
(2) Outline Dawkins's reasoning for thinking that God is 'very, very improbable indeed'.
(3) What is Dawkins's reasoning for thinking that 'the hypothesis that [life] was started by a supernatural creator is superfluous'?
(4) What kinds of *evidence* might lend support to someone's religious beliefs?
(5) What would show the following,
  (i) 'Religion shows a pattern of heredity similar to genetic heredity' is (a) true, (b) false?
  (ii) 'Faith is belief in spite of the lack of evidence' is (a) true, (b) false?

(iii) 'The existence of God is statistically very improbable' is (a) true, (b) false?

II Extracting the arguments from Dawkins's text

To extract the arguments from Dawkins's text we follow the steps described in Chapter 2, so we first circle all the explicit argument indicators. These are not obvious, but they appear to be 'because' (k), 'This is because' (r), 'because' (s), 'for' (t) and finally 'we can safely conclude that' (t). The argument indicators are not obvious partly because there are several phrases which look like argument indicators, but which are functioning differently. Thus, 'because of' in (e), 'because' in (g) and 'the reason is' in (n) are all presenting explanations, not reasons (cf. p. 18 section (iii)). Also 'so' in (j) and (k) are being quoted, not used, i.e., Dawkins is discussing arguments which have been asserted by other people but is not asserting them himself (the notion of 'assertion' is explained on p. 173.)

We next bracket any clearly indicated reasons and underline clearly indicated conclusions using inference indicators to help us. It seems reasonably clear that his main conclusion is,

[God] is very very improbable indeed.

or

Though we cannot prove there is no God, . . . He is very, very improbable indeed.

Some other conclusions which occur earlier in the piece are,

The hypothesis of God offers no worthwhile explanation for anything

Even if the postulation of such an entity [God] explained anything (and we don't need it to), it still wouldn't help

The alternative hypothesis, that [life] was all started by a supernatural creator, is not only superfluous, it is also highly improbable.

and,

The argument that 'although there is no positive evidence for the existence of a God, nor is there evidence against His existence. So it is best to keep an open mind and be agnostic' seems a cop-out.

It is not easy to find conclusions (in the sense of claims which are argued for) in the first half of Dawkins's piece. He asserts that,

> Religion shows a pattern of heredity which I think is similar to genetic heredity

but it is not quite obvious whether he is arguing for that or not. However, if we ask the Assertibility Question, 'What would show this claim to be true?', the natural answer is that we would need to find evidence that nearly everyone adopts the religion of their parents (just as they inherit the genes of their parents) and that is very close to what Dawkins asserts, so it is reasonable to construe that as his reason for his claim.

It is also clear that he disapproves strongly when people appeal to 'faith' to justify their beliefs,

> I will respect your views if you can justify them. But if you justify your views only by saying you have faith in them, I shall not respect them.

but again it is not quite clear how he is arguing against such appeals. His reasoning appears to be that appeals to faith are used (i) to evade the need to evaluate evidence and (ii) to justify some deplorable activities – including both incitement to murder and the cruelty involved in some slaughter practices.

If you accept what has been said so far, you will agree that Dawkins's piece should be marked up somewhat as follows,

(a) As a Darwinian, something strikes me when I look at religion. Religion shows a pattern of heredity which I think is similar to <u>genetic heredity.</u> The vast majority of people have an allegiance to one particular religion. There are hundreds of different religious sects, and every religious person is loyal to just one of these.

    1

    2
    ↓
    1

(b) Out of all the sects in the world, we notice an uncanny coincidence: (the overwhelming majority just happen to choose the one their parents belonged to.) Not the sect that has the best evidence in its favour, the best miracles, the best moral code, the best cathedral, the best stained-glass, the best music: when it comes to choosing from the smorgasbord of available religions, their potential virtues seem to count for nothing compared to the matter of heredity.

    2

(c) This is an unmistakable fact; nobody could seriously deny it. Yet people with full knowledge of the arbitrary nature of this heredity, somehow manage to go on believing in their religion, often with such fanaticism that they are prepared to murder people who follow a different one.

(d) Truths about the cosmos are true all around the universe. They don't differ in Pakistan, Afghanistan, Poland or Norway. Yet we are apparently prepared to accept that the religion we adopt is a matter of an accident of geography.

(e) If you ask people why they are convinced of the truth of their religion, they don't appeal to heredity. Put like that it sounds too obviously stupid. Nor do they appeal to evidence. There isn't any, and nowadays the better educated admit it. No, they appeal to faith. (Faith is the great cop-out, the great excuse to evade the need to think and evaluate evidence. Faith is belief in spite of, even perhaps because of, the lack of evidence.) The worst thing is that the rest of us are supposed to respect it: to treat it with kid gloves.

(f) (If a slaughterman doesn't comply with the law in respect of cruelty to animals, he is rightly prosecuted and punished. But if he complains that his cruel practices are necessitated by religious faith, we back off apologetically and allow him to get on with it.) Any other position that someone takes up can expect to be defended with reasoned argument. But faith is immune. Faith is allowed not to justify itself by argument. Faith must be respected: and if you don't respect it, you are accused of violating basic human rights.

(g) Even those with no faith have been brainwashed into respecting the faith of others. (When so-called Muslim community leaders go on the radio and advocate the killing of Salman Rushdie, they are clearly committing incitement to murder – a crime for which they would ordinarily be prosecuted and possibly imprisoned.) But are they arrested? They are not, because our secular society respects their faith, and sympathizes with the deep hurt and insult to it.

(h) Well I don't. <u>I will respect your views if you can justify them. But if you justify your views only by saying you have faith in them, I shall not respect them.</u> [The argument]

(j) I want to end by returning to science. It is often said . . ⋏ . <u>that although there is no positive evidence for the existence of a God,</u>

3

4a

$$\underbrace{4a + 4b}_{\substack{\text{appeals to faith} \\ \text{are used to} \\ \text{justify} \\ \text{deplorable} \\ 3 + \text{activities}}}$$
5

4b

5

nor is there evidence against His existence. So it is best to keep an   6
open mind and be agnostic.

(k) At first sight that seems an unassailable position, at least in the
weak sense of Pascal's wager. But on second thoughts it seems a   6 (Continued)
cop-out, because (the same could be said of Father Christmas and   7 7
tooth fairies.) There may be fairies at the bottom of the garden. $\downarrow$
There is no evidence of it, but you can't *prove* that there aren't any,   6
so shouldn't we be agnostic with respect to fairies?

(m) The trouble with the agnostic argument is that it can be applied to
anything. There is an infinite number of hypothetical beliefs we
could hold which we can't positively disprove. On the whole, people
don't believe in most of them, such as fairies, unicorns, dragons,
Father Christmas, and so on. But on the whole they do believe in a
creator God, together with whatever particular baggage goes with
the religion of their parents.

(n) I suspect the reason is that most people . . . nevertheless have a
residue of feeling that Darwinian evolution isn't quite big enough
to explain everything about life. All I can say as a biologist is that
the feeling disappears progressively the more you read about and
study what is known about life and evolution.

(p) I want to add one thing more. The more you understand the significance of evolution, the more you are pushed away from the agnostic position and towards atheism. Complex, statistically improbable
things are by their nature more difficult to explain than simple,
statistically probable things.

(q) The great beauty of Darwin's theory of evolution is that it explains
how complex, difficult to understand things could have arisen step
by plausible step, from simple, easy to understand beginnings. We
start our explanation from almost infinitely simple beginnings: pure
hydrogen and a huge amount of energy. Our scientific, Darwinian
explanations carry us through a series of well-understood gradual
steps to all the spectacular beauty and complexity of life.

(r) The alternative hypothesis, that it was all started by a supernatural   8
creator, is not only superfluous; it is also highly improbable. It
falls foul of the very argument that was originally put forward

9   in its favour. [This is because] ⟨any god worthy of the name must have been a being of colossal intelligence, a supermind, an entity of enormous sophistication and complexity. In other words, an entity of extremely low statistical probability – a very improbable being.⟩

11   10   (s) Even if the postulation of such an entity explained anything (and
↓
10   11   we don't need it to), it still wouldn't help [because] ⟨it raises a bigger mystery than it solves.⟩

(t) Science offers us an explanation of how complexity (the difficult)
13   12   arose out of simplicity (the easy). The hypothesis of God offers
↓
12   no worthwhile explanation for anything, [for] ⟨it simply postulates
13   the difficult to explain and leaves it at that.⟩ We cannot prove that
14   there is no God, but [we can safely conclude that] He is very, very improbable indeed.

Though it is not easy to be sure, the overall structure of the argument looks something like the following,

(1) Religious beliefs are inherited (not based on rational thought); appeals to faith do not justify religious beliefs and should not be respected; (6) the argument for agnosticism about God's existence does not justify its conclusion; **and** (8) God is superfluous and a very improbable being **Therefore** [though we cannot prove there is no God] (14) the existence of God is very, very improbable indeed.

III 'Tests for a good argument' applied to Dawkins's arguments

Now that we are as clear as we can be about what Dawkins is arguing, we can ask whether his arguments establish his conclusions. We have already addressed this question in some cases – where we used the Assertibility Question to extract the best reasoning we could find in the text – but there is a good deal more work to do.

Let us look through successive arguments in Dawkins's piece and see what judgements we reach.

IIIa   'Religion is (almost) inherited'

Assuming for the moment that Dawkins is *arguing* that 'religion shows a pattern of heredity which is similar to genetic heredity', does his reasoning establish its conclusion? We must first ask whether his premiss is true and then, if it is true, whether its conclusion could be false judging by appropriate standards. Is it true that the overwhelming majority of people adopt the religion of their parents – the merits of various religions counting for very little? This is a straightforwardly empirical claim and the facts could be checked out. Well, what evidence would be required to establish Dawkins's conclusion? If nearly everyone (worldwide) adopts the religion of their parents, then 'religion does show a pattern of heredity similar to genetic heredity' but if 'enough' people adopt a different religion from their parents, this would undermine the claimed similarity. Clearly, if 99% adopt their parents' religion, Dawkins's claim is strongly supported but if only 50% do, it isn't, though it is hard to draw a line and say what percentages would persuade us for or against Dawkins's claim.

Perhaps, however, we have misconstrued his intention. Perhaps he is not arguing a case here, but is simply asserting a striking analogy, to make the point that most people adopt their religion without thinking much about alternative religions – and certainly without rationally weighing the evidence for and against alternatives. If that is Dawkins's purpose, my hunch is that he is very probably right, though investigation might show otherwise in many cases.

IIIb 'Faith versus evidence'

It is clear that Dawkins disapproves strongly when people appeal to 'faith' to justify their religious beliefs and, as we said earlier, his reasoning appears to be that appeals to faith are used (i) to evade the need to evaluate evidence and (ii) to justify some deplorable activities – including incitement to murder and the cruelty involved in some slaughter practices. Again, to evaluate this reasoning, we need to ask whether the basic claims are true and whether they justify their conclusion (judging by appropriate standards).

Assuming Dawkins's reasoning here has the structure we 'marked up' earlier, let us consider each of his basic claims.

On the cruelty involved in some slaughter practices, we would need to investigate carefully whether cruelty does occur in these cases and whether it occurs more often than in the slaughter practices which involve stunning animals before they are killed. We would then need to decide whether such cruelty (if it occurred) broke the law or was otherwise unjustified. Cruelty is contrary to most moral codes, so on the face of it, slaughter practices which required 'unnecessary' cruelty would not be easy to justify and simple appeals to the requirements of 'faith' would surely not be enough. Furthermore, it is likely that sophisticated defenders of these slaughter practices would be able to show that stunning is often ineffective (so cruelty occurs) and that the justification for using their methods is more subtle than a mere appeal to religious faith. In this case the 'appropriate standard' by which to judge would surely be whether slaughter practices required or involved 'unnecessary' cruelty.

Moving on to the *fatwa* against Salman Rushdie, was this a case of 'incitement to murder' or otherwise unjustified? (Salman Rushdie wrote a book called *Midnight's Children* which was condemned by some Islamic leaders for blaspheming against Islam. As a result, they issued a *fatwa* against him, which authorised and encouraged Muslims to kill Rushdie.) It was certainly an extraordinary thing to do, and one which was regarded very differently by different groups of people. Many Muslims thought it was perfectly proper – and was justified. Many 'liberals' thought it was an appalling thing to do – and was completely unjustified. How should we react? In short, we would have to investigate what 'harm' was done by Rushdie's book (to Islam, its followers and perhaps to others) and whether this could justify issuing a *fatwa* against him. We should have to consider the grounds on which the *fatwa* was issued and how these square with our moral code and that of Islam. It would be a complex matter and surely one where mere appeals to religious 'faith' would not be enough, but, as we said in the previous case, sophisticated defenders would be unlikely to rely on simple appeals to their faith.

Dawkins also claims that people appeal to faith to evade the need to evaluate evidence about their religious beliefs. Suppose we ask the Assertibility Question about a religious belief – for example, 'What argument or evidence would justify me in accepting that a Christian God exists?' Many people claim that religious beliefs are based on all kinds of evidence, including 'sacred' texts, well-established historical events, personal 'religious' experiences, the lives of religious leaders and much more. They may also grant that suffering and 'the existence of evil' are 'problems' for those who believe in a Christian God – that they provide evidence *against* God's existence. These are the kinds of considerations which are normally taken to be relevant to Christians beliefs and it is surely a mistake on Dawkins's part to claim that those who believe in a Christian God do not consider such matters.

IIIc 'Agnosticism about God, fairies, unicorns and dragons'

Moving on to his argument in (j) – (m), we encounter what looks like a very neat move. Dawkins is commenting on the argument that,

> although there is no positive evidence for the existence of a God,
> nor is there evidence against His existence. So it is best to keep an
> open mind and be agnostic.

As Dawkins says, this looks like plausible reasoning (Pascal's wager is the argument presented on p. 2 earlier), but it seems that the same 'pattern' of reasoning would justify us in 'being agnostic' about whether there are fairies, unicorns and Father Christmas, but most people do not keep an open mind about the existence of these. So what is going on here?

Consider the following argument which exhibits the same pattern we are considering,

> there is no positive evidence that Jones committed the murder (though we think he might have), nor can we prove that he didn't (he does not have a cast-iron alibi, etc.). So it is best to keep an open mind and be agnostic (admit we don't know yet).

Surely this is a reasonable argument. If the reasons are true, how could there be anything wrong with the conclusion (judging by appropriate standards etc.)? Equally, surely this would also be a reasonable pattern of argument for a scientist investigating the existence of, say, telepathy, flying saucers, life on other planets or Atlantis; if we believe these things might exist and we can't prove they don't, then shouldn't we keep an open mind and be agnostic?

But this pattern of argument does not persuade us to be agnostic about fairies, unicorns, dragons or Father Christmas, so why doesn't it? In short, the answer seems to be that if you believe you have enough evidence to settle an issue (e.g., that Father Christmas could not exist), the agnostic argument will not give you a reason to change your belief (because you believe that one of the premisses is false). If you accept the premisses (Jones could be the murderer but might not be), the conclusion is reasonable. Most people have made up their minds about unicorns, dragons and Father Christmas (because they believe these are merely fictitious creations) but God's existence is a rather more serious issue (as Pascal saw). Dawkins has already made up his mind that God does not exist, so he is not impressed by the argument for agnosticism with respect to God's existence – but many people are because they simply haven't made up their minds on the subject.

In fact, the argument for agnosticism comes very near to 'begging the question' as philosophers say; it assumes something 'very close' to what is sets out to prove. If you believe God could exist, but His existence is not proven, the argument barely gives you a reason for being agnostic, because you have to be agnostic for it to get started. If you believe the idea of God is absurd and that He couldn't exist (any more than Father Christmas could) the argument for being agnostic about His existence doesn't even get started (because you reject a premiss on which it is based). The same is true for fairies etc. The difference Dawkins draws attention to is explained by the fact that most people have made up their minds about fairies etc. but many haven't about God.

IIId 'God is superfluous and very improbable'

This brings us to Dawkins's four concluding paragraphs, where the reasoning seems to lead first to the conclusion that 'The . . . hypothesis . . . [of] a supernatural creator, is . . . superfluous' and then to 'We cannot prove that there is no God, but we can safely conclude that He is very, very improbable indeed.'

The reasoning for the first conclusion (and its structure) seem to be,

11   ⟨Postulating the existence of God raises a bigger mystery than it solves,⟩ (so) even if the postulation of such an entity explained

10 anything, it still wouldn't help.

13   ⟨The hypothesis of God simply postulates the difficult to explain

12 and leaves it at that⟩ (so) it offers no worthwhile explanation for anything.

⟨The great beauty of Darwin's theory of evolution is that it

15 explains how complex, difficult to understand things could have

arisen step by plausible step, from simple, easy to understand

10 beginnings.⟩ However, ⟨even if the postulation of [God] explained

anything, it still wouldn't help,⟩ but in fact ⟨it offers no worthwhile

12 explanation for anything.⟩

(So) . . . The alternative hypothesis, that it was all started by a supernatural creator, is . . . superfluous (we don't need it).

$$\begin{array}{c} 11 \quad 13 \\ \downarrow \quad \downarrow \\ \hline 15 + 10 + 12 \\ \hline 1^{st} \text{ part of } 8 \end{array}$$

first part of 8

Does this reasoning establish its conclusion (judging by appropriate standards etc.)? If you accept that postulating God's existence 'raises a bigger mystery than it solves' or 'offers no worthwhile explanation for anything', you may conclude that God is superfluous. On the other hand, if you think postulating God's existence, far from creating a bigger mystery than it solves, actually 'makes sense' of something which is otherwise incomprehensible – namely the existence of the universe – you will not conclude that God is superfluous. In short, this looks like another 'question begging' argument – which comes very close to assuming what it sets out to prove.

The other line of reasoning is,

9   any god worthy of the name must have been a being of colossal intelligence, a supermind, an entity of enormous sophistication and complexity.

9
↓   So [though] we cannot prove there is no God, He is very very   2nd part of 8, or
14   improbable indeed.   14

Again, this look like a question begging an argument. Of course 'a being of colossal intelligence (etc.)' is very, very improbable but so is the existence of the universe and some people think it is more probable with a Creator than without.

IIIe To conclude

It is not easy to know how to evaluate the arguments in this passage – or even whether they are arguments. The passage is very engagingly and eloquently written. However, my judgement is that though the material is very well expressed and is rhetorically powerful, its arguments, if that is what they are, carry little persuasive force, because they so often tend to beg the question. In short this is an example of rhetorically forceful writing where asking the Assertibility Question helps you to see just how circular its arguments are – if they are arguments.

SECTION B: AYER

I Ayer: 'all utterances about the nature of God are nonsensical'

A. J. Ayer wrote the following piece in 1935 and it articulates a distinctive view about God which is clearly argued. This view presents a challenge to the Assertibility Question and we consider it here partly for that reason. (The sentences are labelled for ease of subsequent reference.)

> (a) It is important not to confuse [my] view of religious assertions with the view that is adopted by atheists, or agnostics. (b) For it is characteristic of an agnostic to hold that the existence of a god is a possibility in which there is no good reason either to believe or to disbelieve; and it is characteristic of an atheist to hold that it is at least probable that no god exists. (c) And our view that all utterances about the nature of God are nonsensical, so far from being identical with, or even lending support to, either of these familiar contentions, is actually incompatible with them. (d) For if the assertion that there is a god is nonsensical, then the atheist's assertion that there is no god is equally nonsensical, since it is only a significant proposition that

can be significantly contradicted. (e) As for the agnostic, although he refrains from saying either that there is or that there is not a god, he does not deny that the question whether a transcendent god exists is a genuine question. (f) He does not deny that the two sentences 'There is a transcendent god' and 'There is no transcendent god' express propositions one of which is actually true and the other false. (g) All he says is that we have no means of telling which of them is true, and therefore ought not to commit ourselves to either. (h) But we have seen that the sentences in question do not express propositions at all. (j) And this means that agnosticism also is ruled out. (A. J. Ayer, *Language, Truth and Logic*, 2nd edition, Gollancz, 1960, pp. 115–16)

Questions

    (1) What is Ayer's main conclusion in this piece?
    (2) Outline Ayer's argument for thinking that 'there is no God' is non-sensical or meaningless.
    (3) Outline Ayer's argument for thinking 'agnosticism is ruled out'.
    (4) What is the basic assumption underlying Ayer's reasoning?
    (5) What would show the following,
      (i) 'God exists' is true?
     (ii) 'God exists' is false?
    (iii) 'God exists' is meaningless?

II Extracting the arguments from Ayer's text

To extract the arguments from Ayer's text we follow our standard procedure. First we circle all the explicit argument indicators. These are 'for' (sentences (b) and (d)), 'since' (sentence (d)) and 'this means' (sentence (j)). The 'therefore' in sentence (g) is not being used by Ayer as part of his argument but is being quoted by him as part of the agnostic's argument, so we shouldn't circle it (you need to understand the difference between **using** 'therefore' in an argument – when you are *asserting* the reasons which come before it and the conclusion which comes after it – and **quoting** 'therefore' as part of someone else's argument – in which case you, the speaker, are *not* asserting the reasons or the conclusion).

    We next bracket any clearly indicated reasons and underline clearly indicated conclusions, using argument indicators to help us. If we do this we shall identify the following as conclusions,

(1) '[my] view that all utterances about the nature of God are nonsensical . . . is actually incompatible with [atheism] and [agnosticism]'

(2) 'if the assertion that there is a god is nonsensical, then the atheist's assertion that there is no god is equally nonsensical'

(3) 'agnosticism . . . is ruled out'.

To cut to the chase, the reasoning then amounts to something like the following,

(c) All utterances about the nature of God are nonsensical

[**so** the sentence 'there is a god' is nonsensical].

(d) It is only a significant proposition that can be significantly contradicted,

(d) **therefore** if the assertion that there is a god is nonsensical, then the atheist's assertion that there is no god is equally nonsensical.

(g) The agnostic believes that the two sentences 'There is a transcendent god' and 'There is no transcendent god' express propositions [are both meaningful],

(j) **so** agnosticism is ruled out.

(c) **Therefore** '[my] view that all utterances about the nature of God are nonsensical . . . is actually incompatible with [atheism] and [agnosticism]'.

III 'Tests for a good argument' applied to Ayer

Now that we are clear about Ayer's argument, we can ask whether it establishes his conclusion. If it is to do this, its premisses must be *true* and its conclusion must *follow* from them judging by *appropriate standards* of evidence or appropriate standards of what is possible.

If it is true that claims about the nature of God are nonsense, then it is very hard to see how the sentences 'there is a God' and 'there is no God' could be anything but meaningless nonsense. In that case what agnostics and atheists believe is nonsense too. So by the fiercest of logical standards, Ayer's argument is watertight if his initial premiss is true.

The question is whether his initial premiss is correct – whether it is correct to say that 'all utterances about the nature of God are nonsensical'. Ayer takes this position because he has a very narrow view about what evidence could show that God exists. He concludes from this that nothing could show

God does or does not exist and since nothing could settle such claims they are meaningless. So, in a sense, Ayer agrees with the Assertibility Principle (cf. p. 22) but he thinks that nothing could show 'God exists' true or false, so he thinks it must be meaningless. At this point you must consider for yourself what you think of that position, but if you wish to read more about it first you could turn to pp. 165ff.

Further reading

Richard Swinburne. *Is There a God?* Oxford University Press (1995)
Richard Dawkins's Review of Swinburne's *Is There a God?* in *The Sunday Times*, 4 Feb. 1996

7 · How do your mind and body interact?

In this chapter we analyse and evaluate an argument by a famous philosopher, A. J. Ayer, about the connection between (i) electrical impulses in our brains and (ii) thoughts and ideas in our minds. Most of us have a reasonably clear idea about what we mean when we talk about 'thoughts and ideas in our mind' and we know that scientists study how the brain works, how it is constructed, how 'messages' are transmitted within it and so on, but Ayer's piece is about the *connection*, if any, between the two – about how one's brain and mind interact with each other.

If you *conjure up an image* of an elephant in your mind's eye, or *entertain the thought* that 'the moon has a weak gravitational field' or *decide* to raise your arm, you might expect some 'corresponding' activity in your brain – some activity (physical, chemical, electrical or whatever) of a kind that scientists could see, describe and study. But what is the connection between the two? Does one cause the other? Does the 'mental activity' of *deciding* to raise your arm somehow send signals to your muscles which *cause* your arm to raise and, conversely, do electrical impulses in your brain somehow *cause* you to have the image of an elephant in your mind's eye or to *entertain the thought* about the moon's gravitational field? Alternatively, do these two distinct kinds of activities – the mental and the physical – just occur together without causally interacting? No sooner are these questions asked than you realise they raise further questions about what it means to say 'one causes the other' or 'they just occur together'.

We have here what many people would identify as a distinctly *philosophical* question; it is not quite clear how we should try to answer it; we don't quite know what information we should look for or can expect to find which might be relevant to answering it; and we have to try to get clear what is *meant* by various of the claims involved. That is partly why this example is included here, to see how the approach outlined in Chapter 2 might help us in dealing with such arguments.

Freddie Ayer, as he was generally known, is probably most famous for his book *Language, Truth and Logic*, which was first published in 1936, but which continued to be very influential for many years and is still well worth reading, especially for the clarity with which he presents his views. He had a distinguished career as a philosopher – including being Professor of Logic in Oxford University from 1959 to 1978 – and published widely on many philosophical topics. He was a colourful personality, an engaging lecturer and broadcaster and, unusual among philosophers, a life-long and keen supporter of Tottenham Hotspurs football team.

The passage we shall study, called *The Physical Basis of Mind*, was first presented as one of a series of broadcast talks and subsequently published in *The Physical Basis of Mind: A Series of Broadcast Talks* edited by Peter Laslett and published by Basil Blackwell, Oxford, 1957 (pp. 70–4).

I   Extract from *The Physical Basis of Mind* by A. J. Ayer

(Successive paragraphs are labelled to enable easy reference to them later.)

(a) The scientists who have spoken in this series have shown very fully and convincingly, how various mental processes – thinking, feeling, perceiving, remembering – are causally dependent upon processes in the brain, but to some of them at least the character of this connection still appears mysterious. Thus, . . . Professor Adrian . . . says that 'the part of the picture of the brain which may always be missing is of course the part which deals with the mind, the part which ought to explain how a particular pattern of nerve impulses can produce an idea; or the other way round, how a thought can decide which nerve cells are to come into action'.

(b) If this is a genuine problem, it is hard to see why further information about the brain should be expected to solve it. For however much we amplify our picture of the brain, it remains still a picture of something physical, and it is just the question how anything physical can interact with something that is **not** that is supposed to constitute our difficulty . . . It looks, indeed, as if some of the previous speakers were hoping to discover in the brain something describable as the locus of the mind; as if mind and brain could be conceived as meeting at a point in space or as somehow shading into one another: but to me this is not even an intelligible hypothesis. What would it be like to come upon this junction? By what signs would you recognise it if you found it? Descartes had the same problem, and he met it by suggesting that mind and body came together in the pineal gland; but how this conjecture could conceivably be tested he did not explain. The reason he had the problem – the reason why we have it still – is that matter and mind were conceived by him from the outset as distinct orders of being; it is as if there were two separate worlds, such that every event had to belong to one or other of them, but no event could belong to both. But from these premises it follows necessarily that there can be no bridge or junction; for what would the bridge consist of? Any event that you discovered would have to fall on one or other side of it. So, if there is a difficulty here, it is not because our factual information is scanty, but because our logic is defective. Perhaps this whole manner of conceiving the distinction between mind and matter is at fault. In short, our problem is not scientific but philosophical.

(c) Let us consider, then, what can be meant by saying that a particular pattern of nerve impulses 'produces' an idea, or that 'a thought decides' which nerve cells are to come into action. What are the facts on which such assertions are based? The facts are that the physiologist makes certain observations, and that these observations fall into different categories. On the one hand there are the observations which lead him to tell his story about nerve cells and electrical impulses. That is to say, the story is an interpretation of the observations in question. On the other hand there are the observations which he interprets by saying that the subject of his experiment is in such and such a 'mental' state, that he is thinking, or resolving to perform some action, or feeling some sensation, or whatever it may be. It is then found to be the case that these two sorts of observations can be correlated with one another; that whenever an observation of the first type can be made, there is a good reason to suppose that an observation of the second type can be made also . . . It seems to me that when it is asserted that the two events in question – the mental and the physical – are causally connected, that the pattern of nerve impulses 'produces' the sensation, or that the thought 'decides' which nerve cells are to operate, all that is meant, or at least all that can properly be meant, is that these two sets of observations are correlated in the way that I have described. But if this is so, where is the difficulty? There is nothing especially mysterious about the fact that two different sets of observations are correlated;

that, given the appropriate conditions, they habitually accompany one another. You may say that this fact requires an explanation; but such an explanation could only be some theory from which the fact of this correlation could be deduced. And in so far as the theory was not a mere re-description of the facts which it was intended to explain, it would serve only to fit them into a wider context. We should learn from it that not only were these observations correlated, but certain further types of observation were correlated with them. To ask *why* something occurs, it is not simply equivalent to asking *how* it occurs, is to ask what other things are associated with it. Once the facts are fully described, there is no mystery left.

(d) If there seems to be a mystery in this case, it is because we are misled by our conceptual systems; not by the facts themselves but by the pictures which we use to interpret the facts . . . The picture we are given is that of messengers travelling through the brain, reaching a mysterious entity called the mind, receiving orders from it, and then travelling on. But since the mind has no position in space – it is by definition not the sort of thing that can have a position in space – it does not literally make sense to talk of physical signals reaching it; . . . In short, the two stories will not mix . . . But to say that the two stories will not mix is not to say that either of them is superfluous. Each is an interpretation of certain phenomena and they are connected by the fact that, in certain conditions, when one of them is true, the other is true also.

(e) My conclusion is, then, that mind and body are not to be conceived as two disparate entities between which we have to make, or find, some sort of amphibious bridge, but that talking about minds and talking about bodies are different ways of classifying and interpreting our experiences. I do not say that this procedure does not give rise to serious philosophical problems; how for example, to analyse statements about their observable behaviour. But once we are freed from the Cartesian fallacy of regarding minds as immaterial substances, I do not think that the discovery of causal connections between what we choose to describe respectively as mental and physical occurrences implies anything by which we need to be perplexed.

Bearing in mind what we noted earlier, that this is a distinctively *philosophical* argument, the reader may find it instructive to answer the following questions before proceeding. In effect they are answered in the discussion below.

Questions

(1) What is Ayer's main conclusion?
(2) What reasoning does he present for this conclusion?
(3) What are Ayer's starting points – his basic premisses?
(4) What would show the following:
　　(i) 'a particular pattern of nerve impulses causes an idea' is true;
　　(ii) 'a thought decides which nerve cells are to come into action' is true?
(5) Do Ayer's arguments establish their conclusions?

II Extracting the arguments from Ayer's text

To extract the arguments from Ayer's text we follow our standard procedure. First we circle all the explicit argument indicators. These appear to be 'for' (b, line 2), perhaps 'the reason' (b, line 15 twice), 'it follows necessarily' (b, line 19), 'for' (b, line 20), 'so' (b, line 22), 'since' (d, line 6), 'my conclusion is', (e, line 1). The 'because' at (d), line 1 is clearly signalling an explanation (cf. p. 18 above). It is not quite obvious whether 'the reason' (b, line 15 twice) is being used as an argument indicator or whether it signals an explanation, but it looks as though it plays both roles.

We next bracket any clearly indicated reasons and underline clearly indicated conclusions, using argument indicators to help us. Of course, Ayer makes it very clear what is his 'main' conclusion, namely,

> My conclusion is . . . that mind and body are not to be conceived as
> two disparate entities between which we have to make, or find, some
> sort of amphibious bridge, but that talking about minds and talking
> about bodies are different ways of classifying and interpreting our
> experiences.

And perhaps he intends a further conclusion, which could reasonably be expressed as,

> Furthermore, once we are freed from the Cartesian fallacy of
> regarding minds as immaterial substances, I do not think that the
> discovery of causal connections between what we choose to describe

103

respectively as mental and physical occurrences implies anything by which we need to be perplexed.

It is clear from the occurrences of other argument indicators that something very like the following arguments are also part of Ayer's thinking,

> (R) If there is a genuine problem about how minds and brains causally interact, more information about the brain cannot help solve it,
>
> **because**
>
> however much we amplify our picture of the brain, it remains still a picture of something physical, and it is just the question how anything physical can interact with something that is not that is supposed to constitute our difficulty.

> (S) If matter and mind are thought of as distinct orders of being – as if there are two separate worlds, such that every event has to belong to one or other of them, but no event can belong to both,
>
> **it follows necessarily**
>
> that there can be no bridge or junction
>
> **for**
>
> any event that you discovered would have to fall on one side or the other of it.
>
> **So**, if there is a difficulty here, it is not because our factual information is scanty, but because our logic is defective. Perhaps this whole manner of conceiving the distinction between mind and matter is at fault. In short our problem is not scientific but philosophical.

> (T) **Since** the mind has no position in space – it is by definition not the sort of thing that can have a position in space – it does not literally make sense to talk of physical signals reaching it.

After arguing that our way of thinking about the difference between mind and matter is mistaken, Ayer explores (in paragraph (c)) what *'can be meant'* by saying that 'a particular pattern of nerve impulses "produces" an idea', or that 'a thought "decides" which nerve cells are to come into action'. This is a very typical move in philosophy – to ask what some claim *means* or might mean. Answering such a question can sometimes unravel confusion – and that is obviously what Ayer hopes to do in this case. But, how should one proceed to try to clarify the meaning of some expression or claim? In general, it is hard to say, especially when the question occurs in the course of a philosophical discussion. Such a question will not usually be answered simply by checking what a dictionary says of the words involved – though that might give you some initial help. It usually requires some measure of what philosophers call 'analysis' i.e., digging deeper into what the phrase or claim *implies* or *presupposes*, setting the phrase or claim in the context of *related claims* whose meaning is *similar* or *different* in a way which clarifies the original, giving clear *examples* where the phrase applies and where it doesn't, and perhaps considering the *history* of its use – and all this can be a very complex process. It might also require that you take into account whatever information you know about the subject. However, our contention is that if you use the Assertibility Question and the level of understanding you have, you can often get quite a long way.

The Assertibility Principle (p. 23) says that if you understand a claim you must be able to give at least some account of what argument or evidence would show it to be true or false, so what would show it to be true or false that 'a particular pattern of nerve impulses produce an idea' or that 'a thought decides which nerve cells are to come into action'? However little you understand about this issue it seems natural to say of the first phrase something like 'if you observe this pattern of nerve impulses you will also find that the person says they are having such and such an idea (at the same time)' and this is true for different people and on different occasions. And with the second phrase it is surely natural to say 'if someone reports such and such a thought you can also observe certain nerve cells come into action (at the same time)' and this is true for different people and on different occasions. You might also want to say that there also has to be some understandable 'connection' between the two kinds of event, so that you can see how their occurring together is causally linked rather than just coincidental; another way of putting it might be that there has to be some kind of 'mechanism' which you can understand as linking the two kinds of event (as when meshing cog-wheels move each other).

In this case, Ayer does a very neat piece of 'analysis', by asking what are the facts on which claims about 'nerve impulses producing ideas' and 'thoughts causing action' are based and he argues that all that *can* be meant is that the two kinds of observations involved – observations of nerve impulses and observations of ideas – are 'correlated' or 'habitually accompany one another'. On his account, that is all there is to it. Physiologists observe electrical impulses in the brain when their subjects also report thoughts, ideas or impressions of a particular kind – and the two just 'habitually accompany one another'. There is nothing more to it – nothing more to understand – no mystery left, according to Ayer.

This might leave you (the reader) feeling that something is still missing – that somehow you want to understand *why* these events occur together.

You might wonder, for example, why 'ideas and thoughts' occur at all. Why don't the electrical impulses in our nerves just determine actions without the intervention of 'thoughts'? You might wonder what the 'connection' is between electrical impulses and thoughts – what the *mechanism* is by which one affects the other.

Ayer's view is simple. He says that once you have understood that all we *could* mean by saying that 'nerve impulses produce thoughts' etc. is that they 'habitually go together', there is nothing left to explain and *there is no mystery left*. In fact, he adds, explaining this habitual conjunction simply amounts to setting these observations in a larger context – a context of many more such correlations, all of which hang together in a way which makes sense to us in our attempt to understand how the brain and mind function and how they relate to each other. He doesn't think there can be or needs to be a 'connection' or 'mechanism' which is anything more than a set of other related correlations.

So Ayer's argument marked up according to the method of chapter 2 looks somewhat as follows:

(a) The scientists who have spoken in this series have shown very fully and convincingly, how various mental processes – thinking, feeling, perceiving, remembering – are causally dependent upon processes in the brain, but to some of them at least the character of this connection still appears mysterious. Thus, ... Professor Adrian ... says that 'the part of the picture of the brain which may always be missing is of course the part which deals with the mind, the part which ought to explain how a particular pattern of nerve impulses can produce an idea; or the other way round, how a thought can decide which nerve cells are to come into action'.

(b) If this is a genuine problem, it is hard to see why further information
1   about the brain should be expected to solve it. (For) (however much
2   we amplify our picture of the brain, it remains still a picture of some-
↓
1 2 thing physical, and it is just the question how anything physical can
     interact with something that is **not** that is supposed to constitute
     our difficulty.) . . It looks, indeed, as if some of the previous speakers
     were hoping to discover in the brain something describable as the
     locus of the mind; as if mind and brain could be conceived as meet-
     ing at a point in space or as somehow shading into one another: but
     to me this is not even an intelligible hypothesis. What would it be

like to come upon this junction? By what signs would you recognise it if you found it? Descartes had the same problem, and he met it by suggesting that mind and body came together in the pineal gland; but how this conjecture could conceivably be tested he did not explain. [The reason] he had the problem – [the reason] why we have it still – is that (matter and mind were conceived by him from the outset as distinct orders of being; it is as if there were two separate worlds, such that every event had to belong to one or other of them, but no event could belong to both.) But from these premises [it follows necessarily] that there can be no bridge or junction; [for] what would the bridge consist of? (Any event that you discovered would have to fall on one or other side of it.) [So], if there is a difficulty here, it is not because our factual information is scanty, but because our logic is defective. Perhaps this whole manner of conceiving the distinction between mind and matter is at fault. In short, our problem is not scientific but philosophical.

(c) Let us consider, then, what can be meant by saying that a particular pattern of nerve impulses 'produces' an idea, or that 'a thought decides' which nerve cells are to come into action. What are the facts on which such assertions are based? The facts are that the physiologist makes certain observations, and that these observations fall into different categories. On the one hand there are the observations which lead him to tell his story about nerve cells and electrical impulses. That is to say, the story is an interpretation of the observations in question. On the other hand there are the observations which he interprets by saying that the subject of his experiment is in such and such a 'mental' state, that he is thinking, or resolving to perform some action, or feeling some sensation, or whatever it may be. It is then found to be the case that these two sorts of observations can be correlated with one another; that whenever an observation of the first type can be made, there is a good reason to suppose that an observation of the second type can be made also . . . (It seems to me that when it is asserted that the two events in question – the mental and the physical – are causally connected, that the pattern of nerve impulses 'produces' the sensation, or that the thought

107

'decides' which nerve cells are to operate, all that is meant, or at least all that can properly be meant, is that these two sets of observations are correlated in the way that I have described.) But if this is so, where is the difficulty? There is nothing especially mysterious about the fact that two different sets of observations are correlated; that, given the appropriate conditions, they habitually accompany one another. You may say that this fact requires an explanation; but such an explanation could only be some theory from which the fact of this correlation could be deduced. And in so far as the theory was not a mere re-description of the facts which it was intended to explain, it would serve only to fit them into a wider context. We should learn from it that not only were these observations correlated, but certain further types of observation were correlated with them. To ask *why* something occurs, it is not simply equivalent to asking *how* it occurs, is to ask what other things are associated with it. Once the facts are fully described, there is no mystery left.

(d) If there seems to be a mystery in this case, it is because we are misled by our conceptual systems; not by the facts themselves but by the pictures which we use to interpret the facts . . . The picture we are given is that of messengers travelling through the brain, reaching a mysterious entity called the mind, receiving orders from it, and then travelling on. But (since) (the mind has no position in space – it is by definition not the sort of thing that can have a position in space) – it does not literally make sense to talk of physical signals reaching it; . . . In short, the two stories will not mix . . . But to say that the two stories will not mix is not to say that either of them is superfluous. Each is an interpretation of certain phenomena and they are connected by the fact that, in certain conditions, when one of them is true, the other is true also.

(e) [My conclusion is], then, that mind and body are not to be conceived as two disparate entities between which we have to make, or find, some sort of amphibious bridge, but that talking about minds and talking about bodies are different ways of classifying and interpreting our experiences. I do not say that this procedure does not give rise to serious philosophical problems; how for example,

11   to analyse statements about their observable behaviour. But <u>once</u> <u>we are freed from the Cartesian fallacy of regarding minds as</u> <u>immaterial substances, I do not think that the discovery of causal</u> <u>connections between what we choose to describe respectively as</u> <u>mental and physical occurrences implies anything by which we need</u> <u>to be perplexed.</u>

Using the numbering above, we could represent the overall structure of Ayer's argument as something like the following,

3   Assuming the Cartesian view that mind and brain are different substances,

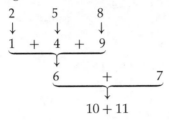

III   'Tests for a good argument' applied to Ayer

Now that we are reasonably clear what Ayer's argument is, we can ask whether it establishes its conclusion(s). If the argument is to do this, its premisses must be *true* and its conclusion must *follow* from them judging by *appropriate standards*. Let us look at Ayer's reasoning in the three arguments we identified above (R), (S) and (T).

IIIa   The 'negative' arguments

(R) In dealing with 'the problem' scientists have identified, Ayer argues (in effect),

1   If there is a genuine problem about how minds and brains causally interact, more information about the brain cannot help solve it,

    because

2   however much we amplify our picture of the brain, it remains still a picture of something physical, and it is just the question how anything physical can interact with something that is **not** that is supposed to constitute our difficulty.

The premiss here seems hard to fault. If we try to learn more about the brain, we investigate things like brain cells, nerves, electrical impulses, behaviours and suchlike phenomena – but these are things which are physically

109

identifiable – unlike ideas and thoughts which, *ex hypothesi*, belong to a non-physical realm. It is hard to see any weakness in his reasoning here; if these two realms – mind and matter – are supposed to be so different, how can more information about one of them help to explain how they interact? (And, again, if these two realms are supposed to be so different, Ayer is surely right to suggest that Descartes' idea that mind and matter meet in the pineal gland simply makes no sense.) On the other hand, who knows what we might discover, in the course of studying the brain or the mind, which might incline us to believe that we understand the link between the brain's activity and our conscious ideas and thoughts? Is it absolutely inconceivable that, in studying the brain, we should learn 'scientific facts' which help us make sense of the interaction between mind and brain? Such scientific study might incline us to view the mind in a much less Cartesian way (i.e., not as a distinctly different kind of substance) and this might lead us to be less puzzled about the way mind and brain interact. Indeed, Ayer suggests that something like this is a possibility ('Once we are freed from the Cartesian fallacy of regarding minds as immaterial substances . . .'). Alternatively, is it inconceivable that we should come to think about the brain and the mind in ways which are different from the Cartesian conception and which remove some or much of our puzzlement? Surely, something like this is happening nowadays, as we learn more and more about computers and how they resemble and differ from brains and minds.

The implication is that this piece of Ayer's reasoning does not really establish the conclusion for which he is arguing. Rather, it establishes,

> If there is a genuine problem about how minds and brains causally
> interact, more information about the brain cannot help solve it,
> unless it leads us to conceive of the mind quite differently.

(However, when Ayer was writing, it was common to believe science and philosophy were utterly different activities and he would not have thought scientific discoveries could change our way of thinking about the mind or that insights in other areas could change our whole way of thinking about brains and minds. That has changed in recent decades, particularly following the work of Kuhn, Rorty, Quine and others. For more on this see Everitt and Fisher, *Modern Epistemology*, McGraw-Hill.)

(S) Part of Ayer's main conclusion (in paragraph (e)) is that,

> mind and body are not to be conceived as two disparate entities
> between which we have to make, or find, some sort of amphibious
> bridge.

If you ask yourself how you might establish such a conclusion (having the Assertibility Question in mind), the obvious answer is that if you do think in this way it leads to absurd results. And this is precisely what Ayer tries to show in argument (S), which is,

> If matter and mind are thought of as distinct orders of being – as if
> 3 there are two separate worlds, such that every event has to belong to one or other of them, but no event can belong to both,
>
> 3
> ↓
> 5 **it follows necessarily**
> ↓
> 4 4 that there can be no bridge or junction
>
> **for**
>
> 5 any event that you discovered would have to fall on one side or the other of it.

If mind and matter are distinct orders of being then clearly nothing can connect the two (since it would have to be one or the other and not both). That is neat and conclusive logic if ever there was such! It is what philosophers call a *reductio ad absurdum* argument; it assumes a position and 'reduces it to absurdity'. We shall say much more about this kind of reasoning in due course.

Notice, however, that Ayer then concludes,

> 6 **So**, if there is a difficulty here, it is not because our factual information is scanty, but because our logic is defective. Perhaps this whole manner of conceiving the distinction between mind and matter is at fault. In short our problem is not scientific but philosophical.

In this remark, Ayer is again making a sharp distinction between science and philosophy. But I have just argued (briefly) against this, so what I said above applies against his conclusion here too.

(T) His third argument for this part of his main conclusion is,

> 8 **Since** the mind has no position in space – it is by definition not the
> ↓
> 9 sort of thing that can have a position in space – it does not literally make sense to talk of physical signals reaching it.

Here, his premiss is that mind is 'by definition' not the sort of thing which can have a position in space. If you try to analyse what you mean when you talk about ideas, thoughts and minds, you may well agree with the Cartesian view that they don't have a position in space. If on the other hand you think that your mind is in your head and that particular thoughts can be identified as belonging to particular places in your brain (perhaps because you have read that brain damage in particular places can result in people being unable to process some kinds of thoughts), then you may disagree. However, this little piece of reasoning is, in effect, prefaced by the assumption, due originally to Descartes, that minds and thoughts don't have any position in space. When philosophers try to characterise what minds are like – on the Cartesian view – this is one of the features of 'mind' that they pick out as distinguishing it from matter. Given that, it is surely reasonable to say that it makes no sense to speak of physical signals reaching the mind.

To conclude my comments on these three arguments, *if* mind and brain are thought of as completely different kinds of substance, as Descartes taught, then Ayer's reasoning is powerful and he is right to reject that conception. However, in my view he makes too fierce a distinction between science and philosophy which weakens his case in some respects.

IIIb   The 'positive' alternative

Let us now look at his positive alternative. Though he says,

> talking about minds and talking about bodies are different ways of
> classifying our experiences

he says very little about what this means, so I shall incorporate my response to this in my comments about his other positive claim, below.

After describing how two phenomena might be regularly observed to occur together, he claims the following,

> (It seems to me that when it is asserted that the two events in
> question – the mental and the physical – are causally connected, that
> 7 the pattern of nerve impulses 'produces' the sensation, or that the
> thought 'decides' which nerve cells are to operate, all that is meant,
> or at least all that can properly be meant, is that these two sets of
> observations are correlated in the way that I have described) [para (c)
> 'when scientists make observations which they interpret by saying
> that such and such nerve cells are undergoing such and such electrical
> disturbances, they can also make observations which are interpreted
> by saying that the subject is having sensations of a certain type
> (and conversely)]. But if this is so, where is the difficulty? There is
> nothing especially mysterious about the fact that two different sets
> of observations are correlated; that, given the appropriate conditions,
> they habitually accompany one another.

Though the reader may be unaware of it, Ayer is in effect adopting David Hume's view about what it *means* to say that event A causes event B. David Hume criticised those who thought there had to be some 'link' between a cause and its effect, saying that all we can *know* is that A-like events and B-like events are constantly conjoined – or, to use Ayer's language, 'they habitually accompany one another' and there is nothing more to it than that. Now, although Hume's view was widely accepted for a very long time, it does seem to leave out the importance of finding things which 'hang together' – which make sense to us as part of a whole picture or 'model' of what is going on in the world.

Looking back to our use of the Assertibility Question, we suggested that when we say 'A caused B' we have in mind some connection or mechanism which makes sense of the correlation for us. It is clear that some pairs of events occur together without there being any causal connection between them, perhaps because both are caused by something else. For example, if you put an iron bar in a hot flame it expands and it changes colour and such changes habitually occur together but the expansion and the colour change are not cause and effect, but are both effects of a common cause.

These considerations lead me to think that Ayer has missed something important in his account of what it is for mind and matter to impact on each other. Perhaps we shall one day have more detailed knowledge of how the brain works and we shall be able in some sense to 'read' from the electrical impulses in the brain what thought or idea the person is having. Alternatively, perhaps we shall come to view both brain and mind so differently (from the Cartesian tradition) that our puzzlement about how brain and mind interact will reduce or evaporate.

To give a partial analogy, just as computer experts can tell us what physical and electrical arrangements in a computer correspond to the sentence or picture shown on its screen, why should we not find something similar with brains – where the scientist becomes able to 'read off' from what his observations of the brain tell him what thought or image the person is having? Alternatively, we might find that our understanding of computers – their hardware and software and the languages in which we describe their activities – lead us to a 'paradigm shift' in the way we think about minds and brains which removes our puzzlement about how they interact, so that we have no more difficulty in understanding this link than we have in understanding how a magnet can make a compass needle swing. In the case of magnetism, we have a picture/model of what is happening which makes sense of a great many associated phenomena and numerous other experiences and predictions fit in well with our picture of how magnetism is caused and causes other events. Perhaps the scientific study of the brain, or the development of computers, or some other new conception will help us make sense of how minds and brains interact.

IV   To conclude

In my view, Ayer's arguments against traditional Cartesian views are well put, but his arguments in favour of his alternative view leave something important out of account. Also, in my view, his absolute division between science and philosophy is a mistake. You will have to decide whether you take the same views. Remember, one of the purposes of our method is to persuade you that you can sort out quite a lot yourself.

Before we leave this argument, there are two things to say about our general method of dealing with arguments. First, in this chapter we had to look carefully at what certain claims *meant* and in effect we have given a bit more guidance here about how to answer the Assertibility Question in some cases. Secondly, it is worth noting that arguments (R), (S) and (T) are all really prefaced on the Cartesian assumption that minds and brains are completely different kinds of stuff and all three are really *reductio ad absurdum* arguments which aim to show that Descartes' idea and those of the scientists who adopted it, were wrong. It might have been easier to make some of the points we have made above if we had treated (R), (S) and (T) as 'suppositional' arguments – which are discussed in the next two chapters. I leave it to the reader to look back in due course to judge whether the ideas and notation introduced in the next two chapters make it easier to see the structure of Ayer's reasoning in this chapter. My view is that it will help you to see the advantages of introducing such ideas and notation, but that is for you to judge.

8 · Suppose for the sake of argument that . . .

I 'Supposition' explained: and how to handle simple cases

In this chapter we deal with a distinctive kind of reasoning – suppositional reasoning. Most informal logic/critical thinking texts make no mention of it at all (although there are some notable exceptions, for example Stephen Thomas's *Practical Reasoning in Natural Language*). This is surprising since this kind of reasoning is elegant, powerful, and extremely common, as we shall illustrate in the next three chapters.

The arguments considered in most texts employ only *assertions*: in speaking of *reasons and conclusions* they are always talking about *asserted* propositions – propositions which their authors have put forward as being true (cf. our remarks on assertion in Chapter 2, p. 23). However, some arguments reach their conclusion *not* by asserting their starting points, but by *assuming* or *supposing* something 'for the sake of argument' as it is often described.

If someone begins an argument by saying 'Suppose that oxygen does not burn' he is not asserting that oxygen does not burn – he is not *presenting this as true*. Indeed he may well know that oxygen burns and he may be setting out on a *reductio ad absurdum* argument to prove that it does. Suppositions then are not assertions.

An atheist who begins to argue her case by saying, 'Suppose there is an omniscient Being of the sort in which Christians believe', is not asserting (claiming) that there is a Christian God (because she doesn't believe that there *is* one). She could just as well have said, 'If there is an omniscient Being of the sort in which Christians believe' and as we pointed out earlier (p. 23), someone who uses such a hypothetical does not assert its antecedent.

A mathematician who presents the standard Euclidean proof that there are infinitely many prime numbers begins by supposing that *there are only finitely many*. He is not asserting (telling us) that there *are* only finitely many primes (because he knows full well that this is false) but he is asking us to consider the proposition with a view to drawing out its implications.

Several of the arguments with which we began this book employed suppositions: the Galileo argument supposed that 'the heavier a body is the faster it falls'; Pascal's Wager considered alternative suppositions about one's beliefs and actions; Hume's argument began 'Suppose four-fifths of all the money in Great Britain to be annihilated in one night'. The reasoning employed by John Stuart Mill in the example of Chapter 5 was based on a supposition: 'Let us suppose . . . that a general reduction of the hours of factory labour, say from ten to nine, would be for the advantage of the work-people'. Similarly with Ayer's argument in Chapter 8.

The essential thing about a supposition is that it is not presented as being true – it is not asserted – it is put forward so that we may consider its implications. Arguments employing suppositions are common enough in theoretical contexts – in mathematics, in the physical sciences, the biological sciences, social studies and philosophy – to name some obvious ones so we must explain carefully how to handle suppositions in argument analysis if we are not to leave a serious gap.

We shall generally speak of *suppositions* in this book, though for most people it would probably be more natural to speak of *assumptions*. In many contexts the words are interchangeable, but many arguments contain *implicit* assumptions – propositions the author takes for granted as true – without bothering to mention them: although the author *does not assert* such assumptions (because he doesn't mention them) he would be prepared to, or would have to, if they were drawn to his attention. For example arguments about nuclear deterrence usually assume – without actually saying it – that your alleged opponent *wants to attack and dominate you*. This implicit assumption is usually taken for granted and needs no explicit mention. We have already encountered various implicit assumptions in Chapter 1 and subsequently. However, in this chapter we are not especially interested in such implicit assumptions. We are interested in the case where someone assumes or supposes something 'for the sake of the argument' in the sense we just explained, so in order to focus attention on this case we shall use the less familiar term *supposition*.

In Chapter 10 we shall deal with scientific *hypotheses*. These are obviously closely related to suppositions in the way they function in reasoning, but we shall reserve the term 'hypothesis' until then, again in order to focus attention at this stage on 'supposing something for the sake of argument'.

We begin to explain how to handle suppositions by looking at a simple example. Consider the following piece of reasoning:

> Suppose Darwin's theory of evolution is true. Then there should be fossil evidence which shows species changing and evolving, but this evidence simply doesn't exist so Darwin's theory must be wrong.

If we now attempt to extract the argument in accordance with the instructions in Chapter 2 (pp. 21f.), it is clear that we must circle (so) and underline what is obviously the main conclusion,

C Darwin's theory must be wrong.

(If the reader is also tempted to circle $\boxed{\text{then}}$ he or she will see in the course of this chapter both what is the source of this temptation and why it should be resisted in a simple case like this and whilst the instructions of Chapter 2 remain unrevised.)

When we ask, 'What immediate reasons are presented in the text for accepting C?' we clearly have one reason in,

(2) this evidence simply doesn't exist

but we may hesitate before seeing how to mark up the remainder. A moment's reflection will show that its meaning is captured correctly if we construe the supposition as the antecedent of a hypothetical, so the argument becomes,

(1) If Darwin's theory of evolution is true then there ought to be fossil
    evidence which shows species changing and evolving
and (2) This evidence simply doesn't exist
therefore
    C Darwin's theory must be wrong

and the result of attempting to mark up this simple example according to the instructions of Chapter 2 will look something like this,

(1) Su̶p̶p̶o̶s̶e̶ ⟨^{If}Darwin's theory of evolution is true. Then there should
    be fossil evidence which shows species changing and evolving,⟩ but $\underbrace{1+2}_{C}$
(2) ⟨this evidence simply doesn't exist⟩ $\boxed{\text{so}}$ Darwin's theory must be
    C wrong.

This example shows how to handle a supposition in a simple case; however, this will not always be the best way to proceed. In more complicated cases it may prove unnatural and laborious to treat suppositions as the antecedents of hypotheticals. We now illustrate this with another example as a preliminary to presenting an alternative way of handling suppositions. Consider the following piece of reasoning, taken from Stephen Thomas's *Practical Reasoning in Natural Language* (2nd edn).

> Suppose that only good researchers can be effective college teachers. In that case it follows that a faculty member will be an effective teacher *only if* he or she is a good researcher. From this it follows that if a faculty member is an effective teacher, then he or she must be a good researcher. Therefore every effective college teacher must be a good researcher. So, if only good researchers can be effective college teachers then every effective college teacher must be

117

a good researcher. Therefore we could ensure that the university will excel in research by basing tenure decisions solely on teaching effectiveness.

If we attempt to treat the supposition here as part of an hypothetical and then re-construe the argument accordingly we get something like,

If only good researchers can be effective college teachers then a faculty member will be an effective teacher only if he or she is a good researcher. And if a faculty member will be an effective teacher only if he or she is a good researcher then if a faculty member is an effective teacher he or she must be a good researcher.

This is awful to read and rapidly obscures the logic of quite simple moves which follow the initial supposition! Not only that, if we are still trying to follow the instructions in Chapter 2, we circle the occurrences of ⌐it follows that⌐ as *conclusion* indicators, which means that we take the sentences to which they refer to be *asserted*, but they are *not* asserted; they are in effect the consequent of a hypothetical.

We shall not continue to describe ways in which standard methods of argument and analysis, including those of Chapter 2, are inadequate for dealing with what we shall call 'suppositional contexts'. Instead we shall revise our method in such a way that we can still do everything we want to do with ordinary (non-suppositional) contexts but which also copes with suppositional contexts. The result clarifies our thinking in both contexts.

It is clear that reasoning does take place with the aid of suppositions – within the 'scope' of suppositions – and any proposed method of argument analysis must cope with this. In fact suppositional contexts are very important and instructive. In traditional logic and in most informal logic texts they have been given too little attention, with the result that conditionals have been misunderstood, though this is not the place to elaborate on such matters. We now revise our method of argument analysis before applying the revised method to an illuminating example.

II   The method of informal argument analysis revised

The key to the revised method is the distinction between an asserted and an unasserted proposition. We already encountered this distinction in Chapter 2 (p. 23) and at the beginning of the present chapter. To recap briefly what we need, the proposition 'oxygen burns' may be *presented as being true* or it may be used in a compound proposition like 'if oxygen burns then the phlogiston theory is wrong', or 'either oxygen burns or nitrogen burns', and in these cases it is *not presented as being true*. If a proposition is presented as being true logicians say (following Gottlob Frege (1848–1925), the founder of modern logic) that it is asserted. Otherwise it is not asserted. This is the distinction we need.

Given this distinction the method of Chapter 2 does not need much revision. We shall need to extend our lists of reason and conclusion indicators (pp. 16, 17). We shall need to re-interpret R → C (p. 19). We shall need to put our earlier remarks about hypotheticals into our new context (cf. pp. 23f.). And we shall have to revise the requirement that the premisses of an argument have to be true in order to establish its conclusion (p. 25).

The language of reasoning: some revisions

In informal logic books it is normal to say that reasoning or arguing consists in giving reasons for conclusions, but the only reasons and conclusions usually considered are asserted. The simplest and most economical way of coping with reasoning which proceeds from suppositions is to call suppositions *reasons* (or premisses) and, similarly, to call what follows from them *conclusions* (which are in turn reasons for *their* conclusions etc.) and to recognise that in suppositional contexts reasons and conclusions are not necessarily asserted – and hence that the occurrence of reason and conclusion indicators does not necessarily imply that what they relate to is asserted. (This may involve some slight distortion of normal usage – in calling a supposition a reason (or premiss) – but let this chapter and the next show whether the resulting simplification is justified.) If we do this our reason and conclusion indicators will include all the ones we gave earlier but the list will need extension in the two following ways.

Firstly, we need a list of 'supposition indicators' to add to our list of reason indicators. These will be such words or phrases as these:

> *Supposition indicators*
> suppose that . . .
> let us assume (for the sake of the argument) that . . .
> imagine that . . .
> consider the hypothesis/theory that . . .
> let us postulate that . . .

As with the usual lists of reason and conclusion indicators, we are not saying that *whenever* these phrases are used a supposition is present. They are markers which have to be used intelligently in the light of our interests and our explanation of what a supposition is.

Secondly, a supposition is presented so that we may consider its implications and it is equally natural to write after it 'it follows that' or 'then' (cf. some of our earlier examples). So we now need to include 'then' among our conclusion indicators – this explains the temptation we mentioned on

p. 117 – and to circle it as such when it occurs in a suppositional context to signal that a conclusion is being drawn from a supposition. Of course if we decide it is simpler to handle this particular context by means of hypotheticals we do not circle 'then'.

All the reservations which were expressed in Chapter 2 about using argument indicators apply with equal force to the extended lists.

The structure of reasoning: some revisions

Some conventions and terminology

We need to be able to mark the distinction between asserted and unasserted propositions now, and we shall 'flag' the occurrence of an unasserted proposition which is functioning as a reason or a conclusion by means of a small raised letter ^{u} (for 'unasserted') placed before it. Thus our example from p. 117 will be marked,

> Suppose that ^{u}(only good researchers can be effective college teachers). In that case it follows that ^{u}(a faculty member will be an effective teacher only if he or she is a good researcher). [etc.]

The simplest way to revise what we said in Chapter 2 about '$\rightarrow$' is as follows. We shall now construe the arrow '$\rightarrow$' to stand for the logical relationship which is assumed to obtain between a reason R and its conclusion C in the context in which it occurs. If a speaker asserts R and also believes that C *follows from* R, or equivalently that R implies C, then he or she naturally says, 'R therefore C' relying on the assumed logical relationship between R and C to justify saying 'therefore C'. We shall still represent such a case thus,

$$R \rightarrow C$$

and read it 'R therefore C' or some idiomatically appropriate equivalent. We might call this a 'categorical' context to distinguish it from a suppositional context.

If, on the other hand, the speaker says, 'Suppose R. Then C will be true' he or she is asserting neither R nor C and we shall represent this either as the hypothetical 'if R then C' or as follows,

$$\text{(Suppose) } ^uR \\ \downarrow \\ ^uC$$

The '(Suppose)' is to remind us that this is the beginning of a suppositional argument. The arrow now stands for the logical relationship which is presented by the speaker as obtaining between R and C and is read 'then' or 'it follows that' or whatever seems idiomatically appropriate: a lengthy suppositional argument,

$$(\text{Suppose})\ {}^{u}R \rightarrow {}^{u}C_1 \ldots \rightarrow {}^{u}C_n$$

might be read, 'Suppose R. Then C_1 follows. So C_2. Therefore C_3. In that case C_4 follows. (Etc. up to the nth conclusion C_n.)'

Note that there is clearly a very close relationship between saying 'if R then C' and saying 'Suppose R. Then C.' For our purposes we take them to be equivalent, and which way to construe a piece of natural language reasoning depends entirely on which seems simplest and most natural.

Except for these revisions everything which is said under the heading 'Some conventions and terminology', p. 19, about reasons and conclusions still obtains: reasons may still be *independent* or *joint* and conclusions may still be *intermediate* or *final* etc. But there are two important additions to argument diagrams. (Again, those who hate notation and diagrams need to grasp the underlying ideas.)

Clearly suppositions can be combined with assertions in argument. The following is a simple example, correctly marked up,

(1) $\boxed{\text{Suppose}}$ ${}^{u}\langle$the Government wants to raise bank interest rates.$\rangle$

(2) $\boxed{\text{Since}}$ $\langle$the Government also wants to keep mortgage rates down$\rangle$

 C ^{u}it will clearly have to issue directives to the building societies.

We write the argument diagram for this argument as follows,

$$\underbrace{(\text{Suppose})\ {}^{u}1 + 2}_{}$$
$$\downarrow$$
$${}^{u}C$$

(Devising a clear linear form is left for the moment as an exercise especially for the reader who dislikes diagrams.)

Notice that, in general, if a reason R is unasserted in the course of some piece of reasoning this unasserted character will, so to speak, 'infect' every proposition P which is taken to follow from it (it will infect it in the sense that the truth and assertibility of P are conditional on the truth and assertibility of R) *except in an important case* which we must now explain. This is inference by 'conditionalisation'.

Conditionalisation

Suppose we have an argument which proceeds from some supposition R to the conclusion C by *logically sound* steps (i.e. the conclusion at each step follows from the reasons given for it) then the soundness of the argument entitles us to infer the *conditional* (hence the name 'conditionalisation'), if R then C.

We have already seen an example of such an inference by conditionalisation: here it is again, marked up for present purposes,

(1) ⸢Suppose⸣ ᵘ(only good researchers can be effective college teachers.)

(2) ⸢In that case it follows that⸣ ᵘ(a faculty member will be an effective teacher only if he or she is a good researcher.) ⸢From this it follows

(3) that⸣ ᵘ(if a faculty member is an effective teacher then he or she must be a good researcher.) ⸢Therefore⸣ ᵘ(every effective college

(4) teacher must be a good researcher.) ⸢So⸣ if only good researchers

C can be effective college teachers then every effective college teacher must be a good researcher.

This argument begins with the supposition (1); on this basis alone it reaches the conclusion (4) by logically sound steps; it then draws the conditional conclusion C, i.e. 'if (1) then (4)'. Notice that, as we mentioned above, the unasserted character of (1) infects all the conclusions which follow from it *except the conclusion C, 'if (1) then (4)'.* If the argument steps from (1) to (4) are sound, 'if (1) then (4)' must be true, *whether (1) is true or not*, and we can *assert* it simply because the soundness of the reasoning guarantees it.

In general if an argument proceeds from supposition R to conclusion C and then concludes 'if R then C' we shall represent this process of conditionalisation in an argument diagram as follows,

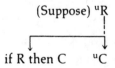

The arrow which is drawn *out from the side of the arrow to C* serves to remind us that the justification for 'if R then C' is the *argument* to C (not C itself). Thus our previous example is diagrammed as follows,

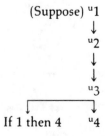

There are two concluding cases we need to mention. An argument may proceed from two (or more) *joint* reasons only one of which is unasserted and it may then conditionalise on that unasserted premiss. Such an argument is diagrammed,

$$\underbrace{(\text{Suppose}) \text{u}1 + 2 + (\ldots)}$$

If 1 then C   uC

Alternatively we may have an argument which contains two (or more) unasserted reasons among its joint basic reasons and which then condition-alises on only one of them. We diagram such a case as follows,

$$\underbrace{(\text{Suppose})\,{}^{\text{u}}1 + (\text{Suppose})\,{}^{\text{u}}2 + (\ldots)}$$

ᵘif 1 then C   ᵘC

and the conclusion 'if (1) then C' is still unasserted because it depends on the unasserted (2). We need develop technicalities of this representation no further here.

The method of extracting arguments revised

The method outlined in Chapter 2 (pp. 21f.) needs only slight revision to cope with suppositional contexts. Inference indicators are circled just as before, except that we must now circle supposition indicators too (since they are rea-son indicators). In underlining conclusions and bracketing reasons we should now mark those which are clearly unasserted thus ᵘ⟨ . . . ⟩, etc. Otherwise everything is as before. (It might be worth mentioning in connection with the use of the Assertibility Question that the answer to the question 'What argument or evidence would justify me in believing "if R then C"?' will often be 'A *sound* argument from R to C.')

It remains true that reasons and conclusions may be logically complex. For example we might have 'Suppose that either A or B' or 'Suppose that A implies B'. Whether to split up logically complex reasons or conclusions (cf. p. 23) is now determined by whatever seems simplest: one just needs to keep a clear head about what is asserted and what is unasserted.

Tests for a good argument revised

Everything which was said in Chapter 2 under the heading 'Tests for a good argument' remains true for the wider class of arguments we are now consid-ering *except that,*

(**A**) premisses which are suppositions do not have to be *true* in order to establish their conclusions, or to put it another way,

(**B**) If we have an argument which proceeds from a supposition R to a conclusion C and then conditionalises to the conclusion 'if R then C', whether this conditional conclusion is established *does not depend* on the truth of R. If the other basic reasons are true and the argument is sound, 'if R then C' is established *whether R is true or false*.

We now 'flesh out' the revised method and show how it works in applying it to an instructive example.

III   An application of the revised method: an example from Galileo

The test of what we have said is whether it works with real arguments – with arguments which have actually been used – so we now apply it to a famous piece of reasoning due to Galileo. We gave a modern version of Galileo's argument on p. 1, but we now look at his original argument. It comes from his *Dialogues Concerning Two New Sciences* and it is given in its full context as exercise 10, pp. 199–202.

In the early seventeenth century there was a tradition deriving from Aristotle (and therefore generally believed) that heavier bodies fell to earth *faster* than lighter ones. As Galileo explains in our example (and speaking of bodies with the same shape),

> Aristotle declares that bodies of different weights in the same medium, travel (in so far as their motion depends upon gravity) with speeds which are proportional to their weights.

This is the claim which Galileo sets out to *refute* and he attempts to do so *not by experimenting with bodies of different weights* but by means of a beautiful piece of reasoning which treats Aristotle's claim as a supposition and which then draws out the implications of that supposition. As a preliminary to his argument Galileo accepts that 'each falling body acquires a definite speed fixed by nature' and he calls this its 'natural speed'. His argument then proceeds as follows,

> If we then take two bodies whose natural speeds are different, it is clear that on uniting the two, the more rapid one will be partly retarded by the slower, and the slower one will be somewhat hastened by the swifter . . .
>
>   . . . But if this is true, and if a large stone moves with a speed of, say, eight while a smaller moves with a speed of four, then when they are united, the system will move with a speed less than eight;

but the two stones when tied together make a stone larger than that which before moved with a speed of eight. Hence the heavier body moves with less speed than the lighter; an effect which is contrary to your supposition. Thus, you see how from your assumption that the heavier body moves more rapidly than the lighter one, I infer that the heavier body moves more slowly.

This is a deceptively difficult piece of reasoning. The reader will see this best if he or she tries to answer the following questions before proceeding.

Questions

    (1) What is the main conclusion of Galileo's argument?
    (2) What is the reasoning for it?
    (3) What would show that,

        'If we take two bodies whose natural speeds are different, on uniting the two, the more rapid one will be partly retarded by the slower, and the slower will be somewhat hastened by the swifter' *is true*? And what would show it to be *false*?

    (4) Does Galileo's argument establish its conclusion?

IV   Extracting the argument from Galileo's text

To extract the reasoning from Galileo's text by our revised method we first circle all the explicit argument indicators. There is an obvious one in the third sentence, 'Hence'. In the last sentence 'Thus' and 'I infer' are nearly as obvious. Least obvious is probably 'then' near the beginning of the first sentence: the reader who misses it at this stage will simply miss a clue to the structure of the argument, but it does not affect the operation of the method. Subsequent attention may well reveal argument indicators which were overlooked at a first reading.

We next bracket any clearly indicated reasons and underline any clearly indicated conclusions using inference indicators to help us. The most obvious conclusion is,

    the heavier body moves with less speed than the lighter.

It is not quite so obvious how to construe his last sentence. Galileo could be saying. There, I have shown you how I draw a conclusion which is contrary to your supposition or he could be conditionalising, saying, 'Thus, from the supposition that the heavier body falls faster, it follows that the heavier body

125

falls slower.' We can decide later which alternative to choose – if it matters. However, it is clear from Galileo's last two sentences that his argument proceeds from a supposition so we should write this in (it immediately becomes clearer that 'then' in sentence (1) is an inference indicator).

We leave the remaining details to the reader. If we look for Galileo's reasoning for the conclusion,

the heavier body moves with less speed than the lighter,

there are several equivalent ways of construing and marking up the passage but the following seems most straightforward,

(1) [Suppose] ᵘ(the heavier body moves more rapidly than the lighter one)]

(2) ᵘ⟨If we [then] take two bodies whose natural speeds are different, it is clear that on uniting the two, the more rapid one will be partly retarded by the slower, and the slower one will be somewhat hastened by the swifter.⟩ ...

(3) ... But if this is true, and ᵘ⟨if a large stone moves with a speed of, say, eight while a smaller one moves with a speed of four, then when they are united, the system will move with a speed less than eight;⟩

(4) but ⟨the two stones when tied together make a stone larger than
C that which before moved with a speed of eight.⟩ [Hence] ᵘthe heavier body moves with less speed than the lighter; an effect which is contrary to your supposition. [Thus] you see how from your assumption that the heavier body moves more rapidly than the lighter one [I infer] that the heavier body moves more slowly.

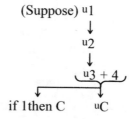

(Suppose)u 1
↓
ᵘ2
↓
ᵘ3 + 4
⎵
ᵘC

If we construe Galileo's last sentence as conditionalising we underline the last sentence and the diagram becomes,

(Suppose) ᵘ1
↓
u2
↓
ᵘ3 + 4
⎵
if 1 then C   ᵘC

Those who hate diagrams may prefer the following linear form,

Suppose

ᵘ(1) The heavier body moves more rapidly than the lighter

it follows that

    ᵘ(2) If we take two bodies whose natural speeds are different, on uniting the two, the more rapid one will be partly retarded by the slower and the slower one will be somewhat hastened by the swifter.

From this it follows that

    ᵘ(3) if a large stone moves with a speed of, say, eight while a smaller one moves with a speed of four, then when they are united, the system will move with a speed less than eight.

But (4) the two stones when tied together make a stone larger than that which before moved with a speed of eight.

Therefore it follows from (3) and (4) that

    ᵘC the heavier body moves with less speed than the lighter.

Therefore by conditionalisation,

    If the heavier body moves more rapidly than the lighter one, the heavier body moves more slowly.

'Reductio ad absurdum': a technicality

A *'reductio ad absurdum'* argument reasons from some initial supposition to an absurd or contradictory conclusion (hence the name) and thus concludes that the initial supposition *must have been false*. The Galileo argument is just such a reductio. The simplest way to construe and diagram such an argument for our purposes is as follows. If a supposition ᵘR yields a conclusion ᵘC *which cannot also be true* we shall diagram it thus,

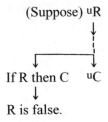

We then evaluate the steps by 'appropriate standards'.

V 'Tests for a good argument' applied to Galileo

Now that we are clear what Galileo's argument is, we can ask whether it is a good argument – whether it establishes its conclusion. Remember that in the previous examples we considered, if an argument was to establish its conclusion it *had to have true premisses* and it had to make sound inferences from them. But in an argument which proceeds from a supposition, the supposition need not be true in order to establish its conclusion. With non-suppositional arguments if a premiss turns out to be false, that is usually fatal to the argument (except in the case of independent premisses) but in the case of a supposition – although we initially assume it true both for the sake of the argument and for the purpose of analysis – if it turns out to be false this need not weaken the argument at all. Indeed in a *reductio ad absurdum* argument, such as Galileo's, the reasoning precisely *aims* at proving the initial supposition/premiss false. It does this by assuming the supposition is true and by drawing out absurd implications from this assumption.

In this example the only asserted premiss,

> (4) the two stones when tied together make a stone larger than that which before moved with a speed of eight

is obviously true. That apart, we need only consider the soundness of each successive inference in order to decide whether the argument establishes its conclusion. So the question is, 'Do we have *good reason* to accept the inferences from (1) to (2), from (2) to (3) etc.?'

In fact the only point of difficulty in the argument is the initial reasoning from (1) to (2), i.e.

Suppose

> ᵘ(1) the heavier body moves more rapidly than the lighter one

it follows that

> ᵘ(2) if we take two bodies whose natural speeds are different, it is clear that on uniting the two, the more rapid one will be partly retarded by the slower, and the slower will be somewhat hastened by the swifter.

The question for us is whether this is a sound inference, whether the premiss could be true and the conclusion false judging by appropriate standards (etc.). Most philosophers would say that (2) does not follow from (1) because if we assume with Galileo that,

> (1) the heavier body moves more rapidly than the lighter one

nothing follows from that about their behaviour *when joined together*: if when joined together they constitute a heavier body then (1) tells us that they will fall faster still but it tells us nothing about how two bodies when joined together will act on each other. (See the Postscript to this chapter on pp. 130–1) for a very clear statement of such an orthodox response.) We shall argue that this response is inappropriate, but since it is the orthodox view, we shall first shore up our defences with an appeal to authority, before presenting our own view!

Sir Karl Popper in *The Logic of Scientific Discovery* describes Galileo's arguments as follows:

> One of the most important imaginary experiments in the history of natural philosophy, and one of the simplest and most ingenious arguments in the history of rational thought about our universe, is contained in Galileo's criticism of Aristotle's theory of motion. It disproves the Aristotelian supposition that the natural velocity of a heavier body is greater than that of a lighter body.

Popper runs through the argument and continues,

> since the Aristotelian supposition was the one from which the argument started it is now refuted: it is shown to be absurd.
>
> I see in Galileo's imaginary experiment a perfect model for the best use of imaginary experiments.

He then discusses the conditions for the 'best use of imaginary experiments' and, for our purposes, the crucial requirement which Popper identifies is that the argument must assume what the author being criticised assumes, or would have had to assume, if it were drawn to his attention. In this case then, Galileo's argument, to be a legitimate criticism of Aristotle's theory of motion, must assume what Aristotle would have assumed (or would have had to assume).

Fortified by Popper's judgement in favour of Galileo's argument let us now return to explaining our reason for thinking that it is a good argument. Remember that on our view, we have to judge whether (1) could be true and (2) false 'judging by appropriate standards of what is possible or appropriate standards of evidence'. So what are the appropriate standards in this case?

What determines the answer to this question is the *model* with which we are operating – the 'picture' lying behind what we say – and the *assumptions* embedded in that model or picture. Whether this model and these assumptions are part of the *meaning* of what is explicitly stated may be arguable but it doesn't matter for our purposes. On our view knowing the meaning of a proposition is a matter of degree – one may have a sketchy or a thorough understanding of something – and knowing the picture or assumptions behind what is said is also something which may be partial or more complete and these may or may not be counted as part of its meaning.

Aristotle's mechanics were based on quite different ideas from Galileo's but it is quite certain that Aristotle would have accepted that the lesser weight would act as a 'brake' on the heavier one, etc., that the rapid one will be partly retarded by the slower, and the slower somewhat hastened by the swifter.

Aristotle's discussions were often about practical things like men pulling a ship through the water or a horse pulling a stone. Aristotle would have accepted it as an 'observed fact' that a man who could run fast would be slowed by having to pull a boat through the water (etc.) and it is basically because Aristotle would have accepted the key move in Galileo's reasoning that Popper regards it as a model argument against Aristotle.

Of course Galileo's picture was quite different. His picture was one in which two bodies joined together may be thought of as *one* body *or* as *two* bodies (or indeed as n bodies where n is any number!) and in which the behaviour of the composite body may be worked out or deduced from the forces at work on the component bodies (and conversely). Given these assumptions Galileo's argument is logically watertight. From these assumptions it follows that heavier bodies must fall with the same acceleration as lighter ones otherwise any given body (which may be thought of as comprising n lighter bodies) would fall at an infinite variety of speeds simultaneously!

Galileo's assumptions were also Newton's. There is no doubt that Galileo's result is provable in Newtonian mechanics: it follows quite easily from the initial definitions and Newton's three laws of motion (see Newton's *Mathematical Principles of Natural Philosophy*, Scholium to the Definitions, Corollary 3). Since most people have learned Newtonian mechanics at school (even if not by that name) and since that picture is now universal knowledge, the picture with which most people operate – the picture due to Galileo and Newton – employs the very assumptions which render Galileo's argument sound so we have every reason to accept that Galileo's argument establishes its conclusion.

There is still a question about the relationship between Galileo's argument and what *actually* happens to falling objects: this is basically the question how we know that our model, picture, theory, assumptions are *correct*. We shall discuss the relationship between theory and fact in such cases at considerable length in Chapter 10, 'Evaluating scientific arguments', but we conclude these remarks by noting that an argument like Galileo's cannot be evaluated out of its proper context, out of the context supplied by what Toulmin has called the 'warrants' and 'background' of a given theory or area of discourse. (See Stephen Toulmin, *The Uses of Argument*.)

Postscript: an alternative view of Galileo's argument

(This note was written by, and is published with permission of, N. Everitt, University of East Anglia.)

Galileo's argument asks us to suppose the following principle, in order to show that it leads to contradiction:

The heavier a body is, the faster it falls.

Let us call this Principle P. P tells us what happens to *a body* when it falls. It does not tell us what happens to *a collection of bodies* (except in so far as what happens to a collection is deducible from what happens to the members); and it does not tell us what happens to *the parts of the body* (except in so far as what happens to the parts is deducible from what happens to the whole).

What we therefore have to decide is whether M + m (the big body and the little body) in Galileo's proof is *a body* or not. If it is, then it is certainly heavier than M by itself, and P therefore predicts that it will fall faster. If it is not a body (but, e.g., a collection of two bodies), then P is not committed to making any prediction about it.

But Galileo's proof that P implies both that M + m will fall faster, and that it will fall slower, than M, equivocates on this point. The proof that M + m will fall faster requires us to view M + m as *a* body: the proof that M + m will fall slower requires us to treat M + m as two bodies, albeit joined by weightless glue. If M + m *is* one body, then P does not tell us anything about the effect that *parts* of M + m have on the behaviour of M + m. P tells us only how those parts *would* behave if they were separated from M + m, i.e. if they each became a body in their own right and thereby ceased to be part of M + m. So we cannot infer that in the one body that is M + m, the m-part acts as a brake on the M-part. We know that the m-part would fall slower than the M-part, if they were separate bodies. But that does not entitle us to infer that *when they are joined together to form one body*, the m-part acts as a brake on the M-part. So Principle P does not commit us to incompatible predictions about the speed of fall of M + m, and Galileo's argument therefore fails.

9 · An example from Karl Marx

In this chapter we apply the method we have outlined so far to a real and quite complicated example due to Karl Marx. The reader should first read the passage through and should then attempt to answer the questions which immediately follow it. Unless one does this it is easy to underestimate the difficulties in Marx's argument.

Those readers who can answer the questions without recourse to the method we have outlined need read no further, but we hope that others will find that the method enables them to answer questions which otherwise defeated them.

Karl Marx: *Value, Price and Profit*

Karl Marx was born in 1818, the son of a lawyer. He studied at the universities of Bonn and Berlin before embarking on a life of journalism and political activism. He was expelled from Prussia in 1849 having been acquitted of high treason. He settled in London where he spent the rest of his life, often in real poverty. He died in 1883 and is buried in Highgate cemetery in North London.

His major work, *Das Kapital*, makes very hard reading, but our extract comes from his *Value, Price and Profit*, which gives a much simpler statement of his ideas. It was originally delivered as a paper to an international congress of working men in 1865. At that time there was 'on the continent a real epidemic of strikes, and a general clamour for a rise of wages', as Marx put it, and the question was whether working people *could* increase their wages by such activity. Citizen Weston, the target of Marx's criticism, had argued that working people could *not* increase their real wages. Even though Weston's argument is over one hundred years old, something very like it is often used today so it is of some interest to see whether Marx is right or wrong. Marx attempted to refute him in the following passage.

I Extract from Karl Marx's *Value, Price and Profit*

I Production and Wages

(a) Citizen Weston's argument rested, in fact upon two premisses: firstly, that the *amount of national production* is a *fixed thing*, a *constant* quantity or magnitude, as the mathematicians would say: secondly, that the *amount of real wages*, that is to say, of wages as measured by the quantity of the commodities they can buy, is a *fixed* amount, a *constant* magnitude.

(b) Now, his first assertion is evidently erroneous. Year after year you will find that the value and mass of production increase, that the productive powers of the national labour increase, and that the amount of money necessary to circulate this increasing production continuously changes. What is true at the end of the year, and for different years compared with each other, is true for every average day of the year. The amount or magnitude of national production changes continuously. It is not a *constant* but a *variable* magnitude, and apart from changes in population it must be so, because of the continuous change in the *accumulation of capital* and the *productive powers of labour*. It is perfectly true that if a *rise in the general rate of wages* should take place today, that rise, whatever its ulterior effects might be, would, by *itself*, not *immediately* change the amount of production. It would, in the first instance, proceed from the existing state of things. But if *before* the rise of wages the national production was *variable*, and not *fixed*, it will continue to be variable and not fixed *after* the rise of wages.

(c) But suppose the amount of national production to be *constant* instead of *variable*. Even then, what our friend Weston considers a logical conclusion would still remain a gratuitous assertion. If I have a given number, say eight, the absolute limits of this number do not prevent its parts from changing their *relative* limits. If profits were six and wages two, wages might increase to six and profits decrease to two, and still the total amount remain eight. Thus the fixed amount of production would by no means prove the fixed amount

of wages. How then does our friend Weston prove this fixity? By
asserting it.

(d) But even conceding him his assertion, it would cut both ways,
while he presses it only in one direction. If the amount of wages is a
constant magnitude, then it can be neither increased nor diminished.
If then, in enforcing a temporary rise of wages, the working men
act foolishly, the capitalists in enforcing a temporary fall in wages,
would act not less foolishly. Our friend Weston does not deny that,
under certain circumstances, the working men *can* enforce a rise of
wages, but their amount being naturally fixed, there must follow
a reaction. On the other hand, he knows also that the capitalists
can enforce a fall of wages, and, indeed, continuously try to enforce
it. According to the principle of the constancy of wages, a reaction
ought to follow in this case not less than in the former. The working
men, therefore, reacting against the attempt at, or the act of, lowering wages, would act rightly. They would, therefore, act rightly in
enforcing *a rise of wages*, because every *reaction* against the lowering of wages is an *action* for raising wages. According to Citizen
Weston's own principle of the *constancy of wages*, the working
men ought, therefore, under certain circumstances, to combine and
struggle for a rise of wages.

(e) If he denies this conclusion, he must give up the premiss from
which it flows. He must not say that the amount of wages is a
constant quantity, but that, although it cannot and must not *rise*,
it can and must *fall*, whenever capital pleases to lower it. If the
capitalist pleases to feed you upon potatoes instead of upon meat,
and upon oats instead of upon wheat, you must accept his will as a
law of political economy, and submit to it. If in one country the rate
of wages is higher than in another, in the United States, for example,
than in England, you must explain this difference in the rate of wages
by a difference between the will of the American capitalist and the
will of the English capitalist, a method which would certainly very
much simplify, not only the study of economic phenomena, but of
all other phenomena.

(f)   But even then, we might ask, *why* the will of the American capitalist differs from the will of the English capitalist? And to answer the question you must go beyond the domain of *will*. A person may tell me that God wills one thing in France, and another thing in England. If I summon him to explain this duality of will, he might have the brass to answer me that God wills to have one will in France and another will in England. But our friend Weston is certainly the last man to make an argument of such a complete negation of all reasoning.

(g)   The *will* of the capitalist is certainly to take as much as possible. What we have to do is not to talk about his *will*, but to enquire into his *power*, the *limits of that power*, and the *character of those limits*.

Questions

(1) What is the argument which Marx attributes to Citizen Weston?
(2) What would show that,
    (i) 'the amount of national production is a fixed thing' is *false*,
    (ii) 'the amount of real wages . . . is fixed' is *false*, and
    (iii) 'working men should not combine and struggle for a rise of wages' is *true*?
(3) Marx claims that,

> According to Citizen Weston's own principle of the *constancy of wages*, the working men ought . . . under certain circumstances, to combine and struggle for a rise of wages.

What is the reasoning which leads Marx to accept this conclusion?
(4) How does Marx criticise Weston's argument and do his arguments successfully refute Weston?
(5) Express Marx's argument in contemporary language.

II   Extracting the argument from Marx's text

The whole passage is a critique of an argument which Marx attributes to Citizen Weston. Paragraph (c) suggests that the argument in question is this (where we write C^w for Citizen Weston's conclusion),

(1) the amount of national production is a *fixed thing*, a constant quantity or magnitude

therefore

1
↓
2
↓
C^w

(2) the amount of real wages, that is to say of wages as measured by the quantity of commodities they can buy, is a fixed amount, a constant magnitude

therefore

C^w working men should not combine and struggle for a rise of wages.

Marx's initial reference to Weston's 'two premises' may suggest that the argument he has in mind is ((1) *and* (2)) therefore C^w. There is no logical significance in the difference between these alternatives. Either way Marx does exactly what he should in order to fault Weston's argument: he tries to show that (1) is *false*, that (2) is *false* (and/or *does not follow* from (1)) and that even if (2) is true C^w still *does not follow*. Given what we said earlier about 'tests for a good argument' it is clear that the structure of Marx's critique is logically impeccable. We must now see what his argument is and whether it succeeds.

To extract the argument from Marx's text we read it through and circle the explicit inference indicators as we go. Notice that we now circle 'suppose' in paragraph (c) and 'then' in (d). The other obvious ones are in (a) 'firstly' and 'secondly', (b) 'because', (c) 'thus', (d) 'therefore' (three times) and 'because'.

The next stage is to underline conclusions and bracket reasons using inference indicators to help your judgement.

We next identify what we take to be the main conclusion. Marx sets out to refute both Weston's premises *and* the logic of his argument, so he reaches several important conclusions but, bearing in mind the argument which is under attack we take the main conclusion to be,

C According to Citizen Weston's own principle of the *constancy of wages*, the working men ought . . . under certain circumstances, to combine and struggle for a rise of wages.

We must now attempt to trace the reasoning for this conclusion. If the reader does not have a clear grasp of the process of conditionalisation it is hard to track down Marx's reasoning; but given such an understanding it is not difficult to see that C is obtained by conditionalisation and it is the *whole* argument in paragraph (d) which is taken to justify it. The paragraph could just as well say 'Suppose what Weston says is true, that wages are constant. This could cut both ways.' It then proceeds, *on that supposition*, to the conclusion that under certain circumstances working men would 'act rightly in enforcing a rise of wages': conditionalisation then yields the main conclusion C. So if we are to find the reasoning for C we must track down this whole argument. (It may be worth remarking that if someone found it hard to see what reasoning was offered by Marx in support of C and got as far in following our method as to ask the Assertibility Question, 'What would show C to be true?' the natural answer would surely be, 'A sound argument from the supposition that wages are constant'.)

If we follow our revised method, using argument indicators as clues, working 'backwards' from the conclusion that,

> they would act rightly in enforcing a rise of wages

asking what immediate reasons are presented in the text for accepting each step and using the Assertibility Question if necessary, it is not too difficult to extract the following line of reasoning from Marx's text;

Suppose)   (*Suppose*)

$^{u}2$
↓ ^{u}(2) the amount of wages is a constant magnitude,

$^{u}3$ *then*
↓ ^{u}(3) it can be neither increased nor diminished,
$^{u}4$
                 therefore

                      ^{u}(4) if the capitalists enforce a fall of wages a reaction ought to follow [their amount being naturally fixed]

$^{u}4$ *therefore*
↓ ^{u}(5) Working men reacting against the attempt at, or the act of lowering wages, would act rightly.
$^{u}5$

                 Furthermore

$^{u}5 + {}^{u}6$ (6) Every reaction against the lowering of wages is an action for raising wages

$^{u}7$ *therefore*

                      ^{u}(7) They [working men] would act rightly in enforcing a rise of wages

                 therefore

(if 2 them 7)   C According to Citizen Weston's own principle of the constancy of wages the working men ought under certain circumstances [those in which the capitalist enforces or tries to enforce a fall of wages] to combine and struggle for a rise of wages.

There are other arguments in this paragraph. For example there is the inference,

> If the amount of wages is a constant magnitude then it can be neither increased nor diminished

therefore

(8) If . . . in enforcing a temporary rise of wages, the working men act foolishly, the capitalists in enforcing a temporary fall in wages, would act not less foolishly.

There are other arguments too and other ways of construing Marx's intentions but we should attempt to extract the best possible reasoning from the text and this is what we have done.

As we mentioned earlier Marx also tries to show that Weston's first premiss (1) is false and that his second premiss (2) does not follow from his first. The arguments are easy to find. Marx's basic argument for rejecting (1) is this,

$\underbrace{9 + 10}$
$\downarrow$
11(1 is false)

(9) Year after year you will find that the value and mass of production increase, that the productive powers of the national labour increase, and that the amount of money necessary to circulate this increasing production continuously changes

and

(10) What is true at the end of the year, and for different years compared with each other, is true for every average day of the year

therefore

(11) The amount of national production changes continuously. It is not a *constant* but a variable magnitude.

There is also an *independent* argument that the quantity of national production *must* change continuously because of,

(12) the continuous change in the accumulation of capital and the productive powers of labour.

The essence of Marx's argument for thinking that (2) does not follow from (1) is this,

13
$\downarrow$
14
$\downarrow$
15

(13) If I have a given number, say eight, the absolute limits of this number do not prevent its parts changing their relative limits.

therefore

(14) If profits were six and wages two, wages might increase to six and profits decrease to two, and still the total amount remain eight.

therefore

(15) The fixed amount of production would by no means prove the fixed amount of wages (i.e. (2) does not follow from (1)).

So Marx's text marked up according to our previous remarks, looks as follows,

I Production and Wages

Citizen Weston's argument rested, in fact, upon two premisses:

(1) ⟦firstly,⟧ ⟨the *amount of national production* is a *fixed thing*, a *constant* quantity of magnitude, as the mathematicians would

(2) say:⟩ ⟦secondly,⟧ that ⟨the *amount of real wages*, that is to say, of wages as measured by the quantity of the commodities they can buy, is a *fixed* amount, a *constant* magnitude.⟩

Now, his first assertion is evidently erroneous. ⟨Year after year

(9) you will find that the value and mass of production increase, that the productive powers of the national labour increase, and that the amount of money necessary to circulate this increasing production

(10) continuously changes.⟩ ⟨What is true at the end of the year, and for different years compared with each other, is true for every average

(11) day of the year.⟩ The amount or magnitude of national production changes continuously. It is not a *constant* but a *variable* magnitude,

(12) and apart from changes in population it must be so, ⟦because⟧ of ⟨the continuous change in the *accumulation of capital* and the *productive powers of labour.*⟩ It is perfectly true that if a *rise in the general rate of wages* should take place today, that rise, whatever its ulterior effects might be, would, by *itself*, not *immediately* change the amount of production. It would, in the first instance, proceed from the existing state of things. But if *before* the rise of wages the national production was *variable*, and not *fixed*, it will continue to be variable and not fixed *after* the rise of wages.

(1) But ⟦suppose⟧ ⟨the amount of national production to be *constant* instead of *variable*.⟩ Even then, what our friend Weston considers a

(13) logical conclusion would still remain a gratuitous assertion. ⟨If I have a given number, say eight, the absolute limits of this number do not prevent its parts from changing their *relative* limits.⟩

(14) ⟦Therefore⟧ ⟨If profits were six and wages two, wages might increase to six and profits decrease to two, and still the total amount remain

(15) eight.⟩ ⟦Thus⟧ the fixed amount of production would by no means prove the fixed amount of wages. How then does out friend Weston prove this fixity? By asserting it.

9 + 10
↓
11(1 is false)

12
↓
11

13
↓
14
↓
15

But even conceding him his assertion, it would cut both ways,
(2) while he presses it only in one direction. If [Suppose] ⟨the amount
(3) of wages is a constant magnitude⟩ [then] ⟨it can be neither increased
(8) nor diminished.⟩ If [then], in enforcing a temporary rise of wages, the
working men act foolishly, the capitalists in enforcing a temporary
fall in wages, would act not less foolishly. Our friend Weston does
not deny that, under certain circumstances, the working men *can*
enforce a rise of wages, but their amount being naturally fixed,
there must follow a reaction. On the other hand, he knows also
that the capitalists *can* enforce a fall of wages, and, indeed, continuously try to enforce it. According to the principle of the constancy of
(4) wages, ⟨a reaction ought to follow in this case⟩ not less than in the
(5) former. ᵘ⟨The working men, [therefore,] reacting against the
(7) attempt at, or the act of, lowering wages, would act rightly. ᵘThey
(6) would, [therefore,] act rightly in enforcing *a rise of wages*, [because]
⟨every *reaction* against the lowering of wages is an *action* for
raising wages.⟩ According to Citizen Weston's own principle of the
C *constancy of wages, the working men ought*, [therefore,] under
certain circumstances, to combine and struggle for a rise of wages.

If he denies this conclusion, he must give up the premiss from
which it flows. He must not say that the amount of wages is a
constant quantity, but that, although it cannot and must not *rise*,
it can and must *fall*, whenever capital pleases to lower it. If the
capitalist pleases to feed you upon potatoes instead of upon meat,
and upon oats instead of upon wheat, you must accept his will as a
law of political economy, and submit to it. If in one country the rate
of wages is higher than in another, in the United States, for example,
than in England, you must explain this difference in the rate of wages
by a difference between the will of the American capitalist and the
will of the English capitalist, a method which would certainly very
much simplify, not only the study of economic phenomena, but of
all other phenomena.

But even then, we might ask, *why* the will of the American capitalist differs from the will of the English capitalist? And to answer
the question you must go beyond the domain of *will*. A person may

(Suppose) ᵘ2
↓
ᵘ3
↓
ᵘ4
↓
ᵘ5 + 6
↓
ᵘ7
↓
C

tell me that God wills one thing in France, and another thing in England. If I summon him to explain this duality of will, he might have the brass to answer me that God wills to have one will in France and another will in England. But our friend Weston is certainly the last man to make an argument of such a complete negation of all reasoning.

The *will* of the capitalist is certainly to take as much as possible. What we have to do is not to talk about his will, but to enquire into his *power*, the *limits of that power*, and the *character of those limits*.

III 'Tests for a good argument' applied to Marx

Now that we are as clear as we can be about Marx's reasoning we can ask whether he succeeds in rebutting Weston's argument. If he is to succeed in this he must either show that Weston's case rests on a false premiss or that his inferences are unsound. In fact Marx sets out, as we have seen above, to do both.

It is not difficult for us nowadays to believe that national production varies continuously and is *not* a fixed thing. We are so used to hearing about the rise or fall in national output that we are likely to find it hard to understand how Weston could ever have believed his first premiss. To decide whether 'the amount of national production is a fixed thing' is true or false one must simply look at the historical record and this is what Marx appears to have done in (9) and (10). On his other argument, we cannot judge whether he is correct to claim that the quantity of national production *must* change because of the 'continuous change in the accumulation of capital and the productive powers of labour', without knowing the underlying economic theory/assumptions.

His argument for thinking that,

(15) the fixed amount of production would by no means prove the fixed amount of wages

is again hard to judge. It doesn't follow simply from the fact that national production is fixed that wages are fixed because proportion can change as Marx makes clear, but there may be further grounds which are implicit and which make the argument watertight (Marx was certainly not above misrepresenting his opponents). Weston might have been operating with a picture like the following: total output is produced by the labour input L, and the capital input C. If half the capital is used up in a year it must be replaced in order to maintain output, so total wages are fixed at half total output. If wages take more, capital will not be replaced and total output will fall, resulting in a fall in wages. If wages take less, total capital can be increased and total output can rise thus enabling total wages to rise. This is a picture – grossly too simple of course – about the way in which wages could be determined by total production. Some correct, well-established, theory might well show that wages are fixed if production is fixed but we cannot tell just by thinking it through.

Let us turn now to the main argument we have attributed to Marx. It is a very elegant critique of Weston's position: it begins by assuming Weston's premiss that,

> the amount of wages is a constant magnitude

and reaches the opposite conclusion to Weston's. The question is whether Marx's argument is correct.

On the face of it Marx's argument is compelling. On any interpretation of his language which comes readily to mind Marx's conclusion seems to follow: if wages are 'constant', but still the capitalists can enforce a 'fall of wages', then it does seem to follow that the workers would 'act rightly' (i.e. in accord with economic forces?) if they combined and struggled to raise wages back to their 'proper' level. (Similarly the capitalists would 'act rightly' if, working men having enforced a rise of wages, the capitalists subsequently enforced a fall of wages.)

Of course, the language of this piece of reasoning is open to different interpretations. For example does 'act rightly' mean 'act in accord with economic forces' as we have suggested? More importantly, the proposition that wages are 'constant' does not seem to mean just that the (total?) wage-bill (in real terms) is (more or less?) the same (in the medium term?); there is also a suggestion that this constant wage level is determined by economic forces which are at least in part independent of the *will* of either workers or capitalists. (There is a suggestion of explanatory theories lying behind what is said.)

Suppose you ask the Assertibility Question, 'What would show that the amount of wages is a constant magnitude?' After clarifying the questions of meaning we just indicated, one would have to look at the historical record and explain it by fitting it into an economic theory which explained many other aspects of economic activity too: it would all have to 'hang together' as we have put it before. No doubt one would then see the scope for – and the limitations upon – effective trade union action for raising wages.

This is not the place to do the careful historical work which would be necessary to establish Weston's and Marx's meaning. Nor do we need to speculate about the economic theories which might buttress Weston's case or vindicate Marx's rebuttal. In the absence of supplementary arguments to show that workers and capitalists are not comparable (that wages 'cannot and must not *rise*', but 'can and must *fall*, whenever capital pleases'), Marx's reasoning is hard to fault however we construe it and that is partly what makes it a fascinating nugget of reasoning.

10 · Evaluating 'scientific' arguments. Some initial examples

Now that we have shown how in general to handle suppositions, we have explained how to extract arguments from their context and how to represent their structure in sufficient detail for us to be able to delve more deeply into the third part of the exercise – evaluating the soundness of an argument – for a wide range of important arguments.

Remember that in order to test whether an argument is sound we have to ask,

> Could the premises be true and the conclusion false judging by appropriate standards of evidence or appropriate standards of what is possible?

and in order to establish the appropriate standards we ask the Assertibility Question,

> AQ What argument or evidence would justify me in asserting the conclusion? (What would I have to know or believe in order to be justified in accepting it?)

Remember furthermore that, as we have insisted from the beginning, anyone can 'play this game': it is *not* just a matter for the 'experts'.

Two initial examples

Suppose we encounter the claim that 'like magnetic poles always repel' (M). What would show that this was true or false (allowing this as a paraphrase of the Assertibility Question)? If you understand the meaning of the claim M you must be able to give some kind of answer to the question (remember principle * p. 23). And if you are to be able to evaluate an argument with M as its conclusion you must be able – in advance of being given the argument – to say what *would be* a good argument. Before continuing, the reader should attempt to answer the question above. (Write down your answer for future reference.)

Someone assures us that he understands M. Suppose he answers our question like this,

> If you take two bar magnets and find their north poles (by letting them swing in space, say) then bring those north poles together, they will 'push away' from each other. This is what always happens in similar cases and this is what shows M to be true. It would be shown to be false if this didn't always happen.

The question is, 'Is his answer correct and will he evaluate an argument to the conclusion M correctly?'

Consider the claim that 'bodies of different mass fall with the same acceleration' (B). What would show that this was true or false? Most people know nothing of Galileo's proof and a typical answer from someone who understands B will probably be something like this,

> If you take bodies of different mass and drop them from the same height they will hit the ground together. This is what always happens in similar cases (etc.).

This is the way we learn at school about falling bodies and that is what determines our response. It might have been different. For example we might have been taught the Galileo response. Again the question is whether this answer is correct and whether someone who gives it will correctly evaluate an argument to the conclusion B. In this example, however, if we take the answer given above to be correct there is the additional problem about how to evaluate the Galileo argument.

Sometimes people are stumped when asked what would show M or B false. This may be because they take them to be *obviously true*, like Malthus's claim 'That food is necessary to the existence of man', and it may also be because they think these claims are in a sense 'theoretical' so that, for example, B might not be simply shown to be false by bodies of different mass hitting the ground at different times, because other factors might be entering the picture. We discussed the first case earlier (pp. 43f.) and our response to the second case will emerge below.

As we said in Chapter 2 there is no escaping epistemological questions if you wish to evaluate the soundness of real arguments and we cannot now avoid a little philosophical background if we are to answer the questions raised by our first two examples.

David Hume: observation and induction

The British empiricist, David Hume (1711–76), had a very simple view of claims like the ones we have been discussing and one which has been of such immense historical importance that we cannot ignore it.

Hume divides everything we know or reason about into two kinds. Firstly, there are the things we can know just by thinking about them, for example geometrical truths, like Pythagoras' Theorem; these are said to be known a priori and Hume calls them *Relations of Ideas*. Secondly, there are the things we learn from experience, from observing the world; Hume calls these *Matters of Fact*. He holds that 'all reasonings concerning matters of fact seem to be founded on the relation of *cause* and *effect*' (*An Enquiry Concerning Human Understanding*, §22) and that 'the knowledge of this relation is not, in any instance, attained by reasonings a priori; but arises entirely from experience, when we find that any particular objects are conjoined with each other' (§23). And provided 'all the objects similar to the first are followed by objects similar to the second' (§60) then we know that the first *causes* the second.

We believe that bread nourishes us, to use Hume's example, because of all the occasions on which we have eaten bread (or something resembling it) in the past and been nourished by it. Similarly we accept that 'like magnetic poles repel' and 'bodies of different mass fall with the same acceleration' because apparently similar cases always have. But these answers give rise to an obvious question, which is 'why this experience should be extended to future times, and to other objects, which, for aught we know, may be only in appearance similar?' (§29). The answer, according to Hume, is that 'all inferences from experience are effects of custom, not of reasoning' (§36). If we are used to being nourished by bread, to finding that like magnetic poles repel, or that bodies of different mass fall with the same acceleration, then we expect such things to continue in what *appear* to be *similar* cases. We do so out of *custom* or *habit* and not because we have *sufficient reason* for such generalisations: that is Hume's view.

On Hume's account then, our reasonings about claims like M and B, which are obviously *Matters of Fact*, 'seem to be founded on the relation of cause and effect', which we know of only by finding that 'particular objects are conjoined with each other'. And on Hume's account, claims like M and B are *universal generalisations* which we are not strictly entitled to make. We have observed things which appeared similar to like magnetic poles on numerous occasions (but this is a *finite* number all the same) and they have always repelled – without exception – so we generalise from these apparently similar *past, observed* cases to all apparently similar *future* and *unobserved* cases as well, in order to arrive at M: similarly for B. Given our conventions for representing arguments, Hume's picture of such 'reasoning' should be diagrammed somewhat as follows,

$$\underbrace{O_1 + O_2 + \ldots + O_n + \text{No exceptions have been observed}}_{\text{Gen}}$$

where $O_1 \ldots O_n$ are the observations, *finite* in number, which have actually been made and Gen is the generalisation about the world reached from them. As we said, on Hume's view we are not strictly entitled to make this inference, we do not have *sufficient reason* for our conclusion, but this is the best evidence we can hope for and in situations like this we *habitually* generalise from the known to the apparently similar unknown because we could not live our lives without doing so.

Hume's writings have been enormously important in the history of philosophy. They provide many remarkable models of clear thinking and elegant argument yet they have also given rise to some intractable problems, two of which arise in our context. Firstly, the division of knowledge into two mutually exclusive and exhaustive categories has proved endlessly problematic, and secondly, Hume gave us no way of deciding which generalisations from past experience are reliable and which are not – the so-called *problem of induction*. Should the chicken which has been fed by the farmer every day, continue to expect to be fed as Christmas approaches, or to be killed and eaten for Christmas (Bertrand Russell's example from *The Problems of Philosophy*)? Should we believe that 'deterrence works' because it *has worked* or does our survival become yearly more precarious (cf. Chapter 4)? Again should we expect like magnetic poles to continue to repel as they have in the past and should we also expect bodies of different mass to fall with the same acceleration as they have in the past?

Philosophers have come to call an argument which infers a generalisation about *all similar* cases from evidence about all *known* cases an inductive argument/inference. Such an argument goes *beyond* the observed cases to make claims about the *unobserved* cases too. Inductive arguments are clearly not *deductively valid* (see pp. 174f.): it does not follow from '*all observed* cases are X' that '*all* cases are X' – the premiss could be true and the conclusion false. It is difficult to tell in general which arguments of this kind are sound. It is hard to find any principle for distinguishing good from bad inductive arguments, any general way of laying down what the 'appropriate standards of evidence' are in such cases. (For an exercise relating to this discussion, see the Reichenbach passage on pp. 210–12.) We put these difficulties to one side for a moment and try to come at them from a different direction, a direction mapped out by Sir Karl Popper.

Karl Popper: conjectures and refutations

Sir Karl Popper denied that there was any such thing as a sound inductive inference. Furthermore, he denied that we arrive at generalisations like M and B from custom or habit, after observing apparent regularities. Indeed he arrived at a quite different account of the structure of our reasoning in such cases, partly by reflecting on the weaknesses in Hume's arguments and partly by reflecting on various *theories* about the world.

The theories which troubled Popper as a young man (from 1919 on) were Marx's theory of history, Freud's psychoanalysis and Alfred Adler's 'individual psychology'. The key theory which impressed him was Einstein's theory of relativity.

What troubled him about the first three theories was precisely what *impressed* most of their adherents. It was the fact that they seemed compatible with the most divergent human behaviour, to explain practically whatever happened within the fields to which they referred. They seemed *irrefutable*. Whatever happened, believers were able to explain it in terms of the theory, to fit it into the theory and to find in it confirmation of the theory and its power. 'A Marxist could not open a newspaper without finding on every page confirming evidence for his interpretation of history' (*Conjectures and Refutations*, p. 35).

By contrast, what impressed Popper about Einstein's theory was the *risk* involved in its predictions. 'If observation shows that the predicted effect is definitely absent, then the theory is simply refuted. The theory is *incompatible with certain possible results of observation* – in fact with results which everybody before Einstein would have expected' (p. 36)

All these theories claimed to be 'scientific' so Popper set out to answer the question, 'When should a theory be ranked as scientific?' He knew that the prevailing view (deriving essentially from Hume) was that science is distinguished from pseudo-science and from metaphysics – and, we might add now in view of its widespread importance, from ideology in the case of the social sciences – by 'its *empirical method* which is essentially inductive, proceeding from observation and experiment' (p. 34). This account did not impress Popper. After all astrology uses such a method and anyway such an account did nothing to allay Popper's worries about Marx, Freud and Adler.

Considering these theories led Popper to some famous conclusions:

(1) It is easy to obtain confirmations, or verifications, for nearly every theory – if we look for confirmations.

(2) Confirmations should count only if they are the result of *risky predictions*; that is to say, if, unenlightened by the theory in question, we should have expected an event which was incompatible with the theory – an event which would have refuted the theory.

(3) Every 'good' scientific theory is a prohibition: it forbids certain things to happen. The more a theory forbids, the better it is.

(4) A theory which is not refutable by any conceivable event is non-scientific. Irrefutability is not a virtue of a theory (as people often think) but a vice.

(5) Every genuine *test* of a theory is an attempt to falsify it, or to refute it. Testability is falsifiability; but there are degrees of testability:

some theories are more testable, more exposed to refutation, than others; they take, as it were, greater risks.

(6) Confirming evidence should not count *except when it is the result of a genuine test of the theory*; and this means that it can be presented as a serious but unsuccessful attempt to falsify the theory. (I now speak in such cases of 'corroborating evidence'.)

(7) Some genuinely testable theories, when found to be false, are still upheld by their admirers – for example by introducing *ad hoc* some auxiliary assumption or by re-interpreting the theory *ad hoc* in such a way that it escapes refutation. Such a procedure is always possible, but it rescues the theory from refutation only at the price of destroying, or at least lowering, its scientific status. (I later describe such a rescuing operation as a *'conventionalist twist'* or a *'conventionalist stratagem'*.)

Popper sums all this up by saying that *'the criterion of the scientific status of a theory is its falsifiability, or refutability, or testability'* (p. 37). Clearly, astrology does not pass the test. Because astrologers make their interpretations and prophecies sufficiently vague, they are able to explain away whatever happens – and nothing refutes the theory. 'It is a typical soothsayer's trick to predict things so vaguely that the predictions can hardly fail: that they become irrefutable.' But because the theory is not refutable it is not scientific either. The same goes for Marx's theory of history.

> The marxist theory of history, in spite of the serious efforts of some of its founders and followers, ultimately adopted this soothsaying practice. In some of its earlier formulations (for example in Marx's analysis of the character of the 'coming social revolution') their predictions were testable, and in fact falsified. Yet instead of accepting the refutations the followers of Marx re-interpreted both the theory and the evidence in order to make them agree. In this way they rescued the theory from refutation; but they did so at the price of adopting a device which made it irrefutable. They thus gave a 'conventionalist twist' to the theory; and by this stratagem they destroyed its much advertised claim to scientific status.

Social scientists are well used to seeing this kind of thing happen to theories. Of course, theories which are non-scientific may have the makings of a scientific theory in them (if they are made refutable – this could be done with astrology) or the makings of a dogma (if they are made irrefutable – which has certainly happened to some political and economic theories).

Besides thinking about theories – and in particular how to characterise scientific theories – Popper also thought carefully about the weaknesses in Hume's arguments. In *Conjectures and Refutations* he gives an excellent critique of Hume's idea that we observe that *apparently similar* cases are regularly conjoined and infer by habit from these (pp. 44–5; it provides a good example for argument analysis itself), and this led him to reject Hume's view of the structure of our reasoning in scientific contexts in favour of a view which is now very widely accepted (p. 46).

> I was led by purely logical considerations [about apparent similarity] to replace the psychological theory of induction by the following view. Without waiting, passively, for repetitions to impress or impose regularities upon us, we actively impose regularities upon the world. We try to discover similarities in it, and to interpret it in terms of laws invented by us. Without waiting for premises we jump to conclusions. These may have to be discarded later, should observations show that they are wrong . . . This was a theory of . . . conjectures and refutations.

Again, in summarising his position he puts it like this on page 53:

(1) Induction, i.e. inference based on many observations is a myth. It is neither a psychological fact, nor a fact of ordinary life, nor one of scientific procedure.
(2) The actual procedure of science is to operate with conjectures: to jump to conclusions – often after one single observation . . .
(3) Repeated observations and experiments function in science as *tests* of our conjectures or hypotheses, i.e. as attempted refutations.

   Thus, Popper stood Hume's view of things on its head. On Popper's account, generalisations about the world – that bread nourishes us, that like magnetic poles repel, that bodies of different mass fall with the same acceleration, that increased money supply causes inflation, that political parties inevitably become oligarchies (etc., etc.) – these are not *conclusions* which we have arrived at by inferring (shakily) from apparently similar *observed* cases, but they are *guesses, conjectures, hypotheses* (or systems of hypotheses – *theories*). Hypotheses are not put forward as being *true* (initially at least); they are, like suppositions, put forward *for consideration*, so that we may see what they imply and *test* them against experience. On Popper's view, what really happens is *not* that we notice a regularity in the world and then use induction to generalise from that observed regularity to our conclusion (and there are logical reasons why this *cannot* be the case): what really happens is that we make a *guess/conjecture/hypothesis* about how things are and then set out to test by observation and experiment whether it is true. Of course, our conjecture is informed by our knowledge of the history of the subject and by relevant observations, but it is still put forward *not* as a conclusion, but tentatively, for critical assessment (i.e. for testing). In order to test our hypothesis we have to work out *what observations it implies could be made.*

149

> the role of logical argument, of deductive logical reasoning, remains all important for the critical [scientific] approach . . . because only by purely deductive reasoning is it possible for us to discover what our theories imply, and then to criticise them [test them] effectively. (p. 51)

Suppose our hypothesis is that 'like magnetic poles always repel'. This is a good, scientific hypothesis. It makes many risky predictions; it implies that like magnetic poles will repel in all sorts of circumstances – even when they are under water, in space, moving, very small (etc., etc.). If we observe like magnetic poles in all these circumstances and they always repel, then our hypothesis has withstood its tests, 'proved its mettle' as Popper puts it. If one of the observations implied/predicted by the hypothesis turns out to be false then the hypothesis is *false*: for example if like magnetic poles turn out not to repel each other on the Moon then they do not 'always repel'. Notice that, although on Popper's view a hypothesis can be shown to be false, nothing can show it to be true – it cannot be *verified*. If a hypothesis withstands its tests it may yet be falsified, so we cannot say it is true. On the other hand, if it makes 'risky' predictions which turn out to be true, then Popper says it is 'corroborated' though not verified. Furthermore, it is perfectly rational, on Popper's view, to accept well-corroborated scientific theories for practical purposes, for the purposes of living our daily lives, provided we adopt a 'critical attitude' to those beliefs, one 'which is ready to modify its tenets, which admits doubt and demands tests' (p. 49) and not the 'dogmatic attitude' which is associated with pseudo-science (and in our case ideology).

> If . . . the term 'belief' is taken to cover our critical acceptance of scientific theories – a *tentative* acceptance combined with an eagerness to revise the theory if we succeed in designing a test which it cannot pass . . . In such acceptance of theories there is nothing irrational. (p. 51)

So the essential structure underlying scientific reasoning, according to Popper, is not, as Hume thought, inductive generalisation from a finite number of apparently similar observations, but hypothesis and attempted refutation. Given our conventions for representing arguments, Popper's picture of such reasoning could be diagrammed as follows,

The *hypothesis* implies that we can make observations $O_1, O_2, O_3, \ldots$ (etc.)   +   The predicted observations are not all realised.

The *hypothesis* is false

In handling real scientific arguments it will often be easier to use our representation for suppositions than to use hypotheticals throughout (cf. pp. 120f.) but this will depend upon the case.

On Popper's account then, a hypothesis can be refuted – a beautiful theory can be destroyed by an ugly fact! – but it cannot be *verified*. However, provided it makes risky predictions which turn out to be true, then it is 'corroborated' and our confidence in it is increased.

It is hard to overestimate the importance of Popper's work in current thinking about science, scientific method and scientific argument. However, since we shall add some different points of emphasis in this book we make some general remarks now as background to a slightly different approach.

Firstly, one may wonder if there is any essential difference between Hume and Popper concerning the relationship between evidence and empirical generalisation. In Popper's case every (riskily predicted) observation which fits the hypothesis fails to refute it and 'corroborates' it – or increases one's confidence in it. But this is just the same on Hume's view. For Popper a counter-example refutes the hypothesis. But similarly it refutes the generalisation for Hume too. So the difference between them doesn't lie there. (A similar point is made by Hilary Putnam, 'The Corroboration of Theories'.) The shortest way of describing the difference is probably to say that Popper puts a stress on using a particular *method* for finding out about the world, the method of conjectures and refutations, the 'critical' method where you look for the evidence *against* your conjectures.

Secondly, whether an 'ugly fact' is taken to destroy a beautiful theory depends upon the case. In short it depends on how deeply committed our current system of beliefs is to that theory. Our system of beliefs is something like a spider's web; some beliefs are very central to our whole conception of things – for example Newton's laws of motion for terrestrial bodies – and some are more peripheral – for example our beliefs about what causes inflation. It is hard to imagine some contrary observations posing a serious threat to Newton's theory now but not so hard to imagine giving up our beliefs about inflation in the face of contradictory evidence. We shall return to this point later. It is enough now to say that what we believe has to be coherent, has to 'hang together'; one piece of evidence is strengthened if it 'fits' with a great deal more we know and believe and is weakened if it doesn't. (For the *locus classicus* of this picture, see W. V. Quine and J. S. Ullian, *The Web of Belief*.)

Thirdly, we must not forget that scientific ideas have a history. The generalisations and theories which we have are informed not only by previous observations and experience but also by previous theories about the subject. Popper says very little about the history of scientific ideas and how important a knowledge of that history is to the proper understanding of current ideas, although its importance is now widely recognised, especially since the remarkable work of Thomas Kuhn. We conclude this survey with a brief account of his contribution to current thinking about scientific reasoning.

Thomas Kuhn: paradigms, normal science and scientific revolutions

A very influential recent view of the structure of scientific theories and the nature of scientific reasoning is brilliantly articulated in Thomas S. Kuhn's *The Structure of Scientific Revolutions*. Kuhn was a physicist who became interested in the history of science and, by looking at the way science *actually* developed, he was led to revolutionary ideas about the nature of scientific activity and the role of reasoning and observation within it.

The key idea in Kuhn's work is the idea of a 'paradigm'.

> A paradigm is what the members of a scientific community share, *and*, conversely, a scientific community consists of men who share a paradigm. (p. 176)

A paradigm is a 'picture' or a 'model' of the way things are in some realm (Kuhn usually prefers to avoid the word 'theory'). For example there was the Aristotelian picture of how bodies moved; we now have the Newtonian picture/paradigm; Einstein has presented us with yet another picture/paradigm. Darwin presented us with a whole picture of evolution: that constitutes a paradigm. Galen provided Europe with a model of the way the body worked for many centuries; most of us no longer know anything about his views and we employ a quite different picture/model/paradigm.

A paradigm comprises many things. It is a picture of the way things are which consists of *some* basic generalisations/natural laws (these often have the character of definitions within the paradigm, e.g. Newton's Second Law of Motion, force = mass × acceleration) (cf. Kuhn, p. 183), *some* ontological or heuristic model 'the molecules of a gas behave like tiny elastic billiard balls in random motion' (p. 184), some preferred methods and goals (e.g. accuracy, simplicity, fruitfulness, etc.) and some key shared examples of solved problems, what Kuhn calls 'exemplars' (see pp. 187f.).

> To an extent unparalleled in most other fields, [the members of a scientific community] have undergone similar educations and professional initiations . . . the members of a scientific community see themselves and are seen by others as men uniquely responsible for the pursuit of a set of shared goals, including the training of their successors. Within such groups communication is relatively full and professional judgement relatively unanimous. (p. 177)

> Paradigms are something shared by the members of such groups. (p. 178)

A given paradigm doesn't answer every question. Indeed it generates many questions, problems and 'puzzles' of its own. And it is the attempt to answer these questions and to solve these problems by members of a scientific community which Kuhn calls 'normal science'.

'normal science' means research firmly based upon one or more past scientific achievements, achievements that some particular scientific community acknowledges for a time as supplying the foundation for further practice. Today such achievements are recounted, though seldom in their original form, by science textbooks, elementary and advanced. These textbooks expound the body of accepted theory, illustrate many or all of its successful applications, and compare these applications with exemplary observations and experiments. Before such books became popular early in the nineteenth century . . . many of the famous classics of science fulfilled a similar function. Aristotle's *Physica*, Ptolemy's *Almagest*, Newton's *Principia* and *Opticks*, Franklin's *Electricity*, Lavoisier's *Chemistry*, and Lyell's *Geology* – these and many more other works served for a time implicitly to define the legitimate problems and methods of a research field for succeeding generations of practitioners. They were able to do so because they shared two essential characteristics. Their achievement was sufficiently unprecedented to attract an enduring group of adherents away from competing modes of scientific activity. Simultaneously, it was sufficiently open-ended to leave all sorts of problems for the redefined group of practitioners to resolve.   (p. 10)

So a paradigm is a 'picture' of the way things are, it's a picture which leaves many questions unanswered and it generates 'normal science' which is the attempt to answer these questions in a prescribed way. Normal science is the attempt to extend the picture, to draw it more fully and to apply it. But paradigms don't live forever. In attempting to extend them normal science encounters difficulties, failures of fit, falsifying evidence, or what Kuhn generally calls 'anomalous experiences'. Kuhn does not think these function in science as Popper does,

[anomalous experiences are] experiences that, by evoking crisis, prepare the way for a new theory. Nevertheless, anomalous experiences may not be identified with falsifying ones. Indeed I doubt that the latter exist. As has repeatedly been emphasized before, no theory ever solves all the puzzles with which it is confronted at a given time; nor are the solutions already achieved often perfect. On the contrary, it is just the incompleteness and imperfection of the existing data-theory fit that, at any time, define many of the puzzles that characterize normal science. If any and every failure to fit were ground for theory rejection, all theories ought to be rejected at all times.   (p. 146)

Indeed, what happens on Kuhn's account is not that theories are simply refuted as Popper suggests, but that a paradigm encounters more and more 'anomalous experiences' which its scientific community lives with as best it

153

can but which in turn give rise to a new paradigm in a scientific revolution. A new picture emerges, incompatible in part or in whole with the old one, and the whole process sets off again.

Kuhn's view of scientific activity is enormously rich and historically well documented and we shall need to keep it well in mind when evaluating scientific arguments. For the present we mention only two general points about it. Firstly, it is important to note that science has *authorities* (because logicians tend to speak too readily of the 'fallacy of appeal to authority'). We accept many things because the *experts* tell us they are so and, given the nature of paradigms, this should not be surprising. Furthermore, although well-tried paradigms eventually filter through to the rest of us (through the education process) from their scientific communities, more recent ones can be very inaccessible given our existing world view. For example much of what Einstein says contradicts 'common sense': e.g. he says that 'the speed of a ray of light is the same from any vantage point; the moving vantage point cannot, in pursuing the light ray, diminish the relative velocity'. (See Quine and Ullian.) Secondly, in general if you are to assess scientific arguments in their full complexity, you need to know their history and current expert opinion – to know, so to speak, the rules of the game. To say this is not to deny what we have claimed throughout this book, which is that anyone who understands P must be able to give at least a partial answer to the question 'What evidence or argument would or could justify me in asserting P?' Understanding P is a matter of knowing that sort of thing and is a matter of degree. The more you understand P the more you will be able to say in answer to the question, the more you will know the usage given to P, but the game we are trying to explain and teach here can be played at any level of understanding.

Two concluding examples: Darwin and Harvey

We conclude this chapter with two examples of scientific reasoning. In each case we attempt to illustrate some general lessons about evaluating scientific arguments. We begin with a famous argument of Darwin's.

Charles Darwin on the instability of the earth

Darwin established (or certainly *believed* that he had established) that land masses have sometimes risen or fallen in relation to sea level over the course of millions of years. Before looking at the evidence ask yourself what *would* show these two claims to be true? What would show that land, which is now above sea level, was once submerged? Suppose you could find – well above sea level – evidence that creatures which could only live under the sea had actually lived there long ago. If the land had always been above sea level you would not *expect* to find such evidence and if you did find it, it would call for explanation (because it was surprising and unexpected). This is certainly what Popper would call a 'risky' prediction and of course it is precisely what Darwin found.

When he was travelling in the Andes in 1834 he discovered a bed of fossil seashells at 12,000 feet and a small forest of petrified pine trees with marine rock deposits around them at 7,000 feet! How else could these things have got high up in the Andes? At one time the land must surely have been submerged below the sea and as the Andes pushed upwards they presumably became at first a series of wooded islands and then a chain of mountains whose cold climate killed and petrified the trees.

Now, of course, this evidence is *not* conclusive, but its strength is best seen by considering the position before we knew Darwin's discoveries. Once we know his evidence the sceptic says, 'Ah, but there could be some other explanation: the evidence could be as Darwin described and yet the conclusion he infers could be false.' The correct reply to the sceptic is, 'True, but then say what would show *you* that land which is now above sea level was once submerged?' and he will either give a reply which is like ours and Darwin's though perhaps requiring *more* evidence and *more detailed* evidence of the same kind, or he will have no answer. In the former case we can simply agree with him that we didn't go far enough, that more evidence is needed, that this theory has to fit coherently into a whole picture we are in the process of building up, and no such argument about the real world is ever going to be deductively conclusive, but there is no essential disagreement. In the latter case he is shown to be a fraud: he is not playing the game: he is not seriously interested in our finding out about the world as best we can.

The crucial point is that if you understand Darwin's claim you must be able to give at least some account of how you would be able to decide whether it is true or false, what evidence or argument would show it to be true or false. What would *count* as evidence must be known *before* it is known whether the evidence exists or not.

Exercise. To see the force of what has just been said the reader should now say what sort of evidence would show that land which is now submerged below sea level was once, long ago, above sea level. Darwin's original answer is given on pp. 212–14.

William Harvey on the circulation of the blood

Put yourself in William Harvey's shoes in the early 1600s – at an early stage in your career and interested in finding out how the heart works. What should you do? No doubt you would already have some idea about current opinion on the subject but presumably the obvious first thing to do is to read the existing literature on the subject and/or to discuss it with acknowledged experts. To do the former you would have to study the works of Galen (AD 130–200)! He was physician to the Roman Emperors at the height of the Roman Empire. He wrote many medical books and his ideas dominated European medicine for 1,300 years!

Galen taught that what we now call the veins and arteries were two largely *independent* systems, the veins carrying 'natural' blood and the arteries carrying 'vital' blood (which was mostly *air*!). Within these two systems the blood was believed to ebb and flow like the tides. Galen also taught that blood was produced in the digestive organs, that it carried *natural spirits* from there to the left ventricle of the heart and that a little passed *through* the heart wall (the septum) from left ventricle to right ventricle where it met with air from the lungs and was transformed into *vital spirits*.

It is hard to believe now that such ideas helped physicians to treat their patients but they were the best ideas available at the time and they were taught and believed until the seventeenth century. They were part of a system of ideas and of deep-rooted preconceptions – a paradigm – which is very remote from anything we believe now.

Galen was *the* authority on medicine for thirteen centuries: his ideas were taught *because* they were 'in Galen'. In Harvey's day students were commonly taught about, say, the heart and blood not by doing dissections themselves but by watching an assistant do dissections while the lecturer read the appropriate passage from Galen. If things turned out as Galen said they should the assistants would be very proud of themselves but if they didn't, still Galen was to be believed. (See Herbert Butterfield, *The Origins of Modern Science 1300–1800*.)

However, Galen's authority did not go unchallenged in Harvey's day. In 1543 Andreas Vesalius (1514–64) published his *On the Fabric of the Human Body*, which is now generally regarded as the foundation of modern anatomy. Vesalius doubted Galen's authority; for example he was sceptical about the movement of blood through the septum because, he said, the septum appeared to be solid. Galen's authority was so enormous that this simply provoked vigorous opposition from the medical establishment and even Vesalius himself said that he couldn't believe his own eyes. Another critic, Servetus (1509–53), argued that the blood went from right ventricle to left ventricle *via* the lungs where it combined with what we would now identify as oxygen. Similar ideas came from Colombo (1516–59) who had observed the heart during vivisections. In 1603 Fabricius (1537–1619) showed that there were valves in the veins which appeared to let the blood flow *only towards* the heart. Vesalius, Colombo and Fabricius had all worked at the University of Padua, Italy. Harvey went to study in Padua so it is quite certain that he knew of these developments – indeed Fabricius was his teacher.

Put yourself in Harvey's shoes again. You have read the literature and found your experts. What more must you do to find out how the heart and blood function? (Since Galen's picture is under challenge you can hardly feel the matter is settled.) Presumably you must find ways of *observing* their action and you must do *experiments* on them. This seems too obvious to need saying nowadays, but it was less obvious in Harvey's day. Then, *the* obvious way to find out about things was to refer to ancient authorities and although what we now recognise as a broadly scientific approach was beginning to be practised – for example Francis Bacon was advocating the virtues of a scientific method as he understood it – still this was a revolutionary change and it was not universally adopted or understood. Many writers of that time 'talked of the importance of seeing things with one's own eyes . . . [but] still could not observe a tree or a scene in nature without noticing just those things which the classical writers had taught them to look for' as Butterfield tells us. Seeing what is before your eyes is not easy, particularly when your head is full of ideas about what ought to be there – as it usually is. Harvey faced numerous difficulties and it is hard for us to grasp now just how unclear things were to him. He was very familiar with the classical paradigm but he also knew that it was flawed – that there were many 'anomalous experiences'. However, he had no clear alternative picture, no sure way of discovering one and no established methodology that he could reliably employ to test or verify any alternative picture he devised. As he says in Chapter 1 of *An Anatomical Disquisition on the Motion of the Heart and Blood in Animals*,

> When I first gave my mind to vivisections, as a means of discovering the motions and uses of the heart, and sought to discover from actual inspection, and not from the writings of others, I found the task so truly arduous, so full of difficulties, that I was almost tempted to think . . . that the motion of the heart was only to be comprehended by God.

The basic method Harvey used was vivisection. He cut open living creatures and watched the action of the heart and he did this with a large variety of animals (though *not* with human beings!).

> by having frequent recourse to vivisections, employing a variety of animals for the purpose and collating numerous observations, I thought I had attained to the truth. (Chapter 1)

> These things are more obvious in the colder animals, such as toads, frogs, serpents, small fishes, crabs, shrimps, snails and shellfish. (Chapter 2)

This enabled him to give a careful description of the way the heart actually moves and this contradicted popular opinion,

157

Hence the very opposite of the opinions commonly received, appears to be true; inasmuch as it is generally believed that when the heart strikes the breast and the pulse is felt without, the heart is dilated in its ventricles and is filled with blood; but the contrary of this is the fact and the heart when it contracts [and the shock is given] is emptied.   (Chapter 2)

The key discovery for Harvey was the amount of blood pumped by the heart: he found that in an hour the weight of blood pumped by a man's heart was greater than his total body weight!

not finding it possible that [the quantity of blood pumped] could be supplied by the juices of the injested aliment without the veins on the one hand becoming drained and the arteries on the other getting ruptured through excessive charge of blood, unless the blood should somehow find its way from the arteries into the veins, and so return to the right side of the heart; I began to think whether there might not be a motion as it were in a circle. Now this I afterwards found to be true; and I finally saw that the blood was forced out of the heart and driven by the beating of the left ventricle through the arteries into the body at large and into its several parts, in the same way as it is sent by the beating of the right ventricle through the [pulmonary artery] into the lungs, and that it returns through the veins into the *vena cava* and so to the right ventricle, in the same way as it returns from the lungs through the [pulmonary vein] to the left ventricle.   (Chapter 8)

Of course, having got the idea (the *hypothesis* as Popper would call it) that the blood might *circulate,* Harvey had to develop it, to work out the details and to test them. He did this in a great variety of ways. We shall not describe what Harvey did to establish his theory but we leave it as an exercise for the reader to answer the Assertibility Question:
'What argument or evidence would justify me in asserting that,

  (a) the blood flows only *out* 'of the left ventricle through the arteries into the body at large' (and does *not* ebb and flow as Galen says)
  (b) the blood flows only *towards* the heart in the veins (and does not ebb and flow as Galen says)
  (c) the *same* blood which flows along the arteries of the arm returns to the heart via the veins of the arm (it is different on Galen's account because the two systems are independent)?'

Harvey's answer to (b) is given on pp. 214–18. The reader should find it all the more persuasive for having tried to answer (b) first. The core of Harvey's argument for the circulation of the blood is presented in Chapters 9 to 13 of *On the Motion of the Heart and Blood* – chapters which are well worth reading after attempting to answer questions (a)–(c) above. (For a good account of Harvey's work and its importance, see A. C. Crombie, *Augustine to Galileo*.)

Like all new paradigms Harvey's *On the Motion of the Heart and Blood* left some problems unsolved. The most notable gap in Harvey's account was that he could not detect the 'connections' between arteries and veins at their extremities (e.g. in fingers and toes); the observation of these capillaries required a better microscope than Harvey had. However, Malpighi did it after Harvey's death.

Harvey's work illustrates beautifully the emergence of a new 'paradigm' in Kuhn's sense. Harvey could see (as others had before him) that Galen's account of the motion of the blood simply did not hang together with various familiar facts, but he found it very difficult to escape from the Galenic viewpoint. He certainly didn't take Galen's theory to be simply refuted. Finding a new way of looking at things required great inventiveness and although Popper would wish us to view Harvey's work as a well-corroborated hypothesis it is easy to see why Harvey called it *true* and *demonstrated* and why *we* should too. We asked the reader earlier to say 'What argument or evidence would justify you in asserting . . .' various parts of Harvey's picture. In general, when we can answer such questions we *are* justified in believing what has been established by the *standards* we have *appropriately* set. It is easier to *see* this if you put yourself in Harvey's shoes (and in Darwin's in our earlier example) but *impossible* to see it if you adopt the sceptical position so common among philosophers.

Harvey's demonstration of the circulation of the blood is easy to follow and makes a convincing, scientific proof. It was absurd then and is totally absurd now to pretend that it is merely a well-corroborated hypothesis, which we must believe only tentatively and critically. It is true, confirmed and well known.

Although William Harvey was a product of the intellectual climate of his time he, like Galileo, Copernicus and many others, contributed to the demise of medieval authoritarianism. Something equally revolutionary is needed now to remove philosophy from the paralysing influence of Cartesian scepticism (see Chapter 11, especially pp. 168–70).

11 · Philosophical assumptions

The method of argument analysis which is developed in this book is distinctive in employing the Assertibility Question. We introduced it in Chapter 2, we explained how to use it and we have illustrated how it works in several examples, but since it underlies our whole approach we must now attempt to answer some questions which may be raised about it. We shall first remind ourselves of our objectives and of how the Assertibility Question functions in attempting to realise those. We shall then explain some ideas about meaning which lie behind our method. We then provide a brief reply to the general challenge of scepticism and finally we explain why we attach relatively little importance to the notion of deductive validity in this whole exercise.

Objectives

Our objective is to describe and demonstrate a systematic method for extracting an argument from its written context and for evaluating it. We want a method which will apply to a wide range of both everyday and theoretical arguments and which will work for ordinary reasoning as expressed in natural language (and not just for those made-up examples with which logicians usually deal). We also want a method which draws on the insights and lessons of classical logic where these are helpful, but which is non-formal and reasonably efficient (both requirements exclude a method which requires us to translate real arguments into the symbolism of classical logic). Besides all this we want a method which is teachable and which combats – to the proper extent – our tendency to rely on experts: as we put it earlier (p. 1 above),

> it is possible to rely too heavily on experts, and this approach to learning and knowledge tends to encourage passivity and receptiveness rather than inventiveness and imagination.

We want to stress with our method how far one can get by *thinking things through for oneself*, what might be called the 'confidence-building' objective.

The Assertibility Question is justified to the extent that it enables us to achieve these objectives.

Extracting the argument

It is now standard practice in the tradition of informal logic which has emerged during the past two decades to employ 'inference indicators', that is to say, key words which indicate the presence of reasons and conclusions. Those who are unfamiliar with this tradition often fail to realise how difficult it can be to extract an author's intended argument from a written natural-language text. Inference indicators are a real and practical help in doing this and our method uses them initially in a standard way, but since authors often omit them for rhetorical and other reasons, some further guidance is needed in dealing with real arguments. This is where the Assertibility Question first comes in.

In extracting an argument from its context by our method, we locate the inference indicators, find the main conclusion and then proceed as follows (see Chapter 2, pp. 22f.):

> Starting with [the main conclusion] C, ask 'What immediate reasons are presented in the text for accepting C?' or 'Why (in the text) am I asked to believe C?' Use inference indicators to help answer the question. If the question is hard to answer because the author's intentions are not transparent (i.e. they are neither explicitly shown by argument indicators nor obvious from the context), then ask the Assertibility Question, (AQ):

> (AQ): What argument or evidence would justify me in asserting the conclusion C? (What would I have to know or believe to be justified in accepting C?)

It is at this point that one so to speak 'looks away' from the text to think about what C means. This is the moment for 'thinking things through', for being reflective and imaginative, for asking, 'What would prove this?' or 'How should I argue for this?' Most people are surprised to discover how far they can get at this point. Having decided what reasons need to be given to support C and to convince you of it, you then,

> see if the author asserts or clearly assumes these same claims (reasons). If he does it is reasonable (and accords with the Principle of Charity) to construe him as having intended the same argument. If he doesn't you have no rational way of reconstructing his argument (on the basis of the text alone).

In outline, this is how the Assertibility Question functions in extracting an argument from its context.

Two points – of clarification and justification – are worth adding. As we said in Chapter 2, p. 22,

(b) inference indicators may make an author's intentions completely clear (quite *certain*); context may do the same; but if this is not the case the only way you can divine the author's intentions (given only the text) is to construct the best argument you can and ask whether the author can be construed as presenting it.

It is worth stressing that if the appropriate language is used – i.e. explicit inference indicators are used – then this shows quite *unambiguously* what argument is intended. Whether it is a good or a bad argument is irrelevant to the question 'What argument is being presented?' and the author's private thoughts are irrelevant too. Examples 1 to 4 in Chapter 1 (pp. 6–11) are just such examples; in these examples there is no room for doubt as to what argument is being presented.

However, there are many other cases where the matter is not so clear, and it is in such cases that we use the Assertibility Question in order to divine the author's intentions. (There are numerous examples of this throughout the book but especially in Chapter 4.) In short the justification for doing this is as follows. In presenting an argument the author is attempting to communicate with others and to convince them of a viewpoint. It is reasonable to assume that the author uses language much as the rest of us do, that she/he means much the same by what she says and how she presents it, that she understands what she is saying and that therefore she takes what verifies it or falsifies it to be much what the rest of us take it to be: we all learn to use language in much the same way.

Of course, the use of the Assertibility Question to extract an author's intended argument is open to sceptical challenge: everything always is. But we are not *normally* sceptical about the possibility of understanding other people, nor is it *appropriate* to be. If the sceptic feels that we assume too much we can only reply here that he grants too little about the way we actually use language. We shall say more in this vein shortly.

Evaluating an argument

We use the Assertibility Question not only in extracting arguments from their context but also in evaluating them. To summarise what we said earlier, if an argument is to establish its conclusion,

(I) its premises must be true (except that if there are independent premises only one need be true and also suppositions need not be true in order to establish their conclusions), and

(II) its conclusion must *follow* from its premises.

The big question is how to decide whether (II) is the case – whether a conclusion does *follow*. The standard test is basically,

> Could the premisses be true and the conclusion false?

but we argued in Chapter 2 (pp. 26f.) that this test leads to scepticism in many areas – in science, in history, in our knowledge of other minds, etc. – and that,

> Such scepticism is quite remote from *normal* – and *appropriate* – standards of argument.

For this reason we revised the standard test so that our test makes explicit reference to such standards. The test we use is,

> Could the premisses be true and the conclusion false judging by appropriate standards of evidence or appropriate standards of what is possible?

and this is where the Assertibility Question comes in a second time, except that this time we use it in order to decide what these 'appropriate standards' are; i.e. in order to decide whether some conclusion C *does* follow from a given train of reasoning we ask,

> (AQ): What argument or evidence would justify me in asserting the conclusion C? (Etc.)

The reader may think that this process is in danger of looking almost circular, as if it says, 'In order to decide whether C *does* follow from the reasons given we must first decide whether it *would* follow.' But, in fact, it is no more circular than scientific method, as conceived by Popper. On Popper's account, the scientist says what evidence would refute the hypothesis, looks to see if this evidence exists and, if it does, concludes that the hypothesis *is* refuted.

The more general point is that the wording of the Assertibility Question is quite deliberate, and paraphrases of it – such as occur in the previous paragraph – can be misleading unless understood in the intended way. There are three aspects of its wording which we should mention at this point.

The first, and most important, is that the Assertibility Question talks about *justified assertion* and *not* about *truth-conditions*. The Assertibility Question asks,

> What . . . would *justify* me in *asserting* C?

or

> What would I have to *know* or *believe* to be *justified* in *accepting* C?

It does *not* ask,

> What would have to be true or false for C to be true or false?

or

> Under what conditions will C be true/false?

This point will be elaborated in the next section.

The second respect in which the wording of the Assertibility Question is important is in the reference to

> *appropriate standards* of evidence or *appropriate standards* of what is possible.

As we explained in Chapter 2, p. 27,

> claims about the past, or about the future, or about causal connections, or about other people's intentions, or about mathematics ... (etc.) ... all these have different *standards of proof*.

Some philosophers like to insist that there is only one standard of proof – deductive validity, say – but this is unhelpful.

Consider the following, arbitrarily chosen, example. A painting is discovered and someone suggests that it was painted by Vermeer. There are tests which can be applied to try to settle the matter: experts will examine the picture to see if it displays Vermeer's characteristic technique and to see if there is any evidence of forgery; they will examine contemporary records for evidence of the picture's existence and so on. There are standard procedures for settling a question of this sort and they will often be decisive, they will often settle the matter beyond doubt. Sometimes, of course, they will be inconclusive and, in some cases, mistakes will be made, but, in general, these are well-established procedures – indeed errors can only be identified by the standards of precisely these procedures. This is not to say, of course, that the standards of proof which are normally employed in some field must be the appropriate ones and are immune from criticism. Art experts, mathematicians, astrologers – or whoever – may or may not employ standards of proof which are appropriate to their task. This depends on what the task is. The point is that these different standards are not reducible to some one formula or standard – say deductive validity – which is common to all good arguments. We shall return to this point – with respect to deductive validity as the standard – shortly.

The third respect in which the wording of the Assertibility Question is deliberate differs from the previous two. These were mainly based on philosophical considerations whereas the present one is also a matter of 'the psychology' of our approach. In short, the use of the personal pronouns 'me' and 'I' are intentional; anyone using the Assertibility Question asks,

> What ... would justify *me* in asserting C?

or

> What would *I* have to know?

If, instead, one asks something like,

> What would prove C to be true?

this tends to make people feel they have to find the *right* answer – an answer which is known to the teacher or the expert – and this inhibits them from getting as far as they can on their own. Our question is meant to make the user think through his or her *own* answers; it is meant to encourage the user to be reflective, imaginative and self-confident (because people discover that they can get surprisingly far). Of course, we do not mean to imply that each individual can give their own answer quite arbitrarily. As we said in Chapter 2, in using our method,

> you have to make a judgement about 'appropriate standards'. That judgement will be *yours*; it is a judgement which requires justification and which is open to criticism. Set too severe a standard and it will seem that nothing can be known with certainty; set too unimaginative a standard and you will be led easily into error. (See p. 27 above)

We might also remark in passing that the Assertibility Question cannot be answered arbitrarily because words don't mean just whatever you choose them to mean; but we shall now return to the first and most important of these points about the wording of Assertibility Question to elaborate on some of the ideas about meaning which lie behind its use.

The Assertibility Question and meaning

The interpretation which has been placed on the Assertibility Question throughout this book, and which partly justifies the use to which it has been put, depends for its fruitfulness on a particular view about meaning. As we said in Chapter 2, the philosophical justification for using the Assertibility Question is based on the assumption that,

> * If you understand a proposition you must be able to give at least some account of how you could decide whether it was true or false, what argument or evidence would show it to be true or false (otherwise you don't understand it at all).

Baldly stated, this principle is obviously open to different interpretations. It may suggest on the one hand a version of the *truth-condition theory of meaning* and on the other a version of *verificationism*. Since it is liable to be misunderstood from both perspectives we shall now attempt to clarify what is intended, and to elaborate our defence of the Assertibility Question and its use, by contrasting what is intended by the principle * with Gottlob Frege's truth-condition theory of meaning and with A. J. Ayer's verificationism.

On Frege's view (similarly for Russell and the early Wittgenstein) the meaning of a proposition is given by stating the conditions which are individually necessary and jointly sufficient for its truth. Now, of course, on anyone's view what *is* true need not be *known*, but on Frege's view, what is true need not be humanly *knowable* either, and is independent of how *we*, human beings, might come to know it. On this view then, the meaning of a proposition P may be known independently of knowing what would justify us in believing it (if anything could): the meaning of P may be known to someone who has no idea what would *show* it true or false, no idea what counts as conclusive reasons or evidence for *us*.

Although there is much to be said for Frege's truth-condition theory this so-called 'realist' conception of truth can't be right. As Dummett puts it in 'Truth', his famous critique of the theory,

> it is part of the concept of truth that we aim at making true statements; and Frege's theory of truth and falsity . . . leaves this feature of the concept of truth quite out of account. Frege indeed tried to bring it in afterwards in his theory of assertion – but too late; for the sense of a sentence is not given in advance of our going in for the activity of asserting

and later,

> if such a statement as 'Jones was brave' is true, it must be true in virtue of the sort of fact we have been taught as justifying us in asserting it. It cannot be true in virtue of a fact of some quite different sort of which we can have no direct knowledge, for otherwise the statement . . . would not have the meaning *we* have given it.

In short, the meaning of a proposition is to be explained in terms of the kinds of things *we could know*, because that is how we learn language.

There remains a question, of course, about what kinds of things we can know. We shall come at this question (negatively as it turns out) from the other perspective we just mentioned as a source of misunderstanding of our principle * – that of verificationism.

The logical positivists held that the meaning of a sentence was to be explained in terms of what would show it to be true or false – what would *verify* or *falsify* it. They also took the view that if nothing would verify or falsify an apparently meaningful sentence (which was neither a tautology nor a contradiction) then it was *meaningless*. A. J. Ayer's *Language, Truth and Logic* contains the classic statement of the logical positivist's conception of verifiability as a criterion of meaningfulness:

The criterion which we use to test the genuineness of apparent statements of fact is the criterion of verifiability. We say that a sentence is factually significant to any given person if, and only if, he knows how to verify the proposition which it purports to express – that is, if he knows what observations would lead him, under certain conditions, to accept the proposition as being true, or to reject it as being false. If on the other hand the putative proposition is of such a character that the assumption of its truth, or falsehood, is consistent with any assumption whatsoever concerning the nature of his future experiences, then, as far as he is concerned, it is, if not a tautology, a mere pseudo-proposition. (p. 35)

Ayer puts this criterion to use in a fierce and famous attack on 'metaphysics' throughout the remainder of the book. Here is a characteristic example of the use to which he puts it (itself an excellent example for argument analysis!):

A good example of the kind of utterance that is condemned by our criterion as being not even false but nonsensical would be the assertion that the world of sense-experience was altogether unreal. It must, of course, be admitted that our senses do sometimes deceive us. We may, as the result of having certain sensations, expect certain other sensations to be obtainable which are, in fact, not obtainable. But, in all such cases, it is a further sense-experience that informs us of the mistakes that arise out of sense-experience. We say that the senses sometimes deceive us, just because the expectations to which our sense-experiences give rise do not always accord with what we subsequently experience. That is, we rely on our senses to substantiate or confute the judgements which are based on sensation. And therefore, the fact that our perceptual judgements are sometimes found to be erroneous has not the slightest tendency to show that the world of sense-experience is unreal. And, indeed, it is plain that no conceivable observation, or series of observations, could have a tendency to show that the world revealed to us by sense-experience was unreal. Consequently, anyone who condemns the sensible world as a world of mere appearance, as opposed to reality, is saying something which, according to our criterion of significance, is literally nonsensical. (p. 37)

This elegant argument not only employs verifiability as a criterion of meaningfulness but also gives the positivist game away since it reveals very clearly that the only things which *count* as verifying or falsifying the proposition are 'observations or series of observations'. The logical positivists were not only verificationists, they also had a very restricted empiricist view of

167

what *counted* for and against a proposition. Dummett makes the point well in his book *Frege: Philosophy of Language,*

> Although [the positivists] regarded sense as determined by the conditions for the verification of a sentence, they insisted on viewing these conditions as consisting solely in the bare impact of the external world upon us, as transmitted through the senses, in abstraction from any activity of ours which enables us to recognise the sentences as having been verified. The result is a notion of verification which bears little resemblance to any procedure we actually employ when we determine the truth-value of a sentence . . . The notion of meaning within a verificationist theory [should explain our grasp on the references and so the uses of words] but when verificationism is construed in the bizarre fashion in which the positivists construed it, it is unable to do so, and thus loses its point altogether.

In short, verificationism was led astray by its association with the mistaken epistemology of the logical positivists. In fact very few of our beliefs are proved or refuted merely by observations. They are mostly part of a larger picture or theory which is tested by observation 'at its edges' (to use Quine's image) and which has to 'hang together' in various ways (which are not just a matter of deductive consistency) so, in general, verification or falsification is a complex mixture of observation and evidence on the one hand and inference and argument on the other. Consider, for example, how one would establish that 'Herbert and Anthony are brothers'. (Cf. Dummett, *Frege: Philosophy of Language*, p. 591.)

It is a pity to lose Ayer's beautiful argument against the possibility of our senses always deceiving us but a properly reconstructed verificationism will rescue it (cf. P. M. S. Hacker, *Insight and Illusion*).

To sum up this section: if we are to understand the philosophical ideas lying behind our use of the Assertibility Question, in particular the principle *, we must separate the truth-condition theory from Frege's realism and we must divorce verificationism from positivist epistemology. This is the direction in which principle * is intended to point. Of course, this still leaves open what kinds of answers are appropriate to the Assertibility Question but that is as it should be for our purposes. In general the right answers are determined by how we learn and use language and this is what anyone knows who understands the language.

The challenge of scepticism

There is a widely held philosophical belief, inspired especially by Descartes, that *certainty* is the impossibility of doubt. On this view if you can imagine *any* circumstances in which the reasons could be true and the conclusion false then the conclusion does not *follow* from the reasons, is not *conclusively* established by them, or, in general, is not *certain*. This view leads to extreme scepticism about what we can know and as we said in Chapter 2,

> Such scepticism is quite remote from *normal* – and appropriate – standards of argument.

Suppose we ask the Cartesian sceptic, 'What would prove that Hitler died in Berlin in 1945?' (cf. p. 193). Suppose that there was a body which was witnessed by many who had known Hitler to be his body (and that these included independent witnesses who had no motive for lying), and suppose that medical records confirmed this. The sceptic will be unimpressed because, 'There is always the possibility that he made a miraculous escape, substituted the body of a double, faked medical evidence, duped witnesses, etc.' Yes, this is a possibility, but does it prevent us from claiming to *know* that Hitler died in Berlin in 1945? What would show this 'possibility' to be true or false? Suppose we have a revelation from 'the real' Hitler now dying in Brazil, with confirming papers, witnesses and other evidence. The Cartesian sceptic will again say, 'But why should we believe all this? Perhaps we are being duped again? (Remember the "Hitler diaries"!)' And so we could go on *ad infinitum* because along the sceptic's road there is *no* certainty, *no* knowledge.

But we don't *normally* talk and reason like this. There *is* a problem about deciding what evidence is sufficient to entitle us to assert and believe that someone died at such a time and in such a place, but this is a matter which is *settled* many times every day without any doubts being entertained (and quite properly so). The sceptic of course believes that all sorts of doubts are possible in every case, but this is nonsense. Doubts are possible only in *some* cases and against a background in which certainty is the norm. It is only in a situation in which we know what would establish P that we can give sense to the idea of doubting P. Consider another example: we go for a walk and find that everywhere is wet – the ground, the trees and the buildings are all wet – so we conclude that 'it has been raining'. The sceptic says, 'Not necessarily. Perhaps the military sprayed everywhere or a film company did it'. For the sceptic, every claim is guilty until proved innocent. But we *don't learn* language like them and we *don't use* it like that and we *couldn't use* it like that. Doubting is essentially a parasitic activity, it is parasitic on *knowing*, on being sure. If the sceptic is to cast doubt on whether we really know P to be true he must understand what P means, but on our account (see previous section) this means that he must be able to say what would show it to be true (or false), what would justify us in asserting (or denying) it, what would entitle us to say that we know it. Otherwise he is not using language as we do and must. (Cf. Hacker.)

Although we do not follow the Cartesian sceptic into a world where there is no certainty and no knowledge, it is right to approach any knowledge claim critically (and even sceptically), but such a claim should be treated as innocent until proved guilty and something which *might* tell against it should *count* as a possibility only if *we could know it to be true*. As with our criticism of the truth-condition theory we are once again stressing the importance of what we can *know*.

To conclude: in normal circumstances (outside the philosophy seminar) we do not use the Cartesian sceptic's standards in extracting and evaluating arguments. Nor should we. If a genuine doubt is to be raised against the soundness of an argument it has to be in terms of something we could know to be true and against the background of a standard which would genuinely establish the conclusion to be true too.

On deduction and induction

The traditional philosophical distinction between deductive and inductive arguments plays almost no role in our method. Some readers may feel that our (revised) test for whether a conclusion *follows* from its premises is too 'open' or too vague and that it would be better to evaluate arguments by the 'well-defined' standard of deductive validity or the well-worked standard of inductive validity. But this would be a mistake.

Although deductive validity is sometimes important it is relatively rare in ordinary, natural-language arguments. Attempting to convert such a non-deductive argument into a deductively valid one, say by specifying the 'appropriate standards', or some other implicit premiss, as extra premisses, will not usually yield a deductively valid argument. The reader who doubts this claim should try to convert some of the examples provided in this book into deductively valid arguments in this way. In general this will not work because the 'pictures'/'models'/'theories' with which we work leave many things unsaid and are incompletely specifiable anyway. Of course, any argument, however unsound, can be converted into a deductively valid argument just by adding the hypothetical premiss, 'If the reasons are all true, the conclusion is' but this does not help at all in evaluating the argument because one still has to decide whether the additional premiss is true.

Inductive validity is not the answer either. There is no *general* standard of inductive validity. The appropriate standard differs in every sort of case and there is no escaping the need to recognise these differences. More importantly, it is usually said in this connection that only a deductively valid argument can establish its conclusion with *certainty* – can be *conclusive* – and that inductive arguments yield only probability. It is clear from our previous discussion that we reject this view and that we claim to be certain of, and to know, many things for which we do not have a deductively conclusive case: we are certain that the blood circulates in the body, that like poles repel, that bodies of different mass fall with the same acceleration and that each of us will die.

Conclusion

We have spent the previous sections clarifying and explaining the philosophical assumptions behind our approach. The philosophical defences we began to erect could be developed in different directions. We could employ Dewey's notion of 'warranted assertibility'. Alternatively, we could use Wittgenstein's notion of 'criteria'. Both are obvious possibilities. But we need to say no more here. Clearly the fundamental justification for our approach – in particular the use of the Assertibility Question – is not a philosophical one, it is that *it works*. Either it helps those who use it to extract and evaluate arguments – or it doesn't and this is something which has to be tested. Testing it is not a simple matter because one has to decide what should count as suitable tests. Although the method has been tried on several hundred students – with positive responses from them – no systematic tests of its utility have yet been made. Devising suitable tests is left for the present as an exercise for the reader.

Appendix · Elementary formal logic

> 'For a *complete* logical argument' Arthur began with admirable
> solemnity, 'we need two prim Misses —'
> 'Of course!' she interrupted, 'I remember that word now. And they
> produce — ?'
> 'A Delusion' said Arthur.
> 'Ye-es?' she said dubiously. 'I don't seem to remember that so well.
> But what is the *whole* argument called?'
> 'A Sillygism.'   Lewis Carroll, *Sylvie and Bruno*

It is likely that anyone who has read this far will be interested in the extent to
which formal logic can help in extracting and evaluating arguments. There is
no doubt that traditional formal logic contains many ideas and insights which
are useful if one is to understand and evaluate arguments. On the other hand
it is clearly difficult to *apply* it to *real* arguments – to arguments of the kind
one finds for example in newspapers, magazines and learned journals.

Elementary classical logic articulates a very clear theory and one which
is quite easy to understand. This Appendix is addressed to the reader who
knows little or no formal logic but who would like a brief introduction to the
subject so that he or she may begin to consider what help logic can give in
argument analysis. There are scores of elementary logic texts which develop
carefully and clearly the material which we review *very* briefly here.

What is argument?

Reasoning, or arguing a case, consists in giving *reasons* for some *conclusion*:
the reasons are put forward in order to *establish, support, justify, prove*
or *demonstrate* the conclusion. Traditional logic *begins* by restricting its
attention to arguments in which the reasons and conclusions are *either true
or false* (and it does not consider moral arguments, for example) so we shall
do the same in this Appendix.

Every argument then contains its reasons and its conclusions: the reasons
presented for a conclusion are usually called the *premisses* of the argument.
The question the logician is interested in is whether they are *good* reasons
for the conclusion; if they are the premisses are said to *entail* or *imply* the

conclusion, and the conclusion is said to *follow from* the premisses or to be *implied* or *entailed* by them. We shall explain in the following pages how classical logic understands these terms.

Propositions

A given sentence, e.g. 'Oxygen burns', may be used to express a conclusion on one occasion and a premiss on another, or it may be used as part of a larger sentence, e.g. 'If oxygen burns, then the phlogiston theory is wrong.' We need a way of referring to what these occasions of a sentence's use have in common and clearly we are not interested in the sentence itself but in what it means – in what it expresses. Logicians usually speak of a *proposition* when referring to the thought expressed by a sentence *on a given occasion of its use* and we shall do the same here.

Notice that the *same* sentence, e.g. 'I have a headache', may be used either by the same person on different occasions or by different persons to express *different* propositions. Notice also that *different* sentences may express the *same* proposition. For example 'Mary loves John' and 'John is loved by Mary' may be used to express the same proposition.

We shall use this notion of proposition without further explanation at present. We are interested in what a sentence *means* on a given occasion of its use and this is what we shall call a proposition.

Assertion

Someone may use the proposition 'Oxygen burns' to say something he takes to be true, or he may use it in a compound proposition like 'If oxygen burns the phlogiston theory is wrong.' Although the same proposition is expressed in both cases, in the first case it is *presented as being true* and this is *not* so in the second case; in the hypothetical the speaker is saying '*If* oxygen burns *then*' but he is not saying that oxygen *does* burn. If a proposition is *presented as being true* logicians say that it is *asserted*. Otherwise it is not asserted. Suppose someone says as the premiss of an argument, 'Either oxygen burns or nitrogen burns'; in doing this he *asserts* the whole proposition but he does not assert 'oxygen burns' and he does not assert 'nitrogen burns'.

If someone begins an argument by saying 'Suppose oxygen does not burn' he is not *asserting* that oxygen does not burn – he is not *presenting this as true*. Indeed he may well know that oxygen burns and he may be setting out on a *reductio ad absurdum* argument to prove that it does. Suppositions then are not assertions.

If someone asks the question 'Does oxygen burn?' he is *asking* whether the proposition 'oxygen burns' is true – but he is not asserting anything. So questions too are contrasted with assertions.

The premises and the conclusion of an argument are *assertions* when they are presented as being true.

The 'validity' of an argument

An argument then contains propositions, some as premises and one as conclusion, and what logic is interested in is whether the conclusion *follows from* the premises. To put it another way, the logician's question is whether one who accepts the premises of an argument *must* accept its conclusion. To put it in yet another way, the question is whether the premises could be true and the conclusion false. If in a given argument the conclusion follows from the premises the argument is said to be (deductively) *valid*: if it doesn't the argument is said to be *invalid*. Logic is often defined as the study or science of valid reasoning.

The classical test for validity is very easy to summarise. However, it has a very distinctive feature to which we should draw attention now. It is this: in order to decide whether a given argument is valid one does *not* consider just that argument alone, with its own peculiar subject matter, but instead, one abstracts from that content and considers the argument's structure or 'logical form'. The logical form of an argument is something it has in common with many other arguments – which are about quite different subjects. We shall elucidate the notion of logical form in the following pages but first we give the classical test for validity.

An argument is said to be valid if it has a valid logical form, and a logical form is valid if there is no argument of that form which has true premises and a false conclusion.

The logical form of an argument

The notion of validity is entirely dependent upon the notion of logical form, so we must now explain this. The idea behind the notion of logical form is that one can distinguish between the 'structure' of an argument and its subject matter – or between its *form* and *content*. The content of an argument is what it is *about* (animals, atoms or whatever) and its form is expressed by means of those words which occur in reasoning about any subject whatever. If we call these the 'logical' words they include such examples as 'every', 'all', 'most', 'some', 'few', 'no', 'if . . . then', 'implies', 'entails', 'follows from', 'because', 'so', 'therefore', 'and', 'but', 'or', 'not', 'is a' and many others. One can easily imagine a collection of arguments about very different subjects – about animals or atoms, about mice or men or music or marriage – which all exhibit the same form when the words which are peculiar to each subject are replaced by the neutral, schematic letters, A, B, C, etc. and one is left only with logical words. For example they might exhibit the form,

No A is a C, because every A is a B
and no B is a C.

And yet again, they might exhibit the form,

If A then B but not B so not A.

The logical form of an argument then is found by abstracting from its particular content. To say this, however, is to leave much to explain as the distinction between form and content is still vague. Clearly, if we are to be able to use the classical test for validity we must have a precise account of logical form and we must be able to display the logical form of arguments. The classical approach to this is to identify the logical words and certain logical categories and to introduce a formal symbolism for them, so that forms may be clearly expressed in this formal and unambiguous notation. Once expressed in this way a method for evaluating such forms is given if that is possible. We shall follow this course in the conventional way beginning with some of the logical words which can connect whole propositions.

Propositions and some logical words which apply to them

Clearly, from given propositions, say P and Q, it is possible to construct further, compound propositions by means of logical words. Some examples are 'P and Q', 'P or Q', 'if P then Q', 'P but not Q' and 'it is not the case that P'. We look now at the logical form of such compound propositions. We give a symbolism for expressing them and a method for evaluating arguments which employ them. This is the fragment of classical logical theory known as 'propositional logic'.

(i) *'not' and negation* Suppose we have a proposition P: 'The Moon is made of green cheese.' We may *negate* P in various ways: we may say 'The Moon is *not* made of green cheese' or 'It is false that the Moon is made of green cheese' or 'It is not the case that the Moon is made of green cheese', etc. There are many ways of negating a proposition in English and one has to be alert to all of these when extracting the logical form of an argument, but we shall symbolise negation by means of the single symbol '¬' and ¬ P will symbolise that proposition which is false if P is true and true if P is false, called the *negation* of P.

(ii) *'and' and conjunction* Suppose we have two separate propositions, P and Q. Suppose P is 'Sir Walter Scott wrote *Waverley*' and Q is 'Socrates taught Plato'; clearly we may form a single proposition by joining these with 'and' to give 'Sir Walter Scott wrote *Waverley* and Socrates taught Plato.' This proposition is called the *conjunction* of P and Q and, using '&' for 'and' is symbolised by P & Q. The conjunction of two propositions is true if each of these propositions (called its *conjuncts*) is true and *only if* they are both true. Again, one has to be alert to other ways of expressing conjunction in English when extracting the form of an argument.

(iii) *'or' and disjunction* Again suppose we have two separate propositions, P and Q. For a change suppose P is 'The tank is empty' and Q is 'The battery is flat.' Clearly we may join these by 'or' or by 'either . . . or . . .' to give 'Either the tank is empty or the battery is flat.'

Sometimes in ordinary English 'P or Q' means 'P or Q *but not both*' (as when the parent tells the child 'You may have fish and chips or you may have hamburgers'); this is called the *exclusive* sense of 'or'. At other times it means 'P or Q and *possibly both*'; this is called the *non-exclusive* or *inclusive* sense of 'or'. In Latin there are different words for the two cases; they are 'aut' and 'vel' respectively: in classical logic a symbol 'v', called 'vel', is introduced to symbolise the non-exclusive case of 'P or Q'. This is called the (non-exclusive) *disjunction* of P and Q and is symbolised as P v Q. The (non-exclusive) *disjunction* of two propositions is true if at least one of these propositions (called its *disjuncts*) is true. Otherwise it is false. The exclusive sense of 'or' can be expressed using 'v' as follows: 'P or Q and not both' is symbolised as $(P \lor Q) \& \neg (P \& Q)$.

(iv) *'if . . . then . . .' and the material conditional* Again suppose we have two separate propositions, P and Q. As an example let P be 'All boiled, red lobsters are dead' and let Q be 'All dead, red lobsters are boiled.' Clearly we may form a single proposition by joining these with 'if . . . then . . .' to give 'If all boiled, red lobsters are dead then all dead red lobsters are boiled.' A proposition of the form 'if P then Q', is called a *hypothetical*, a *conditional*, an *implication* or an *entailment*. (The proposition P, which precedes 'then', is called the *antecedent* of the conditional and the proposition Q, which follows 'then', is called the *consequent* of the conditional.) It is less easy with 'if . . . then . . .' than it was with 'not', 'and', 'or' to say under what conditions 'if P then Q' is true or false. Classical logic avoids complex issues about the 'real' meaning of 'if . . . then . . .' by defining a closely related notion, that of the *material conditional*, which is symbolised by '⊃' and is read as 'if . . . then . . .' The material conditional P ⊃ Q is *defined* to be *false* if P is true and Q is false; otherwise it is defined to be true.

Whether the material conditional corresponds to the use of 'if . . . then . . .' in ordinary English has been the subject of endless debate among philosophers. In short it seems quite reasonable to say that 'if P then Q' is false if P is true and Q is false, but much less reasonable to call it true in all other cases. If P and Q are both true but are not *relevant* to each other (as in our example for conjunction above) isn't it misleading to call 'if P then Q' true? And isn't it misleading to call 'if P then Q' true simply on the grounds that P is false or that Q is true? Construing 'if P then Q' in terms of the material conditional gives rise to the paradoxical results that a false proposition implies *any* proposition and a true proposition is implied by *any* proposition. The classical tradition acknowledges these criticisms but insists that they are not serious; it insists that interpreting ordinary uses of 'if . . . then . . .' in terms of the material conditional does not lead to error in evaluating arguments for validity and this is its essential justification – *it works*. It was originally introduced by Frege and Russell for symbolising mathematical arguments and there is no doubt that it works admirably for such contexts. We shall assume for present purposes that it works for many other contexts too, and that occurrences of 'if . . . then . . .' in arguments should be symbolised by ' . . . ⊃ . . .' when exhibiting their logical form.

(v) *'if and only if' and material equivalence* Let P and Q be the propositions of our material conditional example. We could join these by ' . . . if and only if . . .' to give a single proposition, 'All boiled red lobsters are dead if and only if all dead red lobsters are boiled.' A proposition of the form 'P if and only if Q' is called a *bi-conditional* or *equivalence*. The problems which arose in connection with 'if . . . then . . .' return with ' . . . if and only if . . .' but classical logical again *defines* a related notion, *material equivalence*, which is symbolised by '≡'. The *material equivalence* P ≡ Q is defined to be true if P and Q are either *both* true or *both* false; otherwise it is false.

Translating arguments into logical symbolism

In the preceding paragraphs (i)–(v) we have looked at a number of logical words and we have introduced symbols for them. As we have already pointed out there are several equivalent ways of saying 'not' in English. The same is true for 'and' (e.g. 'also', 'but', 'too', 'furthermore'); the same is true for 'or' (e.g. 'either . . . or . . .', 'alternatively'); the same is true for 'if . . . then . . .' (e.g. 'provided that', 'on the assumption that', 'on condition that', 'implies' 'entails'). In general if one wishes to translate a piece of reasoning from English into logical symbolism, to exhibit the logical form, this will require careful judgement about what the appropriate interpretation is. This is partly because of the variety of English usage and partly because of the definitions of '¬', '&', 'v', '⊃' and '≡' given in sections (i)–(v) above. In general one has to decide whether the meaning of these symbols 'fits' sufficiently closely the meanings of the English words – whether the English can be adequately paraphrased by means of the symbolism. For example in the classical tradition, 'P but Q', 'P moreover Q' and 'P nevertheless Q' are all symbolised by 'P & Q' although this clearly leaves something out. We have already mentioned some of the problems raised by 'if P then Q' and 'P ⊃ Q'. There are other similar problems too (see P. F. Strawson, *Introduction to Logical Theory*, for an extensive discussion), but we shall assume for the present – with classical logic – that these can be overcome and that we can translate some ordinary language reasoning by means of these symbols and thus exhibit, at least in part, its logical form.

One remaining point needs to be mentioned. It is clear that,

Peter ran and Ralph jumped or Sarah fell

is ambiguous. Using the obvious notation, P & R v S does not express an unambiguous logical form: does it mean (P & R) v S or is it P & (R v S)? The ambiguity is easily eliminated by using brackets so we shall need not only the proposition letters, P, Q, R, etc., and the symbols ¬, &, v, ⊃ and ≡, but also brackets to exhibit the logical forms of propositional logic. (We saw an example of this earlier in the expression for the exclusive sense of 'or'.)

Testing the forms of propositional logic

We shall find it convenient in this section to speak of the *truth-value* of a proposition: this is True if the proposition is true and False if the proposition is false (and is independent of whether the proposition is asserted). There are no other truth-values and in classical logic every proposition is taken to be true or false.

The logical words 'not', 'and', 'or', 'if . . . then', ' . . . if and only if . . .' and their associated symbols '¬', '&', 'v', '⊃', '≡', are called *logical* or *propositional connectives* or *operators*. The crucial thing about the logical connectives introduced in sections (i)–(v) above, '¬', '&', 'v', '⊃' and '≡', is that they are all *truth-functional* operators. This means that if one applies them to initial propositions, say P and Q, the truth-value of the resulting proposition, ¬ P, P & Q, P v Q, P ⊃ Q or P ≡ Q *is determined solely by the truth-values of the constituent proposition P and Q.*

We can show what this means by setting out the *truth-conditions* described in sections (i)–(v) in *truth-tables* (writing T, F for the truth-values True and False). These tables display how the truth-value of each compound proposition is determined by the truth-values of its constituent propositions P and Q (for all possible combinations of truth-values of P and Q).

(¬: negation)

¬	P
F	T
T	F

This tabulates the fact that
if P is true, ¬ P is false;
if P is false, ¬ P is true.

(&: conjunction)

P	&	Q
T	T	T
F	F	F
F	F	T
F	F	F

This tabulates the fact that
if P and Q are both true, P & Q is true;

otherwise P & Q is false.

(v: disjunction)

P	v	Q
T	T	T
T	T	F
F	T	T
F	F	F

This tabulates the fact that
if at least one of P, Q is true, P v Q is true;

if P, Q are both false, P v Q is false.

(⊃: implication)	P ⊃ Q	This tabulates the fact that
	T T T	if P is true and Q is false, P ⊃ Q is false;
	T F F	otherwise P ⊃ Q is true.
	F T T	
	F T F	

(≡: equivalence)	P ≡ Q	This tabulates the fact that
	T T T	if P and Q have the same truth-value
	T F F	P ≡ Q is true; otherwise P ≡ is false.
	F F T	
	F T F	

As we said above, the difficulties in translating a piece of English reasoning into classical symbolism are due in part to the truth-functional character of '¬', '&', 'v', '⊃' and '≡'. Whilst this truth-functional character presents a difficulty when symbolising arguments its great virtue is that it yields a very simple and elegant procedure for testing the validity of propositional forms. We now explain this procedure with a simple example. Suppose we have the propositional form (P & (¬P v Q)) ⊃ Q, we can easily construct a truth-table for this form quite mechanically from the basic truth-tables given above. We describe below how to do this:

	P	Q	¬P	¬P v Q	P &(¬P v Q)	(P & (¬P v Q)) ⊃ Q
(i)	T	T	F	T	T	T
(ii)	T	F	F	F	F	T
(iii)	F	T	T	T	F	T
(iv)	F	F	T	T	F	T
	(1)	(2)	(3)	(4)	(5)	(6)

We have to consider all possible combinations of truth-values of P and Q so in this example we need the four lines (i)–(iv) and the combinations displayed in columns (1) and (2). Column (3) is computed from column (1) by the truth-table for ¬; column (4) comes from (2) and (3) by the table for v; column (5) comes from (1) and (4) by &; and (6) comes from (5) and (2) by ⊃. The order in which the steps are conducted is determined by the number of occurrences of proposition letters in the *scope* of each logical connective. The *scope* of a connective consists in the parts of the form to which it applies and is usually indicated by brackets: thus in our example, the scope of ¬ is P; the scope of v is ¬P and Q; the scope of & is P and (¬P v Q); and the scope of ⊃ is (P & (¬P v Q)) and the last Q. The order in which steps are taken in constructing a truth-table is as follows: deal first with the connective(s) with smallest scope and so on up to the connective whose scope is the whole formula – called the *main* connective.

The full truth-table, in our example, may be set out like this (with the steps numbered as before):

	(P	&	(¬	P	v	Q))	⊃	Q
(i)	T	T	F	T	T	T	T	T
(ii)	T	F	F	T	F	F	T	F
(iii)	F	F	T	F	T	T	T	T
(iv)	F	F	T	F	T	F	T	F
	(1)	(5)	(3)	(1)	(4)	(2)	(6)	(2)

Notice that under the main connective, ⊃, *all* lines have the value T (True). This means that there is no possible assignment of propositions/truth-values to P and Q which will make the whole form false. This shows, of course, that *there is no argument* with premisses P and (¬ P v Q) and conclusion Q *which has true premisses and a false conclusion.* Hence it is a *valid* logical form. A propositional logical form which only has Ts under the main connective is called a *tautology*; one which has only Fs under the main connective is called a *contradiction*, and one which has both Ts and Fs under the main connective is called *contingent*. Only tautologies are valid propositional forms.

An example

We now show with a simple example how to apply this classical approach to evaluating an argument. Consider the following argument:

(a) If Black Ice wins then either Jim's Tavern will place or Dual Forecast will place. If Jim's Tavern places then Black Ice will not win. If Saucy Kit places then Dual Forecast will not. So, if Black Ice wins Saucy Kit will not place.

The author of this argument clearly presents all four sentences as true (he asserts them). He clearly intends the first three as his premisses and he clearly takes it that these three together imply his conclusion. Using the notation so far available the logical form of the hypothetical to which he is committed may be exhibited thus:

F(a)   [(B ⊃ (J v D)) & ((J ⊃ ¬ B) & (S ⊃ ¬ D))] ⊃ (B ⊃ ¬ S).

We test the validity of the argument (a) (with its asserted premisses and conclusion) by drawing out the truth-table for the form F(a) of its associated hypothetical. Since there are four proposition letters this truth-table will have sixteen lines ($= 2^4$) lines!

A shorter method is to assume the premisses are true and the conclusion false and then apply the truth-tables to see if this is possible. The numbered steps show how the process forces us into a contradiction

B	⊃	(J	v	D)	J	⊃	¬	B	S	⊃	¬	D	B	⊃	¬	S
T	T	F	T	F	F	T	F	T	T	T	T	F	T	F	F	T
4	1	11	6	12	8	1	7	4	5	1	9	10	2	1	2	3

(the combination 11, 6 and 12 is impossible) which shows that it is impossible for the premisses to be true and the conclusion false.

Logicians have developed other methods which will test the validity of propositional forms and which are equivalent to the two we have just described. One of these is the method of semantic tableaux (or truth-trees) and we explain it briefly now. We do this here because the method expounded in this book was developed with the method of semantic tableaux as a partial model. In the light of our remarks about truth-tables it is quite easy to understand the method of semantic tableaux and it may help the reader to understand our later approach if it is construed as a generalisation of the method.

The method of semantic tableaux

The process of writing out a full truth-table will always decide whether a propositional argument form is valid but it can be a long and cumbersome procedure. Our short truth-table method starts by assuming that the premisses are true and the conclusion false; it then applies the truth-tables to determine the truth-values the constituent propositions *must* have if the assumption is correct. This process leads *either* to an assignment of truth-values which shows that the premisses can be true whilst the conclusion is false *or* to one which shows this is impossible.

The method of semantic tableaux proceeds on the same initial assumption as the short truth-table method and leads to the same alternatives. However, this time one proceeds by means of explicit rules (which are derived from the truth-tables in the classical tradition) and one represents the process as a truth-tree or semantic tableau. The classical rules are as follows:

Name	Rule	How the rule is read
T ¬	T ¬ P F P	If ¬ P is true then P is false
F ¬	F ¬ P T P	if ¬ P is false then P is true
T &	T P & Q T P T Q	if P & Q is true P is true and Q is true
F &	F P & Q F P | F Q	if P & Q is false either P is false or Q is false
T v	T P v Q T P | T Q	if P v Q is true, either P is true or Q is true

181

Appendix

Name	Rule	How the rule is read
F ∨	F P ∨ Q	if P ∨ Q is false P is false and Q is false
	F P	
	F Q	
T ⊃	T P ⊃ Q	if P ⊃ Q is true either P is false or Q is true
	F P | T Q	
F ⊃	F P ⊃ Q	if P ⊃ Q is false P is true and Q is false
	T P	
	F Q	

These rules contain exactly the same 'information' as the truth-tables. To test the validity of a propositional argument form one applies these rules successively to see if the conditions which *must* be satisfied to make the premisses true and the conclusion false *can* be satisfied. We illustrate the process by constructing the semantic tableau for our previous example (p. 180):

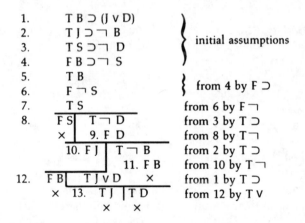

```
1.      T B ⊃ (J ∨ D)      ⎫
2.      T J ⊃ ¬ B          ⎪  initial assumptions
3.      T S ⊃ ¬ D          ⎬
4.      F B ⊃ ¬ S          ⎭
5.      T B                ⎫  from 4 by F ⊃
6.      F ¬ S              ⎭
7.          T S                   from 6 by F ¬
8.      F S│  T ¬ D               from 3 by T ⊃
        × │  9. F D               from 8 by T ¬
          10. F J │  T ¬ B        from 2 by T ⊃
                    11. F B       from 10 by T ¬
12.  F B│  T J ∨ D    ×           from 1 by T ⊃
     ×  13.  T J │ T D            from 12 by T ∨
            ×     ×
```

The tableau is constructed and read as follows: lines (1) to (4) state the assumption that the premisses are true and the conclusion false. The rest of the tableau draws out what must be the case if the initial assumption is correct. Hence lines (5) and (6) must hold if (4) does; if B ⊃ ¬ S is false B must be true and ¬ S must be false. If ¬ S is false, S is true, hence line (7). At line (8) there are two alternatives; if S ⊃ ¬ D is true (line (3)) either S is false or ¬ D is true. However, S cannot be false because in drawing out what conditions must be satisfied if our initial assumption is to be correct we have already discovered at line (7) that S must be true. The × below F S in line (8) shows that that alternative is closed; however, there is still the possibility that ¬ D is true so we continue our search along this 'branch' of the tableau (or truth-tree). Line (9) is obvious. At line (10) again there is a choice; if J ⊃ ¬ B is true then either J is false or ¬ B is true. Again line (11) is obvious, but B cannot be false since we have already found that if our initial assumption is correct B is true (line (5)); hence this alternative is impossible and the fact is marked with an × below F B. The branch which leads to F J is not yet closed so we continue our search here. Again at line (12) we have two alternatives. Again FB is impossible by line (5) so that leaves only T J v D. If J v D is to be true then either J must be true or D must. But neither is possible, by lines (10) and (9) respectively. Hence it is impossible to find an assignment of truth-values which makes the premisses true and the conclusion false so the argument form is valid.

We note in conclusion that the rules for constructing a semantic tableau may also be read 'upwards' as well as 'downwards'; for example

$$T \supset \quad \frac{T \quad P \quad \supset \quad Q}{F \quad P \quad | \quad T Q}$$

may be read not only as 'if P ⊃ Q is true then either P is true or Q is false' but also as 'if either P is true or Q is false then P ⊃ Q is true'. If what is above the line is true what is below the line is true too *and conversely*. In other words the rule states *necessary* and *sufficient conditions* for P ⊃ Q to be true. (The Assertibility Question, AQ, in Chapter 2 partly generalises this idea.)

Some valid propositional forms

Some arguments are valid in virtue of their propositional form so we now list some of the commonest and most important valid propositional forms for ease of reference later. The reader may easily check them by the foregoing methods.

(i) P implies Q and P is true,
    therefore Q is true   (*Modus ponens*)

(ii) P implies Q and Q is false,
    therefore P is false   (*Modus tollens*)

(iii) P implies Q and Q implies R,
    therefore P implies R   (*Transitivity of implication*)

(iv) P implies Q and P implies not Q,
    therefore P is false   (*Reductio ad absurdum*)

(v) Either P or Q and Q is false,
    therefore P is true

Concluding remarks on propositional logic

Let us summarise the position we have reached.

An argument gives *reasons* for a conclusion. Logic studies whether the reasons *entail* or *imply* the conclusion or, equivalently, whether the conclusion *follows from* the reasons given. On the classical view which we have been expounding, whether a conclusion does follow from its reasons is determined by the argument's logical form. The conclusion follows from the reasons *if and only if the argument exhibits a valid logical form, i.e. if and only if there is no argument of that form which has true premisses and a false conclusion*. Thus, to evaluate our argument one must first display its logical form in a suitable notation and one must then test that logical form by some appropriate means.

In our example on p. 180 above there was no difficulty about translating the argument into symbolic notation (because it is a logician's example – made up for the purpose) and the three methods given yield a decision on the validity of the form quite mechanically.

But if we look now at another (logician's) example we shall see that we have a long way to go yet. Consider the following argument:

> No councillor is eligible because every councillor is a rate-payer and
> no rate-payer is eligible.

The conclusion of the argument is obviously 'no councillor is eligible' (call it R) and the premiss is the conjunction after 'because' (call it (P & Q)). If we take this to be the logical form of the argument, '(P & Q) therefore R' it is easy to see that there are arguments of that form with true premisses and a false conclusion so it is not a valid logical form. However, it is equally clear to anyone who understands English that the argument is a good one and that if the premiss (P & Q) is true the conclusion R must be true too.

To deal with an example like this we shall need to go more deeply into its logical structure and to do this we shall need to extract and exhibit the logical form of the propositions P, Q and R. This takes us into what is generally known as *predicate* or *quantificational* logic.

Introducing predicate logic

If we look again at our example and remember our introductory remarks about the 'form' and 'content' of arguments (p. 174) it will be clear that this argument is *about* councillors, rate-payers and eligibility; replacing these terms by the schematic letters (see p. 174), A for 'councillor', B for 'ratepayer' and C for 'eligible' leaves us with words which may *occur in reasoning about any subject whatever*:

> *No* A *is* C *because every* A *is* B *and no* B *is* C.

To deal with an example like this classical logic looks not at the way propositions may be built up from other propositions, but at the way propositions may be built up from *names, quantifiers* and *predicates* – where these are *logical* notions (just as *proposition* was).

Names, quantifiers and predicates

What counts as a *name* in traditional logic is very like what the grammarian counts as a proper name, e.g. Plato, Athens, Greece, etc., but there are restrictions. In short, for something to be a logical name it must refer to *one* thing only in the world (*one* person, place, time, number or whatever it might be) and there *must be* some object to which it refers. The second restriction means that proper names of fictitious characters or places do not count as logical names and the first means that an ordinary proper name which applies to many people, like 'John Smith', is not a logical name; it functions as a logical name if and only if context or some other device shows that it picks out one and only one individual on a given occasion of its use. In short a name, in classical logic, is a term which refers to exactly one object in the world.

A quantifier is a word of *quantity*: it tells us *how many* objects of some kind we are talking about – *all* of them, *none* of them, *some* of them, *most* of them, *exactly two* of them, *at least five* of them, etc. In these brief remarks we shall deal with only some of these quantifiers, namely 'all', 'every', 'some', 'no' and 'none'.

To explain briefly what a *predicate* is consider the following simple sentences:

(1) Plato was a philosopher

(2) Athens is a city

(3) Greece exports oil

If we remove the names, Plato, Athens and Greece, we are left with what logicians call 'open sentences' or *predicate expressions,*

. . . was a philosopher

. . . is a city

. . . exports oil

These three predicate expressions each have one 'gap' left by the removed name. It is easy to think of predicate expressions which would have two, three or more 'gaps' if names were removed from simple propositions involving them, e.g.

. . . is taller than . . .

. . . is between . . . and . . .

Predicate expressions are phrases like these examples, which have at least one 'gap' such that if one inserts names of individuals into the gaps, the resulting sentence expresses a proposition – which is true or false.

185

Predicate logic compared with propositional logic

Just as we needed a formal symbolism for propositions and propositional connectives, so we do for names, predicates and quantifiers. There are numerous logic texts which introduce a suitable notation for these categories and which show how to express predicate logic forms. We shall not present such a notation because it is relatively complicated and we do not need it. We simply note that in most respects displaying and evaluating predicate logic forms is very like doing so for propositional forms – but more complicated. For example we can generalise the method of truth-tables or the method of semantic tableaux to decide whether many predicate logic forms are valid. The two major respects in which predicate logic differs from propositional logic are (1) we cannot always decide by a mechanical routine like truth-tables whether a predicate logic form is valid (this is Church's Theorem) and (2) the forms identified at the predicate level of analysis can look much less like the original sentence than happens with propositional logic, for example the form of 'No councillor is eligible' is the same as 'It is not the case that there exists something which is a councillor and is eligible', and the form of 'Every councillor is a rate-payer' is the same as 'Everything is such that if it is a councillor then it is a rate-payer'.

These two points mean that it can be quite difficult to paraphrase an argument into the notation of predicate logic and that even when this has been successfully completed there may be no mechanical routine for deciding its validity. However, predicate logic enables us to deal with a huge range of arguments whose validity depends on their predicate logic form. In particular it works extremely well for much of mathematics and physical science. Having said this there are two concluding points to make about the depth of analysis we have sketched so far.

Concluding remarks on logical form

Firstly, predicate logic still analyses logical form at a relatively superficial level. Consider the following three examples.

(1) Since Mary is taller than Tom and Tom is taller than Jill, Mary is taller than Jill.

(2) Since it is *true* that men have walked on the Moon, it *must* be *possible*.

(3) George IV wished to know if Scott was the author of *Waverley* and since Scott was the author of *Waverley*, George IV wished to know if Scott was Scott.

On the classical view these arguments are valid if and only if they exhibit a valid logical form. To show that (1) is valid then we shall have to go into the logical form of the relation '. . . is taller than . . .' since that is the idea on which its validity hinges. To show that (2) is valid we shall have to go into the logical form of statements of 'necessity' and of 'possibility' – into modal logic as it is called. To deal with (3) and similar examples we shall need to explore the logic of 'intensional' verbs like 'wish' and 'know'. So the classical tradition has to go much deeper into the notion of logical form if its general approach is to be carried through with even quite simple examples. Classical logic has gone much further in many of these directions but there is still much to be done.

The last point is more of a challenge. Those who believe that the best way to evaluate an argument is via its logical form should show how such an approach works, not on the usual, logicians', made-up examples, but on *real* arguments of the kind exemplified in this book.

Exercises

The following passages are provided so that the reader can try out the approach of this book to see if it is helpful. The exercise in each case is the same: it is to extract the argument and to evaluate it using the methods and principles explained in the preceding pages. The author's experience is that students have difficulty in being clear-headed about these and similar (theoretical and argumentative), passages, but that the methods expounded earlier are a genuine help. The teacher will no doubt wish to supply further exercises which are particularly suited to his or her students: the following examples are provided only as a starting point.

1

An argument is considered in Chapter 1 which relates to this exercise (see p. 13). The Campaign for Nuclear Disarmament (CND) campaigns for unilateral nuclear disarmament for Britain. It does so on various grounds and the 'nuclear winter' evidence has been used widely by CND in *support* of its campaign. However, the following appeared in the *Eastern Daily Press* newspaper in October 1984. A similar position was taken by some prominent politicians.

> The 'nuclear winter' conclusions undermine the unilateral nuclear disarmament case in Britain. If the scientists are right the population of this country would be virtually eliminated in a nuclear war between the super powers *even if no nuclear weapons were situated on our territory*. We might escape a direct nuclear attack, but in addition to the radioactive fall-out we would also suffer the darkness, the sub-freezing temperatures and the starvation of a nuclear winter.

2

Newspaper letter columns are a good source for concise pieces of argument which deserve careful thought and analysis. A few days after publishing Caspar Weinberger's letter (see Chapter 4) the *Guardian* newspaper carried several letters from readers responding to his case. Here is one of them,

Sir, – Caspar Weinberger has recently been attempting to defend US policy on nuclear warfare against a growing chorus of critics. But as has become typical of the Reagan White House, the Secretary of Defence stands condemned by his own words.

He claims that the US Administration does not endorse the concept of protracted nuclear war or nuclear warfighting: when his words are read carefully, they undermine his claim.

Mr. Weinberger's letter to the editors of newspapers in NATO countries states: 'Whatever they (the Soviets) claim their intentions to be, the fact remains that they are designing their weapons in such a way and in sufficient numbers to indicate to us that they think they could begin, and win, a nuclear war.'

This is not US policy, he claims. Yet in the next paragraph he writes: 'We must make the steps necessary to match the Soviet Union's greatly improved nuclear capability.'

In short, Mr. Weinberger is saying that the US Administration is seeking to match a capability which it believes – rightly or wrongly – is designed for nuclear 'warfighting'. So much for the attempted defence of Administration policy.

But on one matter Mr. Weinberger is surely correct, and that is in his claims that the aim of the new proposal is to strengthen deterrence. What the US Administration is doing is converging with the long-criticised Soviet nuclear doctrine of deterrence based on the threat of serious 'warfighting' (compared with 'mutual assured destruction').

The question is: Are we worse off as a result? The answer is almost certainly yes. A 'warfighting' doctrine, even more than deterrence, leaves no satisfactory answer to the question: 'How much is enough?' More than ever, the arms race will be openended. The capabilities which will be collected will erode the nuclear/conventional distinction, as will the attitudes of mind which will inform the new doctrine.

In sum, the old taboo against nuclear war will lose its force. In addition, Soviet defence planners will inevitably be provoked: any 'moderates' in their policy process will be undercut.

The irony of all this is that current US nuclear strategy is not the result of 'crazy' theorists. It is the logical outcome for those nuclear strategists who rejected deterrence based on mutual civilian destruction. The rejection of MAD, leads by impeccable strategic logic to what Colin Gray, a US State Department adviser calls 'A theory of victory'. Strategic logic is gained at the price of political wisdom.

In a different context Samuel Butler once wrote: 'Logic is like the sword – those who appeal to it shall perish by it.' His words have a chilling ring with this fresh twist in the evolution of nuclear strategy.

Ken Booth.

Department of International Politics,
The University College of Wales,
Aberystwyth, Dyfed, Wales

3

The following extract is taken from an article entitled 'How to Think Sceptically About the Bomb'. It was written by Bernard Williams, former Professor of Philosophy, King's College, Cambridge, and it was published in *New Society*. The whole article deserves careful attention, but the following extract can be considered alone:

Is deterrence 'immoral'?

Some moral authorities, including – remarkably – the Bishop of London, think that there are situations in which it would be legitimate actually to use nuclear weapons. Perhaps there might be some, though I doubt that they include situations we are likely to be faced with. However, I am concerned with the other part of the nuclear argument, the morality of deterrence. Western defence policy, and our possession of nuclear weapons, is supposed to be justified in terms of deterrence. But if one couldn't be justified in *using* such a weapon, can one be justified in *possessing* it as a deterrent, and in basing one's policies on threatening to do what one wouldn't be justified in doing? There is an argument which some people think shows that one couldn't be morally justified in such a policy.

It probably influenced the Church of England group which recently said that deterrence is immoral. This is supposed to be an absolutely general argument of principle about the morality of intentions.

Suppose someone is justified in intending to do a certain thing if certain circumstances arise. For instance, he's justified in carrying a gun, and intending to use it if he's attacked by bandits. Now if that is so, then – the argument says – it must follow that if he were to be attacked, he would then be justified in using the gun. So with nuclear deterrence.

The principle of deterrence is based on having a certain kind of intention: that if we were attacked, we would then retaliate with nuclear weapons. That is the intention we in the west announce to the world in declaring this policy.

But now the same argument about intentions is supposed to apply. If we are justified in intending to let off nuclear weapons if attacked, then (the argument goes) it must be that if we were attacked, we would then be justified in actually letting off nuclear weapons. But if no one is ever justified in letting off nuclear weapons, then this can't be so. The strategy based on such threats must itself be immoral. That is the simple moral argument.

I agree with it to this extent – that if deterrence is to be credible, then there has to be a genuine intention behind it. The strategy involves there being people who do intend actually to let off nuclear weapons if the conditions of the threat were met.

I accept the factual basis of the simple moral argument. But I do not think that things can be as simple as this argument makes out. It implies, after all, that there is no moral difference between running a deterrent strategy on the one hand, and intentionally – indeed, wantonly – starting a nuclear war on the other, so that the first is as totally evil as the second. Moreover, we are supposed to be able to see this absolutely in the abstract, without any reference to what we are trying to deter, or other facts about the world in which we are doing all this.

I simply cannot believe that; I think that, on reflection, one can see that, purely in the abstract, the argument does not follow. What about probability, for instance? If it were *certain* that threatening some dreadful thing would prevent some great crime or suffering, would that really leave the threat as morally no better than the dreadful deed which I wouldn't need to perform? I am not suggesting that such certainty exists in the case of nuclear deterrence. The point is simply whether the argument works in the abstract.

In fact, the people who use the argument often do not seem to think that it does work purely in the abstract. Rather, they start to bring in various considerations about Russian intentions, about American crimes, about how tolerable conditions under communism are, and so on – which does show that other considerations make a difference. And if other considerations do make a difference, then the very short argument about the morality of deterrence can't be as good as it looks. That argument either settles the question very quickly, or it does not settle it at all. I think it doesn't settle it.

4

The following passage comes from St Augustine's *Confessions*. It is discussed in R. J. Fogelin's *Understanding Arguments*.

I turned my attention to the case of twins, who are generally born within a short time of each other. Whatever significance in the natural order the astrologers may attribute to this interval of time, it is too short to be appreciated by human observation and no allowance can be made for it in the charts which an astrologer has to consult in order to cast a true horoscope. His predictions, then, will not be true, because he would have consulted the same charts for both Esau and Jacob and would have made the same predictions for each of them, whereas it is a fact that the same things did not happen to them both. Therefore, either he would have been wrong in his predictions or, if his forecast was correct, he would not have predicted the same future for each. And yet he would have consulted the same chart in each case. This proves that if he had foretold the truth, it would have been by luck, not by skill.

5

The following passage is cited in M. C. Beardsley's *Practical Logic*. The evidence summarised in it is taken from *The Last Days of Hitler* by Hugh Trevor-Roper. The problem with this passage is not so much to extract the argument as to evaluate it.

The Death of Hitler

Whatever myths may grow or be built upon the extraordinary circumstances of Adolf Hitler's last days, there can be no reasonable doubt that he died in his bunker, more than fifty feet below the old Chancellery in Berlin, about half past three in the afternoon of April 30, 1945, while Russian shells were falling on the city.

First, there are numerous witnesses to the conference of April 22, which Hitler held in the bunker after his orders for an all-out counter-attack by the troops in Berlin (the so-called 'Steiner attack') had come to nothing. Those who were present agreed, at least, on this: that Hitler denounced everyone as traitors and deserters; that he said his mission was at an end; and that he resolved to stay and die in the bunker when the Russian troops overcame Berlin.

By Hitler's orders, this decision was announced to the people of Berlin on the next day. As long as telephone connections with the bunker remained open, during the succeeding days, many followers and officials begged him to reconsider his decision and fly south, to continue the fight among the Bavarian Alps. To each of them, so far as is known, he gave the same answer; and, indeed, there is no record of Hitler's ever having changed his mind, once it was made up.

During the final week, there were various people with Hitler in the bunker, including Goebbels, who had come at Hitler's invitation, with his wife and six children. Several others, living in nearby bunkers, were constantly in and out of Hitler's bunker.

Early in the morning of April 29, Hitler married Eva Braun, and wrote his final testaments, both political and personal. Three copies of these were smuggled out of the bunker, and later found; in them he announced his marriage; declared that his wife would die with him in the bunker, as she had wished; and added that their bodies would be burnt immediately after their deaths, to prevent their falling into the hands of the Russians.

That afternoon, Hitler had his favourite Alsatian dog destroyed, and in the evening he said good-bye to all but those closest to him. The next morning 180 litres of gasoline were procured. Shortly after three in the afternoon, Hitler and Eva Braun bade farewell to those in the bunker and went into their suite. A single shot was heard by those outside the suite, and when they entered, Hitler was lying dead on the sofa, which was soaked with blood. He had shot himself through the mouth, and Eva Braun had taken poison.

The most important witnesses of the final events, who left the bunker on May 1 and managed to be captured without being killed, agree on certain facts. Artur Axman, Hitler Youth leader, testifies that he saw the two bodies lying in Hitler's suite. Kenipka, Hitler's chauffeur, testifies that he saw the two bodies (Hitler's was wrapped in a blanket, but it was identifiable by the black trousers) being placed in the garden and set afire. Another guard, Karnau, testifies that he recognized the two bodies and saw them burst into flames. Mansfield later saw a rectangular hole evidently dug for burying the corpses. Their bones have never been found, but were perhaps broken up and mingled with other bodies (of German soldiers) that the Russians later dug up in the Chancellery garden.

Those who were not eyewitnesses of these events, but were present in the bunker and later escaped, were convinced of Hitler's death by the fact that everyone began to smoke in the late afternoon. This had never been permitted by Hitler.

6

The following extract comes from an article under the title 'Riddles of Public Choice' published in *The Times Higher Education Supplement*. The authors are Martin Hollis, Robert Sugden and Albert Weale, and the rest of their article considers possible solutions. (Their problem is obviously related to the J. S. Mill argument considered in Chapter 5.)

Riddles of public choice

Take a party so crowded that the noise is unbearable. Each of us wants to hear and be heard. So each of us talks a little louder than those around. But those around have the same desire and talk a little louder still. We all end up hoarse and uncomprehending.

A similar tale goes for other cases. Self-interest bids each of us leave our litter on the beach, rather than trouble to carry it home. The sum of our choices is a mess none of us wants. We each come to the seminar having left the preparatory work to others, and the seminar fails. We each see the advantages of thrift, and collectively so depress the economy that we are all the losers.

So enlightened self-interest says 'Spend', 'Talk normally', 'Prepare', 'Take your litter home'? No, crucially, that is not the rational alternative for any one of us. Talk normally and you will not be heard. Your litter makes no real difference to your enjoyment of the beach. You benefit only if others change their ways; and, if they do, you do better still by not changing yours. To be more precise and formal about it, even enlightened self-interest is self-defeating, when your order of preference for the outcomes is this:

1 You do X, others do Y.
2 You do Y, others do Y.
3 You do X, others do X.
4 You do Y, others do X.

Whatever X and Y may be (talking louder v softer; not preparing v preparing), self-interest demands X. For, if others will do Y, you should choose X, since you would rather have your first choice; and if others will do X, you should again choose X, to avoid your fourth choice. So it makes no difference to you what others will do: X is the dominant choice. If we all reason like this, we all get our third choice, although we would all prefer our second.

This classic 'problem of collective action' turns up in several disciplines. It is particularly familiar to economists as the 'problem of public goods'. Public goods are goods that, if supplied to one member of a group, are necessarily supplied to all. Take street lighting: you cannot have the benefit of lighting on the streets around your home unless your neighbours do so too. Or take the control of infectious diseases, or the preservation of open countryside.

Once a public good is supplied, anyone can enjoy it whether he pays anything towards the costs or not; so why would anyone pay? This is a collective action problem where X stands for 'not paying' and Y for 'paying'. For any individual it is always better not to pay. The result – that the public good is not supplied at all – may be one that nobody wants.

7

The passage below comes from C. S. Lewis's *Miracles*. As usual the reader should attempt to extract and evaluate the argument. In Chapter 2, Lewis explains what he means by a 'Naturalist': 'Some people believe that nothing exists except Nature: I call these people *Naturalists*. Others think that, besides Nature, there exists something else: I call them *Supernaturalists*.' By the 'Total System' Lewis appears to mean the whole natural order.

> We may in fact state it as a rule that *no thought is valid if it can be fully explained as the result of irrational causes*. Every reader of this book applies this rule automatically all day long. When a sober man tells you that the house is full of rats or snakes, you attend to him: if you know that his belief in the rats and snakes is due to *delirium tremens* you do not even bother to look for them. If you even *suspect* an irrational cause, you begin to pay less attention to a man's beliefs; your friend's pessimistic view of the European situation alarms you less when you discover that he is suffering from a bad liver attack. Conversely, when we discover a belief to be false we then first look about for irrational causes ('I was tired' – 'I was in a hurry' – 'I wanted to believe it') . . . All thoughts which are so caused are valueless. We never, in our ordinary thinking, admit any exceptions to this rule.
>
> Now it would clearly be preposterous to apply this rule to each particular thought as we come to it and yet not to apply it to all thoughts taken collectively, that is, to human reason as a whole. Each particular thought is valueless if it is the result of irrational causes. Obviously, then, the whole process of human thought, what

we call Reason, is equally valueless if it is the result of irrational causes. Hence every theory of the universe which makes the human mind a result of irrational causes is inadmissible, for it would be a proof that there are no such things as proofs. Which is nonsense.

But Naturalism, as commonly held, is precisely a theory of this sort. The mind, like every other particular thing or event, is supposed to be simply the product of the Total System. It is supposed to be that and nothing more, to have no power whatever of 'going on its own accord'. And the Total System is not supposed to be rational. All thoughts whatever are therefore the results of irrational causes, and nothing more than that.

8

Galileo's *Dialogues Concerning Two New Sciences* is full of neat arguments which provide excellent and instructive exercises for our purposes. Here is a short extract from *First Day*.

> Aristotle declares that bodies of different weights, in the same medium, travel (in so far as their motion depends upon gravity) with speeds which are proportional to their weights, [assuming that they have the same shape]; . . . [but] if it were true that, in media of different densities and different resistances, such as water and air one and the same body moved in air more rapidly than in water, in proportion as the density of water is greater than that of air, then it would follow that any body which falls through air ought also to fall through water. But this conclusion is false

Is Aristotle's thesis refuted by this argument? (The reader will find that the original context draws out many lessons from this argument.)

9

In Chapter 8 we considered a remarkable argument taken from Galileo's *Dialogues Concerning Two New Sciences*: if one assumes that the lighter a body is the faster it falls one gets a similar contradiction, so it follows that bodies of different mass must fall with the *same* acceleration. Here is another argument, this time from *Third Day*, which shows – if it is successful – that the velocity of a falling body *cannot be proportional to the distance fallen*.

If the velocities are in proportion to the space traversed, or to be traversed, then these spaces are traversed in equal intervals of time; if, therefore, the velocity with which the falling body traverses a space of eight feet were double that with which it covered the first four feet (just as the one distance is double the other) then the time-interval required for these passages would be equal. But for one and the same body to fall eight feet and four feet at the same time is possible only in the case of instantaneous motion; but observation shows us that the motion of a falling body occupies time, and less of it in covering a distance of four than of eight feet; therefore it is not true that its velocity increases in proportion to the space.

Another version of this argument is as follows:

Suppose the velocity of a body falling under gravity is proportional to the distance it has fallen. Suppose also that after falling 16 metres it is travelling at 32 metres/second (though the exact figures do not matter). In that case it must have fallen the last *eight* metres in more than $1/4$ second (because the average velocity over that eight metres was slower than 32 metres/second). By a similar argument it must have fallen the previous *four* metres in more than $1/4$ second. By a similar argument it must have fallen the previous *two* metres in more than $1/4$ second. Similarly with the previous *one* metre, the previous *half-metre* . . . and so on for ever. So the body could never *start* falling, which is absurd. So it is *impossible* for bodies to fall under gravity with a velocity proportional to the distance fallen.

Both arguments are elegant, puzzling and hard to fault. Even if you cannot fault either argument you may feel that there *must* be something wrong with them because they both pretend to *prove* something which we could only know by actually *observing* what happens in the world. Surely we can't know how bodies *actually* fall or *cannot* fall just by thinking about it – surely we have to go and look? Surely from the observed fact that motion/falling *takes time* it doesn't follow that the velocity of a falling body cannot be proportional to the distance fallen? On the face of it there seems no reason why a car starting from rest should not pull away and increase its speed in proportion to the distance travelled. The graph of its motion would be a straight line graph like this,

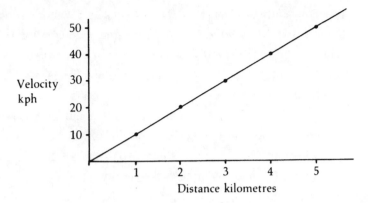

As usual the exercise is to be clear what the arguments are, and whether they prove their conclusions. It will be interesting to compare them with the Galileo argument in Chapter 8.

10

The reader who has already studied the Galileo argument, presented in Chapter 8, might find it instructive to consider the argument in its original context. It was presented originally, in his *Dialogues Concerning Two New Sciences* as follows:

> SALVATIO. I greatly doubt that Aristotle ever tested by experiment whether it be true that two stones, one weighing ten times as much as the other, if allowed to fall, at the same instant, from a height of, say, 100 cubits, would so differ in speed that when the heavier had reached the ground, the other would not have fallen more than 10 cubits.

> SIMPLICIO. His language would seem to indicate that he had tried the experiment because he says: 'We see the heavier'; now the word 'see' shows that he had made the experiment.

> SAGREDO. But I, Simplicio, who have made the test can assure you that a cannon ball weighing one or two hundred pounds, or even more, will not reach the ground by as much as a span ahead of a musket ball weighing only half a pound, provided both are dropped from a height of 200 cubits.

> SALV. But, even without further experiment, it is possible to prove clearly, by means of a short and conclusive argument, that a heavier body does not move more rapidly than a lighter one provided both

199

Exercises

bodies are of the same material and in short such as those mentioned by Aristotle. But tell me, Simplicio, whether you admit that each falling body acquires a definite speed fixed by nature, a velocity which cannot be increased or diminished except by the use of force (*violenza*) or resistance.

SIMP. There can be no doubt but that one and the same body moving in a single medium has a fixed velocity which is determined by nature and which cannot be increased except by the addition of momentum (*impeto*) or diminished except by some resistance which retards it.

SALV. If then we take two bodies whose natural speeds are different, it is clear that on uniting the two, the more rapid one will be partly retarded by the slower, and the slower will be somewhat hastened by the swifter. Do you not agree with me in this opinion?

SIMP. You are unquestionably right.

SALV. But if this is true, and if a large stone moves with a speed of, say, eight while a smaller moves with a speed of four, then when they are united, the system will move with a speed less than eight; but the two stones when tied together make a stone larger than that which before moved with a speed of eight. Hence the heavier body moves with less speed than the lighter; an effect which is contrary to your supposition. Thus you see how, from your assumption that the heavier body moves more rapidly than the lighter one, I infer that the heavier body moves more slowly.

SIMP. I am all at sea because it appears to me that the smaller stone when added to the larger increases its weight and by adding weight I do not see how it can fail to increase its speed or, at least, not to diminish it.

SALV. Here again you are in error, Simplicio, because it is not true that the smaller stone adds weight to the larger.

SIMP. This is, indeed, quite beyond my comprehension.

SALV. It will not be beyond you when I have once shown you the mistake under which you are laboring. Note that it is necessary to distinguish between heavy bodies in motion and the same bodies at rest. A large stone placed in a balance not only acquires additional weight by having another stone placed upon it, but even by the addition of a handful of hemp its weight is augmented six to ten ounces according to the quantity of hemp. But if you tie the hemp to the stone and allow them to fall freely from some height, do you believe that the hemp will press down upon the stone and thus accelerate its motion or do you think the motion will be retarded by a partial upward pressure? One always feels the pressure upon his shoulders when he prevents the motion of a load resting upon him; but if one descends just as rapidly as the load would fall how can it gravitate or press upon him? Do you not see that this would be the same as trying to strike a man with a lance when he is running away from you with a speed which is equal to, or even greater, than that with which you are following him? You must therefore conclude that, during free and natural fall, the small stone does not press upon the larger and consequently does not increase its weight as it does when at rest.

SIMP. But what if we should place the larger stone upon the smaller?

SALV. Its weight would be increased if the larger stone moved more rapidly; but we have already concluded that when the small stone moves more slowly it retards to some extent the speed of the larger, so that the combination of the two, which is a heavier body than the larger of the two stones, would move less rapidly, a conclusion which is contrary to your hypothesis. We infer therefore that large and small bodies move with the same speed provided they are of the same specific gravity.

SIMP. Your discussion is really admirable; yet I do not find it easy to believe that a bird-shot falls as swiftly as a cannon ball.

SALV. Why not say a grain of sand as rapidly as a grindstone? But, Simplicio, I trust you will not follow the example of many others who divert the discussion from its main intent and fasten upon some statement of mine which lacks a hair's-breadth of the truth and, under this hair, hide the fault of another which is as big as a ship's cable. Aristotle says that 'an iron ball of one hundred pounds falling from a height of one hundred cubits reaches the ground before a one-pound ball has fallen a single cubit'. I say that they arrive at the same time. You find, on making the experiment, that the larger outstrips the smaller by two finger-breadths, that is, when the larger has reached the ground, the other is short of it by two finger-breadths; now you would not hide behind these two fingers the ninety-nine cubits of Aristotle, nor would you mention my small error and at the same time pass over in silence his very large one. Aristotle declares that bodies of different weights, in the same medium, travel (in so far as their motion depends upon gravity) with speeds which are proportional to their weights; this he illustrates by use of bodies in which it is possible to perceive the pure and unadulterated effect of gravity, eliminating other considerations, for example, figure as being of small importance (*minimi momenti*), influences which are greatly dependent upon the medium which modifies the single effect of gravity alone. Thus we observe that gold, the densest of all substances, when beaten out into a very thin leaf, goes floating through the air; the same thing happens with stone when ground into a very fine powder. But if you wish to maintain the general proposition you will have to show that the same ratio of speeds is preserved in the case of all heavy bodies, and that a stone of twenty pounds moves ten times as rapidly as one of two; but I claim that this is false and that, if they fall from a height of fifty or a hundred cubits, they will reach the earth at the same moment.

11

The following is a very famous argument which David Hume considers in his *Dialogues Concerning Natural Religion*:

Look round the world, contemplate the whole and every part of it: you will find it to be nothing but one great machine, subdivided into an infinite number of lesser machines, which again admit of subdivisions to a degree beyond what human senses and faculties can trace and explain. All these various machines, and even their most minute parts, are adjusted to each other with an accuracy which ravishes into admiration all men who have ever contemplated them. The curious adapting of means to ends, throughout all nature, resembles exactly, though it much exceeds, the productions of human contrivance – of human design, thought, wisdom, and intelligence. Since therefore the effects resemble each other, we are led to infer, by all the rules of analogy, that the causes also resemble, and that the Author of nature is somewhat similar to the mind of man, though possessed of much larger faculties, proportioned to the grandeur of the work which he has executed. By this argument *a posteriori*, and by this argument alone, do we prove at once the existence of a Deity and his similarity to human mind and intelligence.

The reader should identify the reasons and conclusion and should attempt a critique of the reasoning. Things are known either *a priori* or *a posteriori*: what is known *a priori* is known just by thinking about it, by reflection and without observing the world around us, e.g. mathematics; what is known *a posteriori* is based upon our experience of the world, e.g. scientific knowledge.

The teacher can extend the exercise/discussion by explaining Hume's views on the relation between cause and effect, how this is known *a posteriori* and how we infer from one to the other.

12

Hume also considers a 'simple and sublime argument *a priori*' for the existence of God:

Whatever exists must have a cause or reason of its existence, it being absolutely impossible for anything to produce itself or be the cause of its own existence. In mounting up, therefore, from effects to causes, we must either go on in tracing an infinite succession, without any ultimate cause at all, or must at last have recourse to some ultimate cause that is *necessarily* existent. Now that the first supposition is absurd may be thus proved. In the infinite chain or succession of causes and effects, each single effect is determined to exist by the power and efficacy of that cause which immediately preceded; but the whole eternal chain or succession, taken together, is not determined or caused by anything, and yet it is evident that it requires a cause or reason, as much as any particular object which begins to exist in time. The question is still reasonable why this particular

succession of causes existed from eternity, and not any other succession or no succession at all. If there be no necessarily existent
being, any supposition which can be formed is equally possible; nor
is there any more absurdity in *nothing's* having existed from eternity than there is in that succession of causes which constitutes the
universe. What was it, then, which determined *something* to exist
rather than *nothing*, and bestowed being on a particular possibility, exclusive of the rest? *External causes*, there are supposed to be
none. *Chance* is a word without a meaning. Was it *nothing*? But that
can never produce anything. We must, therefore, have recourse to
a necessarily existent Being who carries the *reason* of his existence
in himself, and who cannot be supposed not to exist, without an
express contradiction. There is, consequently, such a Being – that is,
there is a Deity.

As usual the reader should display the reasoning and attempt to evaluate it. Something is *necessarily* the case if its denial is a self-contradiction
('expresses a contradiction' as Hume says), e.g. $2 + 2 = 4$. Something is *absurd*
if it is self-contradictory. The text which surrounds this extract will provide
the teacher with many suggestions for extending this exercise/discussion.

13

Here is a final example from Hume's *Dialogues Concerning Natural
Religion*:

And it is possible, Cleanthes, said Philo, that after all these reflec-
tions, and infinitely more which might be suggested, you can
still persevere in your anthropomorphism, and assert the moral
attributes of the Deity, his justice, benevolence, mercy, and recti-
tude, to be of the same nature with these virtues in human creatures?
His power, we allow, is infinite; whatever he wills is executed; but
neither man nor any other animal is happy; therefore, he does not
will their happiness. His wisdom is infinite; he is never mistaken in
choosing the means to any end; but the course of nature tends not
to human or animal felicity; therefore, it is not established for that
purpose. Through the whole compass of human knowledge there are
no inferences more certain and infallible than these. In what respect,

then, do his benevolence and mercy resemble the benevolence and mercy of men?

Epicurus' old questions are yet unanswered.

Is he willing to prevent evil, but not able? then is he impotent. Is he able, but not willing? then he is malevolent. Is he both able and willing? whence then is evil?

In this context 'anthropomorphism' means simply ascribing to God characteristics resembling those of human beings.

14

The following passage from Karl Marx's *Value, Price and Profit* is quite long. It can be given as an exercise as it stands or, alternatively, it can be used to provide the background and the context for two shorter exercises. The first short exercise is to extract and evaluate the argument in the paragraph beginning 'All his reasoning amounted to this'. This paragraph is a summary of the argument analysed in Chapter 9 and the exercise may be attempted before or after reading Chapter 9. The second, short exercise is to extract and evaluate the argument in the paragraph beginning 'You arrive, therefore, at this dilemma'. (Remember that Marx is considering the effect of a general rise in *money* wages.) The passage given here is followed in Marx's original text by further extensive argument – in particular he discusses a good deal of *empirical*, historical evidence about movements in wages, prices and profits – and this could provide the interested teacher or student with numerous further exercises and examples. Indeed *Value, Price and Profit* as a whole is full of excellent examples for those interested in political economy.

II   Production, Wages, Profits

The address Citizen Weston read to us might have been compressed into a nutshell.

All his reasoning amounted to this: If the working class forces the capitalist class to pay five shillings instead of four shillings in the shape of money wages, the capitalist will return in the shape of commodities four shillings' worth instead of five shillings' worth. The working class would have to pay five shillings for what, before the rise of wages, they bought with four shillings. But why is this the case? Why does the capitalist only return four shillings' worth for five shillings? Because the amount of wages is fixed. But why is it fixed at four shillings' worth of commodities? Why not at three, or two, or any other sum? If the limit of the amount of wages is settled by an economical law, independent alike of the will of the capitalist and the will of the working man, the first thing Citizen Weston had to do was to state that law and prove it. He ought then, moreover, to have proved that the amount of wages actually paid at every given moment always corresponds exactly to the necessary amount of wages, and never deviates from it. If, on the other hand, the given limit of the amount of wages is founded on the *mere will* of the capitalist, or the limits of his avarice, it is an arbitrary limit. There is nothing necessary in it. It may be changed by the will of the capitalist, and may, therefore, be changed *against* his will . . .

By what contrivance is the capitalist enabled to return four shillings' worth for five shillings? By raising the price of the commodity he sells. Now, does a rise and more generally a change in the prices of commodities, do the prices of commodities themselves, depend on the mere will of the capitalist? Or are, on the contrary, certain circumstances wanted to give effect to that will? If not, the ups and downs, the incessant fluctuations of market prices, become an insoluble riddle.

As we suppose that no change whatever has taken place either in the productive powers of labour, or in the amount of capital and labour employed, or in the value of the money wherein the values of products are estimated, but *only a change in the rate of wages*, how could that *rise of wages* affect the *prices of commodities*? Only by affecting the actual proportion between the demand for, and the supply of, these commodities.

It is perfectly true that, considered as a whole, the working class spends, and must spend, its income upon *necessaries*. A general rise in the rate of wages would, therefore, produce a rise in the demand for, and consequently in the *market prices of, necessaries*. The capitalists who produce these necessaries would be compensated for the risen wages by the rising market prices of their commodities. But how with the other capitalists who do *not* produce necessaries? And you must not fancy them a small body. If you consider that two-thirds of the national produce are consumed by one-fifth of the population – a member of the House of Commons stated it recently to be but one-seventh of the population – you will understand what an immense proportion of the national produce must be produced in the shape of luxuries, or be *exchanged* for luxuries, and what an immense amount of the necessaries themselves must be wasted upon flunkeys, horses, cats, and so forth, a waste we know from experience to become always much limited with the rising prices of necessaries.

Well, what would be the position of those capitalists who do not produce necessaries? For the *fall in the rate of profit*, consequent upon the general rise of wages, they could not compensate themselves by a *rise in the price of their commodities*, because the demand for those commodities would not have increased. Their income would have decreased, and from this decreased income they would have to pay more for the same amount of higher-priced necessaries. But this would not be all. As their income had diminished they would have less to spend upon luxuries, and therefore their mutual demand for their respective commodities would diminish. Consequent upon this diminished demand the prices of their commodities would fall. In these branches of industry, therefore, *the rate of profit would fall*, not only in simple proportion to the general rise in the rate of wages, but in the compound ratio of the general rise of wages, the rise in the price of necessaries, and the fall in the price of luxuries.

What would be the consequence of *this difference in the rates of profit* for capitals employed in the different branches of industry? Why, the consequence that generally obtains whenever, from whatever reason, the *average rate of profit* comes to differ in different spheres of production. Capital and labour would be transferred from the less remunerative to the more remunerative branches; and this process of transfer would go on until the supply in the one department of industry would have risen proportionately to the increased demand, and would have sunk in the other departments according to the decreased demand. This change effected, the general rate of profit would again be *equalized* in the different branches. As the whole derangement originally arose from a mere change in the proportion of the demand for, and supply of, different commodities, the cause ceasing, the effect would cease, and *prices* would return to their former level and equilibrium. Instead of being limited to some branches of industry, *the fall in the rate of profit* consequent upon the rise of wages would have become general. According to our supposition, there would have taken place no change in the productive powers of labour, nor in the aggregate amount of production, but *that given amount of production would have changed its form.* A greater part of the produce would exist in the shape of necessaries, a lesser part in the shape of luxuries, or what comes to the same, a lesser part would be exchanged for foreign luxuries, and be consumed in its original form, or, what again comes to the same, a greater part of the native produce would be exchanged for foreign necessaries instead of for luxuries. The general rise in the rate of wages would, therefore, after a temporary disturbance of market prices, only result in a general fall of the rate of profit without any permanent change in the prices of commodities.

If I am told that in the previous argument I assume the whole surplus wages to be spent upon necessaries, I answer that I have made the supposition most advantageous to the opinion of Citizen Weston. If the surplus wages were spent upon articles formerly not entering into the consumption of the working men, the real increase of their purchasing power would need no proof. Being, however, only derived from an advance of wages, that increase of their purchasing power must exactly correspond to the decrease of the purchasing power of the capitalists. The *aggregate demand* for commodities would, therefore, not *increase,* but the constituent parts of that demand would *change.* The increasing demand on the one side would be counterbalanced by the decreasing demand on the other side. Thus the aggregate demand remaining stationary, no change whatever could take place in the market price of commodities.

Marx is considering the effect of a general rise in (money) wages. He summarises his argument as follows:

You arrive, therefore, at this dilemma: Either the surplus wages are equally spent upon all articles of consumption – then the expansion of demand on the part of the working class must be compensated by the contraction of demand on the part of the capitalist class – or the surplus wages are only spent upon some articles whose market prices will temporarily rise. Then the consequent rise in the rate of profit in some, and the consequent fall in the rate of profit in other branches of industry will produce a change in the distribution of capital and labour, going on until the supply is brought up to the increased demand in the one department of industry, and brought down to the diminished demand in other departments of industry. On the one supposition there will occur no change in the prices of commodities. On the other supposition, after some fluctuations of market prices, the exchangeable values of commodities will subside to the former level. On both suppositions the general rise in the rate of wages will ultimately result in nothing else but a general fall in the rate of profit.

15

There is a famous argument, due to Wittgenstein, which attempts to prove that there can be no such thing as a private language, i.e. a language which only one person *could* know. The original argument is articulated in Wittgenstein's *Philosophical Investigations*, especially §§243–74 where it is *very* difficult to grasp his reasoning. We give below a very neat version of the argument which is to be found in James W. Cornman, Keith Lehrer and George S. Pappas, *Philosophical Problems and Argument: An Introduction*. In their text, Cornman *et al.* display the reasoning in our extract and then give a lengthy evaluation of it. A related argument to show that there cannot be reports of private mental events is similarly treated. The evaluation of both arguments is *very* difficult, but the teacher could use the Cornman text to guide advanced students in handling these arguments. It is our contention that the methods and principles explained in the text are useful even with such hard arguments. For example, the Assertibility Question, which says in short 'what would show X true or false?' helps the student to see what needs to be asked about the premiss 'If at most one person A, can know any rules for the use of "E" then no-one, including A, can distinguish the difference between obeying the rules and merely thinking that he is obeying the rules.' Clearly, what would show this claim false would be a description of a way in which A *could* make the distinction (his *memory* is an obvious candidate): a proof that this is impossible (given the hypothesis that at most A can know the rules) would show it true.

Of course, an argument like this raises many questions about exactly what is *meant* (which is typical of philosophical examples) but still our principles apply – it is just that much of the work of analysis consists in considering *alternative* possible meanings. This is shown very clearly in the text by Cornman *et al.* which is a very careful piece of philosophical analysis.

> Let us assume that 'E' is an expression of a private language of one person, A. That is, at most A can know the rules for the correct use of 'E'. But if at most one person can know such rules, then no-one, including A, can distinguish the difference between obeying the rules and merely thinking that he is obeying the rules. Furthermore, if no-one can make this distinction, then no-one can know whether he is obeying the rules. And because someone can know how to apply an expression correctly only if he can obey the rules for its correct use, it follows that there are no meaningful expressions of a private language, that is, there are no private languages.

16

The following is an elegant example of philosophical argument. The passage comes from Wesley C. Salmon's *The Foundations of Scientific Inference* and in it Salmon is explaining Hans Reichenbach's solution to Hume's 'problem of induction' (cf. p. 146). As usual the exercise is to identify what the argument is and to evaluate it, except that this example is discussed at length by Stephen Thomas in his *Practical Reasoning in Natural Language* (2nd edn) and the reader can therefore compare answers with Thomas.

> Of all the solutions and dissolutions proposed to deal with Hume's problem of induction, Hans Reichenbach's attempt to provide a pragmatic justification seems to me the most fruitful and promising. This approach accepts Hume's arguments up to the point of agreeing that it is impossible to establish, either deductively or inductively, that any inductive inferences will ever again have true conclusions. Nevertheless, Reichenbach claims, the standard method of inductive generalization can be justified. Although its *success* as a method of prediction cannot be established in advance, it can be shown to be superior to any alternative method of prediction.

The argument can be put rather simply. Nature may be sufficiently uniform in suitable respects for us to make successful inductive inferences from the observed to the unobserved. On the other
hand, for all we know, she may not. Hume has shown that we cannot prove in advance which case holds. All we can say is that nature
may or may not be uniform – if she is, induction works; if she is not,
induction fails. Even in the face of our ignorance about the uniformity of nature, we can ask what would happen if we adopted some
radically different method of inference. Consider, for instance, the
method of the crystal gazer. Since we do not know whether nature
is uniform or not, we must consider both possibilities. If nature is
uniform, the method of crystal gazing might work successfully, or
it might fail. We cannot prove a priori that it will not work. At the
same time, we cannot prove a priori that it will work, even if nature
exhibits a high degree of uniformity. Thus, in case nature is reasonably uniform, the standard inductive method *must* work while
the alternative method of crystal gazing *may or may not work*. In
this case, the superiority of the standard inductive method is evident.
Now, suppose nature lacks uniformity to such a degree that the standard inductive method is a complete failure. In this case, Reichenbach argues, the alternative method must likewise fail. Suppose it did
not fail – suppose, for instance, that the method of crystal gazing
worked consistently. This would constitute an important relevant
uniformity that could be exploited inductively. If a crystal gazer
had consistently predicted future occurrences, we could infer inductively that he has a method of prediction that will enjoy continued
success. The inductive method would, in this way, share the success
of the method of crystal gazing, and would therefore be, contrary
to hypothesis, successful. Hence, Reichenbach concludes, the standard inductive method will be successful *if any other method could
succeed*. As a result, we have everything to gain and nothing to lose
by adopting the inductive method. If any method works, induction
works. If we adopt the inductive method and it fails, we have lost
nothing, for any other method we might have adopted would likewise have failed. Reichenbach does not claim to prove that nature is

uniform, or that the standard inductive method will be successful. He does not postulate the uniformity of nature. He tries to show that the inductive method is the best method for ampliative inference, whether it turns out to be successful or not.

17

From *Darwin and the Beagle* by Alan Moorehead.

It was in the Cocos islands that Darwin resolved another matter which had been on his mind for a long time. Back on the Chilean coast he had conceived the notion that if the crust of the earth could be elevated then it could also be depressed, that in fact while the Andes had been rising the floor of the Pacific Ocean had been gradually sinking. Already in October 1835, while they were on their way from the Galapagos to Tahiti, he had made a note on coral islands: '. . . we saw several of those most curious rings of coral land, just rising above the water's edge, which have been called Lagoon Islands . . . These low hollow coral islands bear no proportion to the vast ocean out of which they abruptly rise; and it seems wonderful, that such weak invaders are not overwhelmed, by the all-powerful and never-tiring waves of that great sea, miscalled the Pacific.'

Now was the time to test Lyell's theory that coral atolls represent coral-encrusted rims of submerged volcanic craters. Darwin believed that the coral polyp, the little animal that built up the reefs in tropical waters, would throw some light on the matter. The polyp could not live at a greater depth than 120 feet, and it had always been said that it had to perch itself close to a mainland shore or around volcanic islands. *But suppose*, he had asked himself, *it was found that these reefs went down a very long way, and that all the coral below the 120-foot mark was dead – would not that be a proof that the floor of the ocean had been gradually sinking, and that the coral polyp had kept pace with this sinking by building the reefs up to the surface* [our italics]? This was a theory that he could now put to the test.

He went out with FitzRoy in a small boat to the outer reef and carefully took numerous soundings on the steep outside of Keeling atoll. They found that up to the 120-foot mark the prepared tallow of the lead came up marked with the impression of living corals, but perfectly clean; as the depth increased the impressions became fewer, until at last it was evident that the bottom consisted of a smooth sandy layer. This suggested to Darwin that coral formations were the end products of aeons of slow reciprocal processes: the uplifting of an island by submarine volcanic action, the colonising of its slopes by myriad coral polyps, and finally the gradual subsiding of the island into the sea. He worked out that there were three different varieties of coral formations: barrier reefs and fringing reefs, all part of the same evolutionary process stretching over millions of years. The growth of the coral must keep pace with the subsidence beneath it, and so form first a barrier reef and then an atoll: 'Mountains of stone accumulated by the agency of various minute and tender animals.' He reckoned that the birth of an atoll required not less than a million years. As evidence of the subsidence of these reefs he noted the coconut trees falling in on all sides of the lagoon. 'In one place the foundation posts of a shed which the inhabitants asserted had stood 7 years just above high-water mark, was now daily washed by every tide.' It was a dramatic and brilliant demonstration of his theory of the instability of the earth.

The following illustrations show the three stages of coral development by means of section drawings of the same island. They show how, as the island subsides, the fringing reef builds up into a barrier reef and then becomes an atoll as the land itself sinks below sea-level.

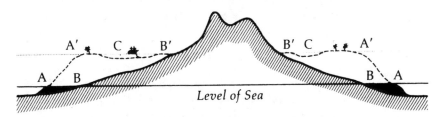

Level of Sea

AA – Outer edges of the fringing-reef, at the level of the sea.   BB – The shores of the fringed island.   A'A' – Outer edges of the reef, after its upward growth during a period of subsidence, now converted into a barrier, with islets on it.   B'B' – The shores of the now encircled island.   CC – Lagoon-channel.

N.B. In this and the following figure, the subsidence of the land could be represented only by an apparent rise in the level of the sea.

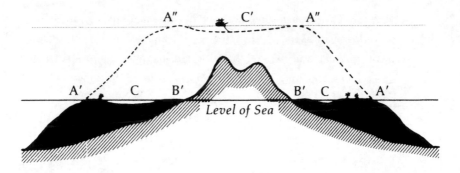

A'A' – Outer edges of the barrier-reef at the level of the sea, with islets on it. B'B' – The shores of the included island. CC – The lagoon-channel. A"A" – Outer edges of the reef, now converted into an atoll. C' – The lagoon of the new atoll.

N.B. According to the true scale, the depths of the lagoon-channel and lagoon are much exaggerated.

(Based on illustrations from Darwin's *Journal of Researches* taken from Alan Moorehead's *Darwin and the Beagle*)

18

The following passage comes from William Harvey's *An Anatomical Disquisition on the Motion of the Heart and Blood in Animals.* In this extract Harvey is discussing the function of the valves which are to be found in the veins and,

which consist of raised or loose portions of the inner membranes of these vessels, of extreme delicacy, and a sigmoid or semilunar shape.

The discoverer of these valves did not rightly understand their use, nor have succeeding anatomists added anything to our knowledge: for their office is by no means explained when we are told that it is to hinder the blood, by its weight, from all flowing into inferior parts; for the edges of the valves in the jugular veins hang downwards, and are so contrived that they prevent the blood from rising upwards; the valves, in a word, do not invariably look upwards, but always towards the trunks of the veins, invariably towards the seat of the heart . . .

Let it be added that there are no valves in the arteries [save at their roots], and that dogs, oxen, etc., have invariably valves at the divisions of their crural veins, in the veins that meet towards the top of the os sacrum, and in those branches which come from the haunches, in which no such effect of gravity from the erect position was to be apprehended.

... the valves are solely made and instituted lest the blood should pass from the greater to the lesser veins ... the delicate valves, while they readily open in the right direction, entirely prevent all such contrary motion ...

And this I have frequently experienced in my dissections of the veins: if I attempted to pass a probe from the trunk of the veins into one of the smaller branches, whatever care I took I found it impossible to introduce it far any way, by reason of the valves; whilst, on the contrary, it was most easy to push it along in the opposite direction, from without inwards, or from the branches towards the trunks and roots. In many places two valves are so placed and fitted, that when raised they come exactly together in the middle of the vein, and are there united by the contact of their margins; and so accurate is the adaptation, that neither by the eye nor by any other means of examination can the slightest chink along the line of contact be perceived. But if the probe be now introduced from the extreme towards the more central parts, the valves, like the floodgates of a river, give way, and are most readily pushed aside. The effect of this arrangement plainly is to prevent all motion of the blood from the heart and vena cava, whether it be upwards towards the head, or downwards towards the feet, or to either side towards the arms, not a drop can pass; all motion of the blood, beginning in the larger and tending towards the smaller veins, is opposed and resisted by them; whilst the motion that proceeds from the lesser to end in the larger branches is favoured, or, at all events, a free and open passage is left for it.

But that this truth may be made the more apparent, let an arm be tied up above the elbow as if for phlebotomy (A,A, fig. 1). At intervals in the course of the veins, especially in labouring people and those whose veins are large, certain knots or elevations (B,C,D,E,F) will be perceived, and this not only at the places where a branch is received (E,F) but also where none enters (C,D): these knots or risings are all formed by valves, which thus show themselves externally. And now if you press the blood from the space above one of the valves, from H to O, (fig. 2,) and keep the point of a finger upon the vein inferiorly, you will see no influx of blood from above; the portion of the vein between the point of the finger and the valve O will be obliterated; yet will the vessel continue sufficiently distended above that valve (O,G). The blood being thus pressed out, and the vein emptied, if you now apply a finger of the other hand upon the distended part of the vein above the valve O, (fig. 3), and press downwards, you will find that you cannot force the blood through or beyond the valve; but the greater effort you use, you will only see the portion of vein that is between the finger and the valve become more distended, that portion of the vein which is below the valve remaining all the while empty (H,O, fig. 3).

It would therefore appear that the function of the valves in the veins is the same as that of the three sigmoid valves which we find at the commencement of the aorta and pulmonary artery, viz., to prevent all reflux of the blood that is passing over them.

Farther, the arm being bound as before, and the veins looking full and distended, if you press at one part in the course of a vein with the point of a finger (L, fig. 4), and then with another finger streak the blood upwards beyond the next valve (N), you will perceive that this portion of the vein continues empty (L,N), and that the blood cannot retrograde, precisely as we have already seen the case to be in fig. 2; but the finger first applied (H, fig. 2, L, fig. 4), being removed, immediately the vein is filled from below, and the arm becomes as it appears at D C, fig. 1. That the blood in the veins therefore proceeds from inferior or more remote to superior parts, and towards the heart, moving in these vessels in this and not in the contrary direction, appears most obviously. And although in some places the valves, by not acting with such perfect accuracy, or where there is but a single valve, do not seem totally to prevent

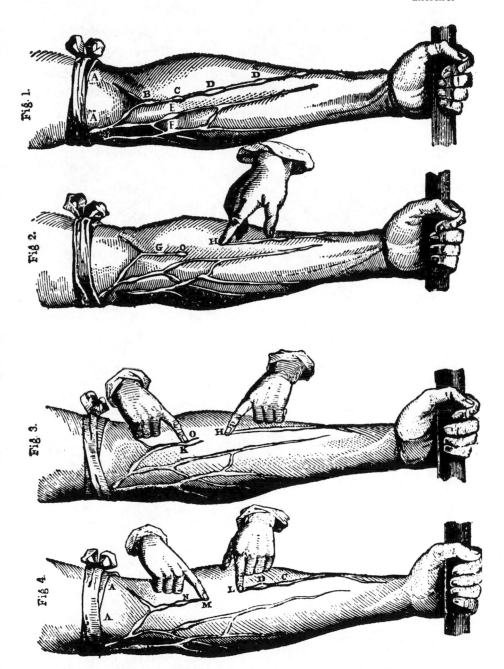

(Taken from William Harvey's *An Anatomical Disquisition on the Motion of the Heart and Blood in Animals*)

the passage of the blood from the centre, still the greater number of them plainly do so; and then, where things appear contrived more negligently, this is compensated either by the more frequent occurrence or more perfect action of the succeeding valves or in some other way: the veins, in short, as they are the free and open conduits of the blood returning *to* the heart, so are they effectually prevented from serving as its channels of distribution *from* the heart.

Bibliography

Austin, J. L. *How To Do Things With Words*, Oxford University Press, 1962

Beardsley, Monroe C. *Practical Logic*, Prentice Hall, 1950, p. 558

Blair, J. Anthony and Johnson, Ralph H. (eds.). *Informal Logic: The First International Symposium*, Edgepress, 1980

Boulding, Kenneth. Foreword to Malthus's *Population: The First Essay*, University of Michigan Press, 1959

Butterfield, Herbert. *The Origins of Modern Science 1300–1800*, G. Bell & Sons, 1949, p. 32 and Chapter 3

Cornman, James W., Lehrer, Keith and Pappas, George S. *Philosophical Problems and Argument: An Introduction*, 3rd edn, Collier Macmillan, 1982, pp. 85f.

Crombie, A. C. *Augustine to Galileo*, Falcon Educational Books (first published 1952), Heinemann, 1980, Vol. II, pp. 221–38

Dawkins, Richard. Review of Swinburne's *Is There a God?*, in *The Sunday Times*, 4 February 1996

Everitt, Nicholas and Fisher, Alec. *Modern Epistemology: A New Introduction*, McGraw-Hill, 1995

Fogelin, Robert J. *Understanding Arguments*, Harcourt Brace Jovanovich, 1978, p. 96

Hacker, P. M. S. *Insight and Illusion*, Oxford University Press, 1972, p. 304

Meek, Ronald L. (ed.). *Marx and Engels on Malthus*, Lawrence and Wishart, 1953, pp. 59, 63

Olson, Mancur. *The Logic of Collective Action*, Harvard University Press, 1965, pp. 2, 3

Popper, Sir Karl. *The Logic of Scientific Discovery* (translated by the author with the assistance of Dr Julius Freed and Lan Freed), Hutchinson & Co., 1959, Appendix xi, pp. 442f.

Putnam, Hilary. 'The Corroboration of Theories' in Schlipp, Paul A. (ed.), *The Philosophy of Karl Popper*, Open Court Publishing Co., 1974, Vol. I, pp. 221–40, §4

Quine, W. V. and Ullian, J. S. *The Web of Belief*, Random House, 1970, p. 62

Russell, Bertrand. *The Problems of Philosophy*, Oxford University Press, 1967, p. 63

Samuelson, Paul A. *Economics: An Introductory Analysis*, McGraw-Hill, 1980

Scriven, Michael. *Reasoning*, McGraw-Hill, 1976

Strawson, P. F. *Introduction to Logical Theory*, Methuen, 1952

Bibliography

Swinburne, Richard. *Is There A God?*, Oxford University Press, 1996
Thomas, Stephen. *Practical Reasoning in Natural Language*, 2nd edn, Prentice
    Hall, 1981, pp. 156, 296–323
    Practical Reasoning in Natural Language, 3rd edn, Prentice Hall, 1986
Toulmin, Stephen. *The Uses of Argument*, Cambridge University Press, 1958

Further reading

A great deal has been, and is being, written on informal logic and critical thinking. The journal *Informal Logic* is a good source for recent work. (It is edited by R. Johnson and A. Blair, the University of Windsor, Ontario, Canada.) Among the many other sources which could be recommended for further reading the following short list makes a good start.

Blair, J. Anthony and Johnson, Ralph H. (eds.). *Informal Logic: The First International Symposium*, Edgepress (1980) [An instructive collection of papers from the first international symposium on informal logic.]

Fisher, Alec. *Critical Thinking: An Introduction*, Cambridge University Press, 2001

Fogelin, Robert J. *Understanding Arguments*, Harcourt Brace Jovanovich (1978) [A thoughtful text which also has an instructor's manual.]

Govier, Trudy. *A Practical Study of Argument*, Wadsworth (1985) [A good and widely used text.]

McPeck, John E. *Critical Thinking and Education*, Martin Robertson (1981) [Probably the most noteworthy attack on the 'critical thinking movement' so far.]

Perelman, C. and Olbrechts-Tyteca, L. *The New Rhetoric: A Treatise on Argumentation*, University of Notre Dame Press (1969) [A classic in the tradition of rhetoric.]

Scriven, Michael. *Reasoning*, McGraw-Hill (1976) [A classic in this field.]

Thomas, Stephen. *Practical Reasoning in Natural Language*, Prentice Hall, 2nd edn (1981), 3rd edn (1986) [A good text with a very carefully worked approach.]

Toulmin, Stephen. *The Uses of Argument*, Cambridge University Press (1958) [An historical classic.]

Index